THROUGH
JAUNDICED
EYES

THROUGH JAUNDICED EYES

How the Media View Organized Labor

William J. Puette

ILR Press
Ithaca, New York

Cover design by Marcelle Toor

Library of Congress Cataloging-in-Publication Data

Puette, William J.
    Through jaundiced eyes : how the media view organized labor /
William J. Puette.
        p.   cm.
    Includes bibliographical references and index.
    ISBN 0-87546-184-0 (acid-free paper). — ISBN 0-87546-185-9
(pbk.: acid-free paper)
    1. Trade-unions and mass media—United States.   2. Trade-unions
in the press—United States.   3. Industrial relations in the press—
United States.   4. Employees—United States—Public opinion.
5. Trade-unions—United States—Public opinion.   I. Title.
P96.T7P84   1992
331.88′0973—dc20   91-46351

Copies may be ordered through bookstores or from

ILR Press
School of Industrial and Labor Relations
Cornell University
Ithaca, NY 14853–3901

Printed on acid-free paper in the United States of America
5   4   3   2   1

Contents

Acknowledgments

The encouragement and support of Professors David Stannard, Floyd Matson, Robert Weyeneth, Edward Beechert, and Ron Brown of the University of Hawaii, and Teresa Bill of Brown University helped make this book possible. I thank them for their invaluable advice and direction.

In addition, I am grateful for the generous contributions of time and research assistance provided by Ethel Miyachi of the Hawaii State AFL-CIO; Paul Clark of Pennsylvania State University; the Annenberg Television Script Archive, Annenberg School of Communications, University of Pennsylvania; Sharon Black, archivist at the Annenberg School of Communications, and her staff, including bibliographic specialist Elizabeth Moersh and archive assistant Margaret Ann Morris; Bob Walther, reference librarian at Van Pelt Library, University of Pennsylvania; the United Mine Workers of America, especially Joe Corcoran and F. Kirsten Smith; William Hoynes and David Croteau of the Sociology Department at Boston College; the Hawaii State Teachers Association and Joan Husted; Linda Helt of Maui High School; George Butterfield of Kalani High School; Justin Wong of Radford High School; the George Meany Memorial Archives and archivist Lynda DeLoach; Al Hamai, education director for the American Federation of State, County and Municipal Employees in Hawaii and member of the Honolulu Media Council; Elaine Wells, Chief Steward of Local 9415 of the Communications Workers of America; Nancy Naganuma of Fullerton, California; reference librarian Florence Fitzgerald of the Fullerton Public Library;

reprographic artist George Bacon of Honolulu; Robert Hasegawa, Nancy Fujii, and Jo Ann Tomita of the University of Hawaii's Center for Labor Education and Research; Walter Kupau of Carpenters' Union, Local 745; Richard A. Desmond of International Longshoremen's and Warehousemen's Union, Local 142, and People's Fund of Honolulu, Hawaii, for their grant, which partially funded the cost of my travel to the Annenberg School.

For permission to reprint the various cartoons included in chapter 5, I acknowledge my appreciation to the following: Brandeis University for figure 1; the Public Affairs Press and M. B. Schnapper for figures 3, 5, and 6; the George Meany Memorial Archives and Gibson M. Crockett for Figure 7; the *Honolulu Advertiser* for figures 8, 9, and 10; the *Honolulu Star-Bulletin* for figures 11 and 12; Paul Conrad and the Los Angeles Times Syndicate for figure 13; Don Wright and the *Palm Beach Post* for figure 14; the Washington Post Writers' Group and Berke Breathed for figures 15–18; Garry Trudeau and the Universal Press Syndicate for figure 19; the North American Syndicate and Johnny Hart for figures 20 and 21; Jerry Bittle and the Universal Press Syndicate for figure 22; Grimmy, Inc., for figure 23; and W. B. Park and United Feature Syndicate, Inc., for figure 24.

THROUGH
JAUNDICED
EYES

Introduction

Unions, Liberals, and the Media

For most of its history the American labor movement has taken adverse media coverage for granted. In 1977 Albert Zack, director of the AFL-CIO Department of Public Relations, delivered the best known and most official complaint about the media's treatment of the labor movement. His article in the federation's national newsletter described what most unionists have long understood as the prevailing press bias against labor. Zack took his examples primarily from mid–1970s coverage, though the history of the labor movement is replete with similar examples. One of the oldest recorded complaints in a similar vein appeared in a 1922 issue of the *International Molders' Journal*, which decried the unsympathetic treatment the American press gave to strikes: "Grasping this fine opportunity for news the big dailies get busy and start to lash the strikers through the blatant columns of their unreliable news sheets for the inconvenience and suffering they have brought upon the public."[1]

Labor views its treatment by the media over the years as uniformly negative. Noted labor historians Derek C. Bok and John T. Dunlop have recorded the pervasively unfavorable image of organized labor projected in the communications media. Though this negative media portrayal has dogged the labor movement nearly since its inception, its effect has been most grievous in the last few decades, when the impact and influence of the media have grown to exceed practically any other source of public opinion. According to John Tebbel's history of the media in America, by the mid–1970s, 95 percent of American homes had televisions, although only about 11 percent of the population over age twenty-five had graduated from college and about two-thirds had not even completed high school.[2] In earlier times people were more likely to form their values and opinions as well as class and party allegiances under the influence of family, neighbor, teacher, preacher, and co-worker, but the educational role of such diverse influences has been increasingly co-opted by the media at a rate that has, in fact, accelerated since 1975. From 1950 to 1988 the time the average American household spends watching television increased from four and a half hours daily to just over seven hours.[3] It would, of course, be an exaggeration to say that public opinion is now entirely the product of media images; yet as V. O. Key first noted, "The media may be especially influential in the formation of opinion . . . about substantive issues and events which are remote from the experience of people and to the appraisal of which they can bring no applicable general convictions."[4] Today only about 15 percent of the nation's work force is unionized, which means that organized labor is a remote experience to the vast majority of Americans, while the presence of the media has become an even more immediate part of our lives. The effect of even a slightly biased portrayal of labor, or any other component of our national makeup, is more apt to control the prevailing public opinion than it was in the days when the union movement was larger and the media were less invasive.

For decades, commercial advertisers have been aware of the essentially nonlogical nature of persuasion. Relying on techniques little different from those of the ill-reputed propagandists of World War II, the strategies of public relations for the advertiser or the propagandist remain essentially the same. Jacques Ellul correctly believed that "propaganda must be total. The propagandist must utilize all of the technical means at his disposal—the press, radio, TV, movies, posters, meetings, door-to-door canvasing. . . . Each usable medium has its own particular way of penetration—specific, but at the same time localized and limited."[5] Indeed, a defender of any one of the media, confronted with evidence of its bias, will fall back to the position that one medium alone can hardly be responsible for such an overwhelming public opinion, and that the other media are perhaps worse. Such diversion may be an effective way to defuse criticism of specific instances of bias, which taken alone may seem minimally significant, but it is the net effect of such instances as they combine with similar jabs and insults that point to a larger, endemic form of institutional bias affecting all the media.

Labor's Public Image

Despite this long-standing media antipathy, public opinion has not always been antagonistic to organized labor. The classic study of a midwestern town at the turn of the century by Robert and Helen Merrel Lynd described how the town's lawyer and superintendent of schools happily addressed an open meeting of the Knights of Labor, and that Samuel Gompers was dined in the mayor's home, while the local press was "agitating for stricter local enforcement of the weekly pay law."[6] By 1920, though, that attitude had changed. The Lynds suggest this change of opinion was part of a growing class schism affecting Middletown, like much of America, as a result of the advent of the town's industrial economy. Craft unionism that limited its reach to trade workers, who were perceived more as local artisans than laborers in America's largely rural nineteenth-century economy, was not so easily vilified as its twentieth-century industrial counterpart.

Even so, according to the *Gallup Report*, public approval of labor unions since the 1930s, when Gallup first began to ask about it, has hovered generally between 55 percent and 75 percent and reached its lowest ebb in 1981. Seymour Martin Lipset observed that approval of unions was high during the New Deal, then declined moderately during the war years. Strangely, these data show that union approval peaked during the supposedly conservative Eisenhower administration. The reason, Lipset believes, is that fluctuations in the Gallup polls tend to reflect public confidence in national institutions in general. But he notes another significant pattern that may be even more germane: "What is important about the public's sentiments toward organized labor is that they have moved virtually in tandem with changes in union strength."[7] Public approval shifted away from unions at about the same time the labor movement decreased in size and success in winning representation elections. Lipset also shows, through other polls and surveys, that the decline in union approval can be attributed to a well-defined set of impressions that have emerged and constitute the negative public image of organized labor.

Roughly the same images emerged in a sampling of high school students in Hawaii that was collected in 1989.[8] When asked to describe their basic impressions of labor unions, students responding to this survey raised ten themes: unions are always going on strike; unions are too powerful; unions are corrupt; unions are greedy and selfish; unions are ruining the country; union leaders (bosses) are overpaid; union dues are too high; unions are undemocratic and un-American; unions protect bad workers; and unions are no longer needed.

More disturbing yet was the parallel finding from the same survey that basic information about the history, comparable size, and purpose of the American labor movement was inaccurate or unknown (see Appendix A). The overwhelming majority of the respondents (70 percent) believed that in the United States a greater part of the work force is unionized than in other industrialized countries, when, in fact, unionization of the U.S. work force is among the lowest of all industrial economies. Similarly, 83 percent of those surveyed estimated a much higher annual average of strike activity than the 2 percent or less that occurs in an average year.

Since only a small percentage of these students had any formal instruction in labor relations and their responses correspond with Lipset's analysis of public opinion polls, these responses appear to reflect the current image of labor unions common to the general public as communicated through the popular media. The problem is not only that this public view of organized labor is so negative but that it appears to be premised to a large extent on incorrect information.

This study raises the question of the extent to which the negative portrayal of organized labor may be considered intentional or institutional bias. Given the express ethical purpose of journalists to value accuracy above all else and given the media's ability to broadcast information far and wide, it is hard to understand how labor's image can be so consistently distorted unintentionally. Indeed, as the following chapters will reveal, often enough there is evidence of deliberate "union animus" or conscious anti-union sentiment, but, more often, the negative portrayal appears to be representative of an institutional bias built into the various media's systems and structures for gathering, producing, and disseminating news or entertainment.

Are the Media Liberal or Conservative?

The way organized labor is portrayed by the American media is also related to the larger question of the media's alleged liberal bias. As Robert Cirino noted in his 1971 study of media bias, the allegation that the press has a liberal bias can be traced to Spiro Agnew's speech in Des Moines, Iowa, on November 13, 1969, before the Mid-West Regional Republican Committee. For at least thirty years, the media had been criticized by liberals and progressives for presenting news or censoring it to favor wealthy advertisers and media moguls. In one speech, with no supporting research or documentation, the vice-president turned the tables on the news media, not only diverting attention from the Nixon administration's support of the Vietnam war but permanently shifting fronts in the growing popular notion of media bias from a liberal to a conservative perspective. Though skillfully avoiding use of the label *liberal*, Agnew left no doubt as to the target of his tirade:

> We do know that to a man these commentators and producers live and work in the geographical and intellectual confines of Washington, D.C., the latter of which James Reston terms the most unrepresentative community in the entire United States.
> Both communities bask in their own provincialism, their own parochialism.[9]

In 1971, Joseph Keeley applied Agnew's critique specifically to television in his book *The Left-Leaning Antenna*. Pointing particularly to Columbia Broadcasting System (CBS) and National Broadcasting Company (NBC) news specials, Keeley employed the word *liberal* to identify a clearly defined political agenda, directly and deliberately opposed to the Nixon administration.

Statistical support for Agnew's charge was soon sought out by a variety of media critics. Edith Efron found that network coverage of Vietnam, civil rights, and the Humphrey-Nixon campaigns was "biased in favor of the liberal, Democratic, left axis of opinion." What appeared to be the most damning evidence came a decade later, when a team of social scientists at George Washington University surveyed journalists in 1980. The Rothman-Lichters surveys, as they are known, revealed that many journalists considered themselves liberal and that most voted Democratic in presidential elections. But media analyst Herbert Gans argued that the Rothman-Lichters analyses and conclusions were more influenced by their own political agenda than by the data collected. He notes, for instance, that the Rothman and Lichters report makes conclusions based on the surveyed journalists' opinions of Marxian doctrine even though the interviews they conducted included no question about such doctrines.[10] Most telling of all is Gans's observation that the entire premise of the Rothman-Lichters study is based on an analysis of the journalists' attitudes compared to a baseline of responses obtained from a similar survey of corporate managers, who were alleged to represent mainstream American values. Nevertheless, in 1986 the initial Rothman-Lichters analysis was expanded and popularized in their book *The Media Elite*. The original data base was essentially the same: interviews with about 240 journalists from the *New York Times*, *Wall Street Journal*, *Washington Post*, *Time*, *Newsweek*, and *U.S. News and World Report*, as well as members of the news departments of the American Broadcasting Company (ABC), CBS, NBC, and the Public

Broadcasting System (PBS). Though the Rothman-Lichters surveys were limited to journalists, conservative critics wasted no time applying their findings to the rest of the media as well.

More recently, William A. Rusher, publisher of the *National Review*, has described what he maintains is a liberal bias that pervades the "media elite." One of Rusher's arguments for asserting this bias is his observation that liberals compose the one political group that almost never protests unfair treatment of the media. "On the contrary," he writes, "liberals are usually quick to praise the media, deny that the media are biased, and defend the media's claimed prerogatives against all challengers."[11]

It is not the purpose of this book to support either side in the ongoing debate over the question of the media's alleged liberal or conservative bias. Rather, it is my intent to analyze and understand the nature of the media portrayal of organized labor as it can be seen in a cross section of the most influential of the media, particularly the movies, newspapers, and television. This portrayal will be considered in the context of the media's reputed liberal bias to ascertain the extent to which the fate of the labor movement may or may not be a concern of the liberal agenda. The book further proffers a framework for understanding and interpreting typical media treatment of organized labor, including case studies of the extended coverage surrounding local and national labor stories, and a review of labor's current efforts to form a viable response to this treatment. I have not included reviews of magazines or radio programs, though both certainly contain abundant examples of anti-union portrayals, because both are targeted to narrowly defined audiences rather than to the general public.

C. Wright Mills observed in 1945 that the so-called liberal left in America was often as unsympathetic to organized labor as were the country's business interests: "Leftwing intellectuals and business executives have often thumbed the same dictionaries of abuse trying to find suitable language with which to characterize the trade union leader."[12] Forty-five years later, the situation appears to be essentially the same, and Mills's thesis comes closest to pointing out the probable underlying cause—power. The "leftwing intellectual" of Mills's description is comfortable crusading for the downtrodden and aggrieved worker but is uncomfortable relating to the working-class union leader and the well-paid union worker. There may well be a deep-seated class antipathy at the bottom of this long-standing intellectual disdain for unions that has colored the media portrayal of labor for over fifty years.

This class-antipathy thesis is supported, significantly, by the absence of any references, in either the Rothman-Lichters work or William Rusher's study of supposed liberal bias, to the media's treatment of labor unions or labor leaders. Certainly that glaring absence suggests that the pattern of labor coverage in the media does not support their thesis. Cirino's *Don't Blame the People* (1971) and Michael Parenti's *Inventing Reality: The Politics of the Mass Media* (1986), however, both of which find evidence of a conservative media bias, likewise devote entire chapters to the anti-labor images typical of media portrayal.

In a recent article weighing the arguments in the on-going debate over the liberal-conservative bias of the national media, Aaron Wildavsky applies *Webster's* definition of bias: "systematic error . . . encouraging one outcome or answer over others."[13] Setting aside the issue of malicious intent, then, Wildavsky rightly focuses instead on the adverse impact of such systematic error in an effort to establish the existence of bias.

To do justice to the truly systematic scope of the media portrayal of organized labor, this book attempts to provide a representative sampling of the three most influential of the mass media. Both local and national sources for each medium as well as the more subtle forms of bias are considered. Harold Laski wrote in *The American Democracy*, "The real power of the press comes from its continuous repetition of an attitude reflected in facts which its readers have no chance to check, or by its ability to surround those facts by an environment of suggestion which, often half-consciously, seeps its way into the mind of the reader and forms his premises."[14] Research by Doris Graber in *Processing the News* (1988) substantiates Laski's proposition and identifies "schemata" or stereotypes that become a framework that enables the average person to arrange and understand the onslaught of contemporary media information.

Since it is the purpose of this book to reveal and analyze the portrayal of labor unions commonly encountered in American media, the framework for this analysis includes representative samples of both news and entertainment media and shall focus on the most popular, current, and, therefore, influential media. Cirino's "catalogue of hidden bias" tactics provides a useful guide for the consideration of news as well as entertainment media:

Bias in the Source of News
Bias Through Selection of News
Bias Through Omission of News
The Art of Interviewing
Bias Through Placement
Bias Through "Coincidental" Placement

Bias in the Headlines
Bias in Words
Bias in News Images
Bias in Photographic Selection
Bias in Captions
The Use of Editorials to Distort Facts
The Hidden Editorial[15]

Though Cirino originally limited his "catalogue" to the devices ordinary only to newspapers, its thoroughness provides a systematic approach by which to compare and evaluate the methods of the other media.

I also use Parenti's seven basic "generalizations" typifying media treatment of labor struggles:

1. Portrayal of labor struggles as senseless, avoidable contests created by unions' unwillingness to negotiate in good faith.
2. Focus on company wage "offers" omitting or underplaying reference to takebacks and employee grievances, making the workers appear irrational, greedy and self-destructive.
3. No coverage given to management salaries, bonuses or compensation and how they are inconsistent with concessions demanded of the workers.
4. Emphasis on the impact rather than the causes of strikes, laying the blame for the strike totally on the union and detailing the damage the strike does to the economy and the public weal.
5. Failure to consider the harm caused to the workers' interests if they were to give up their strike.
6. Unwillingness or inability to cover stories of union solidarity and mutual support.
7. Portrayal of the government (including the courts and the police) as a neutral arbiter upholding the public interest when it is rather protecting corporate properties and bodyguarding strike-breakers.[16]

Although Parenti limited himself to media portrayal of labor disputes, most of his generalizations apply equally well to the reporting of such other union activities as organizing, electioneering, and political action. These generalizations together with Cirino's "catalogue" form a convenient matrix for starting a multimedia analysis. Taken together, their conclusions form the most viable model for understanding and interpreting typical media treatment of organized labor.

The first chapter surveys the portrayal of unions in the movies, tracing the images of organized labor primarily in Hollywood and major studio films from the 1930s to the present. Chapters 2 and 3 examine television images of labor unions as presented in network and local/affiliate news and in nationally produced dramatic series. The analysis of press coverage of unions in chapter 4 is focused on local (city) newspapers, using the two Honolulu dailies, the *Honolulu Advertiser* and the *Honolulu Star-Bulletin*, as representative of average American metropolitan publications whose portrayal may be regarded as indicative. Chapter 5 analyzes the image of organized labor most often portrayed in newspaper syndicated and editorial cartoons. And chapters 6 and 7 consider two case studies of the extended coverage surrounding a local and a national labor dispute.

The final two chapters conclude the study with a consideration of labor's response to its negative media images and a return to the questions raised above regarding the relationship between liberalism, neoliberalism, and the relative effect of these political-social belief systems in the American media.

1. The Movies

Labor Framed

LELAND: As long as I can remember, you've talked about giving the people their rights; as if you could make them a present of liberty . . . as a reward for services rendered.
KANE: Jed.
LELAND: Remember the working man?
KANE: I'll get drunk too, Jedidiah, if it'll do any good.
LELAND: Aw, it won't do any good. Besides, you never get drunk. You used to write an awful lot about the working man. But he's turning into something called organized labor. You're not going to like that one little bit when you find out it means that your working man expects something as his right, not as your gift. When your precious underprivileged really get together . . . Oh boy! That's going to add up to something bigger than your privilege; then I don't know what you'll do. Sail away to a desert island, probably, and lord it over the monkeys.
—*Citizen Kane*

Jedidiah Leland's remarks in *Citizen Kane* were spoken to the fictitious press mogul patterned after William Randolph Hearst. They capture the essential principle behind the American media bias against labor unions that has colored the Hollywood depiction of unions since the 1930s. As long as labor could be viewed as an underprivileged, generally helpless and disfranchised object of pity, the media were glad to take up its banner. But as Jed Leland astutely remarks, the motive was always self-serving, and it turned around when these same workers' unions were sufficiently organized to begin exerting the very power the media had formerly advocated.

American films about labor fall into two major categories: the downscale, usually 16mm, educational film about labor history or giving a union profile; and the Hollywood, feature-length entertainment film. The former were usually produced by unions or sympathetic agencies to be used as training or public relations materials and tend to follow the basic documentary style. Many are of very high quality, but they have not, unfortunately, enjoyed wide release. Though such films as the

Amalgamated Clothing and Textile Workers Union's *The Inheritance* (1964), *With Babies and Banners* (1975), *Harlan County, U.S.A.* (1976), *The Wobblies* (1979), *Rosie the Riveter* (1980), and others present mostly inspirational accounts of the early history of the American labor movement, their limited availability to the public at large prevents them from being seriously considered as media.

The media are most effective, most convincing, and most powerful when they reach most deeply into the culture and when their bias is least obvious. Thus, when Hollywood is attempting to be its most entertaining and least pedagogic, it is capable of having a profound effect on public values and attitudes. In examining the portrayal of unions in the movies, it is important to distinguish those films that deal most directly or overtly with organized labor as part of their basic plot from those movies that refer to unions only in a peripheral, tangential way.

Although the list of movies that deal directly and primarily with labor unions is not extensive, the number of films in which some casual, even flippant, remark reflecting on unions is made is legion. And the cumulative effect of such peripheral commentary has done much to mold the public's, particularly the young moviegoing audience's, feelings about the worth and function of labor unions.

The history of organized labor in America goes back to the eighteenth century with the emergence of craft unions based loosely on the old European guild system. But the distinctly American trade union, organized to protect workers from employer abuses such as unsafe working conditions and substandard wages, grew up in the postbellum period as the country began to industrialize. Yet laws were not passed to recognize workers' rights until Franklin D. Roosevelt's New Deal in the 1930s.

Early Portrayals of Labor

Films about labor date back to the open-shop drive in the first decade of the twentieth century. As Philip Foner has discovered, from 1907 to 1911 scores of anti-labor films were produced, allegedly with the support of the National Association of Manufacturers.[1] With titles such as *Lulu's Anarchists, Gus—The Anarchist, Lazy Bill and the Strikers, The Long Strike, The Riot*, and *Good Boss*, these early silent films were blatant anti-union propaganda. They made heroes out of scabs and depicted union leaders as self-serving, foreign agitators who deserted the workers after a strike and cared nothing for the havoc they caused in the lives of the native populace. Not until D. W. Griffith's *Intolerance* (1916) do we see anything of the spirit of Progressivism in the cinematic treatment of labor unions.

The four plots of *Intolerance* were strongly influenced by the Progressive movement, particularly "The Modern Story," with which the film begins and ends. It is the story of a strike by mill workers, protesting a cut in wages, which the owner of the mill, Jenkins, has made, ironically, to finance his charitable activities. The father of the hero is killed when Jenkins calls on the state militia to break the strike, and "the Boy," as he is called in the subtitles, is forced into a life of crime when he is unable to find work. The hero and his wife, "the Dear One," are depicted as pitiful victims of the tyranny of the powerful capitalist, Jenkins. The three other plots of *Intolerance* provide historical analogies to "The Modern Story" in depicting other infamous tyrants who held the same life-and-death power over their laborers.[2]

But Griffith's sympathetic portrayal was far from the ordinary treatment accorded labor organizing in the early cinema. A decade later, even Walt Disney would be attacking the Wobbly organizers in his *Alice in Cartoonland* series. In an animated short entitled *Alice's Egg Plant* (1925), the character "little Red Henski" is shown leading a strike of the hens at Alice's Egg Factory.[3] Perfecting the stereotype of the foreign, communist agitator, Disney loaded this caricature with the sinister images that had emerged since the films of the open-shop drive that had begun twenty years earlier.[4]

Nor would the moviemakers' image of labor organizers improve much until the Depression and the reemergence of a long-suppressed labor movement. Only after decades of labor strife did the U.S. Congress in 1935 pass the Wagner Act, which finally required private sector employers to recognize and bargain with their workers. That year, Hollywood produced a variety of films on the plight of the industrial worker. Certainly the most famous and best remembered was Charlie Chaplin's *Modern Times*. Originally called *The Masses*, Chaplin's film, featuring the pathetic Tramp being run through the cogs of a gigantic machine, had to be retitled to pass the censors. Though not specifically a union film, it does convey a sympathetic attitude toward factory workers. The strike scenes in *Modern Times*, not unlike those in *Intolerance*, though they criticize the power of capitalism, portray the hero and heroine as hapless victims unable to control the force of the employer or the direction of the strike. This theme—that the average worker is victimized as much by the strike as by the employers' abuses—was to dominate American films about organized labor into the 1980s.

The first major film to deal directly with labor unions was the 1935 Warner Brothers production of *Black Fury*. Starring Paul Muni as the immigrant coal miner Joe Radek, the film describes a sympathetic character caught up in a hopelessly failed strike. As a contemporary reviewer described the plot:

> Mr. Muni is the ignorant and jovial Hunky miner, Joe Radek, whose popularity with his comrades causes him to be singled out as the dupe of the strike-breaking gangsters. Joe is an innocent among the wolves. Having lost his girl, he drowns his sorrow in the whiskey bottle. Without understanding the issues involved, he makes a drunken appearance at a union meeting at the psychological moment to cause a split between the conservative and radical factions. During the subsequent strike, Joe's best friend is brutally murdered by the coal and iron police, and the poor fellow suddenly understands the enormity of his sin. The helpless miners are anxious to return to work on the company's terms, which means that they have lost the Shalerville agreement that the union leaders have struggled so hard to win for them. Joe thereupon barricades himself in the mine and conducts a one-man strike, insisting that he will destroy himself and the entire property unless the company restores the agreement. After a protracted siege, during which the police are unable to dislodge him, the operators give in, allowing the miners to go back to work with all the privileges which they enjoyed before the strike.[5]

This film reveals Hollywood's apparent ambivalence toward the labor movement. Just after the film's release, Albert Maltz, author of a play entitled *Black Pit*, about the plight of similar coal miners, bitterly denounced the movie as anti-union propaganda because it connected the workers' drinking to their decision to picket and showed mine shafts and tunnels that did not come close to resembling the grimness of the real thing.[6] The scene at the end, however, when government officials lay the blame for the incident on the mine owners and the strikebreakers they hired, can be taken as evidence of the film's pro-union stance. But in view of Jedidiah Leland's reproach, a truer conclusion would be that the film attempts overtly to be pro-worker while subtly suggesting that the union effort was misguided and futile; in other words, all for "the working man," but against "organized labor."

The film's seeming ambivalence toward labor unions, as it turns out, was no accident. As Francis R. Walsh discovered in 1986, the script of the film was drastically revised from the original story written by Pennsylvania Justice Michael A. Musmanno while he was a state legislator. That script, entitled *Black Hell*, described a plot by mine owners to infiltrate the union, force a strike, and use hired goons and scabs to break the union. But, as Walsh revealed, the Musmanno script was completed on the eve of the establishment of the Production Code

Administration Office under Joseph I. Breen. Acting on a complaint from the National Coal Association, Breen wrote to Hal Wallis at Warner Brothers, who subsequently ordered the rewrite with the specific direction, "we should bend over backwards to eliminate anything unfavorable to the coal mining industry."[7] Not only was the resulting script an example of what Cirino called "bias by omission," but the characterization of Radek as a "bohunk" is arguably an example of a larger class bias against unskilled blue-collar workers. This class bias commonly operates in the media in concert with the anti-union bias, and, in this case both were being enforced by the Production Code Administration and the studios as well. Unfortunately, this watered-down labor plot would become the stereotype in movie portrayals of organized labor for the next twenty years and more.

In what might be considered a spin-off of *Black Fury* later that year, MGM produced a comedy entitled *Riffraff*, which tells the story of an arrogant fisherman, played by Spencer Tracy, who celebrates his marriage to the fair Hattie (played by Jean Harlow) by calling his fellow workers out on strike. As in *Black Fury*, the battle is lost; the hero is discredited and forced to try to save face. And like *Black Fury*, *Riffraff* popularizes the notion that Parenti observed: that labor struggles are senseless, avoidable contests generally caused for the personal gratification of ignorant and incapable union leaders.[8] *Riffraff*, however, is even more biased than its predecessor because, as a comedy, it trivializes as well as demeans the workers' plight.

A film that comes as close to offering a pro-union message as was likely to be found at that time is William Wyler's *Dead End* (1937). Drina, the film's unionist, is portrayed heroically and sympathetically as she demands better wages and a better way of life. But the labor dispute is a secondary plot, and Drina's efforts are admired because they reflect her desire to escape the slums into which fate had cruelly consigned her. Not unlike Sam Wood's *The Devil and Miss Jones* (1940), *Dead End* shows Hollywood's soft spot for labor organizing undertaken by women and minorities. Into the 1980s, the ordinarily bad portrayal of labor is not infrequently offset by a sympathetic depiction of women or egregiously abused minorities martyred or overcome by superior force in a doomed attempt to organize themselves. This sympathy is not extended to the efforts of white, blue-collar males or to impoverished workers as a class but is meted out selectively to groups that are unrepresentative of the majority, permitting us to believe that the majority of the work force is not being abused.

By the end of the decade the dominant motif in the depiction of ordinary labor unions was revealed in Warner Brothers' *Racket Busters* (1938), in which Humphrey Bogart plays a mobster infiltrating the trucking and produce industry in New York. He assaults business as well as labor, but most of the story is focused on the takeover of the truckers' association. George Brent as the scrappy trucker who is the unofficial leader of the truckers is much like Muni's Joe Radek and Tracy's fisherman, the charismatic leader who is basically unworthy of trust and unequal to the task.

But *Racket Busters* goes beyond its predecessors by playing on the mob connection. Although at first the union truckers are portrayed as victims of mob terror and intimidation, Brent's character, Denny Jordan, gives in soon enough, and the citywide strike that ensues is a manifestation of the mob's plan to compound its extortionate demands upon the innocent denizens of the city. The real hero of the film is the special prosecuting attorney who persuades the courts to force frightened witnesses and suspected mob figures alike to testify or be held in contempt of the grand jury.

Proclaiming in the credits its debt to actual court records and testimony taken in rackets investigations, *Racket Busters* is the first film to demonstrate what would become Hollywood's fixation on the theme of union corruption and organized crime. In many ways it prefigures the films of the 1950s and 1970s that were based on government investigations of well-known and seamy, though essentially unrepresentative, instances of labor corruption.

After an initial burst of concern, occasioned by the passage of the Wagner Act, cinematic interest in the labor movement declined. World War II put a stop to all thoughts of social reform for the next decade, though Twentieth Century-Fox's *Grapes of Wrath* hinted at what might have been. John Ford's epic production of John Steinbeck's novel focuses attention on America's poor farmers and agricultural workers. The labor movement is only a subplot, but it is at least treated with the same compassion as the workers. Casy (John Carradine), a former preacher who has lost his faith, becomes a labor organizer and is murdered for his efforts. But many Americans no doubt perceived his labor activities as a fall from grace and his murder as a just reward.

In *Meet John Doe* (1941), the same year as Orson Welles's *Citizen Kane*, the bias Leland reproached is first expressed as such. The John Doe Clubs depicted were, in many respects, a loose "non-labor" union, large but free of corruption and free of specific leadership or class consciousness. Real unions were, in director Frank Capra's view, then so powerful as to constitute a working part of the system. In the film, Mr.

Kinnell (played by James Gleason) tells the title character that the country's labor leaders are joining the political bosses to pervert the John Doe Convention and elect an "iron hand" to lead the country.

Indeed, even before the war, it seemed that Hollywood had only two images of the labor leader: a misguided dupe or martyr and a power-corrupted union boss. The Hollywood concern for social reform did not long consider the labor movement as worthy of representation. In a film adaptation of Wessel Smitter's novel *F.O.B. Detroit*, Paramount director William Wellman turned a grim social depiction of the plight of automotive workers into a boisterous romantic comedy. As Bosley Crowther of the *New York Times* noted in his review, the film *Reaching for the Sun* (1941) "managed to smear a thick coat of goo over what was originally a harsh and decidedly unsweetened industrial story. All suggestion of Labor conflict has been carefully left out."[9] The attitudes of the workers toward their employers and the numbing effect of the assembly line on their lives, which gave the novel depth of theme and purpose, were deliberately excised.

The development of another 1941 film establishes the intentionality of this bias. Darryl Zanuck, the head of Twentieth Century-Fox, after paying a record $300,000 for the film rights to Richard Llewellyn's *How Green Was My Valley*, required five rewrites of the script before he was satisfied that the labor struggles inherent to the original plot had been sufficiently excised.[10]

Zanuck complained to his script writers that the mine owners were portrayed as villains and that the "English capitalist class" was being criticized at a time when it was already under attack by the German Nazis. As a result, by the time the final script was approved, all the violent clashes between the strikers and the army had been dropped; the minister's stirring defense of the right to strike had been deleted; and the original suggestion that the two Morgan brothers had been fired because of their union activities had been changed to blame their discharge on a surplus of labor in the coalfields.[11] Virtually all criticism of the mine owners and any approbation of the union organizers had been systematically eliminated.

During the war, of course, attention was focused on victory. Workers were admonished to serve unselfishly and tirelessly (as if they had been particularly selfish and lazy before). And unions, in the main, accepted the new regimentation in the spirit of patriotism. Near the end of the war, Metro-Goldwyn-Mayer (MGM) released *An American Romance* (1944) directed by King Vidor. Though its primary purpose was to glorify the traditional "bootstrap" myth that an immigrant worker who was industrious and ambitious could still reach the top of the economic system, the story actually portrays the autoworkers' union as a reasonable development of modern labor-management relations. Incredibly, however, the union spokesman is the owner's son, played by Horace McNally, and the writers seem to have gone to extraordinary lengths to avoid the words *union* and *strike*. In the last thirty minutes, the film devolves into a thinly veiled government training piece plugging New Deal labor law to both unions and employers so more planes and war supplies could pour off the nation's assembly lines. The ideal of labor and management as one happy family was always the theme whenever labor's rights were portrayed at all.

Ironically, when Ayn Rand's novel *Fountainhead* was finally brought to the screen in the 1949 Warner Brothers film directed by King Vidor, these themes of conformity and rigid social cohesion were ridiculed. Now that individualism was being touted, labor was no longer depicted as a radical or antisocial force but as just one more stifling structure preventing true self-expression. In *Fountainhead* Howard Roark, played by Gary Cooper, is a visionary architect, who, in an improbable plot, is set upon by Ellsworth Toohey, the newspaper's architectural critic and chief villain, who despises individualists, calling them "egoists." Toohey is the archetypical "organization man" who has somehow obtained control of the press unions and is able to instigate a strike protesting the publisher's approval of Roark's unusual architectural style. Roark, the publisher, and the woman they both love struggle heroically against Toohey and the overpowering "men on the street" whom Toohey leads. Even the word *brothers*, a word ordinarily associated with union membership, is derided as a corrupting and mindless epithet. At the end of the film Roark valiantly defends his individualism in a bizarre courtroom scene capped by a not so thinly veiled attack on labor unions and the principle of union solidarity: "There is no such thing as a collective brain.... Look at history. Every horror and destruction came from attempts to force men into a herd of brainless soul-less robots without personal rights, without personal ambition, without will hope or dignity."

In the 1950s, the theme changed again. *The Whistle at Eaton Falls*, released by Columbia in 1951, pits a young, newly elected labor leader (played by Lloyd Bridges) in the dilemma of choosing between labor-saving machinery and his fellow workers' jobs. Offsetting the decent and upright figure that Bridges portrays is the antagonistic union agitator (Murray Hamilton); the moral of the story is clearly that nonconfrontation is the truer, more courageous path. The mill owner is also an object of sympathy and admiration, a sensible widow played by Dorothy Gish. Though the plight of the laid-off workers is also depicted empathetically, the film is almost preachy about its theme.

For the most part, though, after the war, the long years of the McCarthy era's red-baiting kept Hollywood entirely away from labor films. Ideals that had been admired as social liberalism in the 1930s were abhorred as bolshevik communism after the war. In Congress the House Committee on Un-American Activities (HUAC) relentlessly singled out Hollywood directors and writers, blacklisting any who stood in its way.

The Stereotype Entrenched

HUAC's rampage through Hollywood in the 1950s caused a set of unusual cinematic duels that resulted in two of the most outstanding films about unions ever produced. In 1954 Elia Kazan, together with screenwriter Budd Schulberg, both of whom had appeared before the committee as "friendly witnesses," wrote and produced the Academy Award-winning *On the Waterfront*. In the same year, blacklisted director Herbert Biberman, with the help of other banished moviemakers, struggled to produce *Salt of the Earth* against nearly overwhelming opposition that delayed and finally crippled its release and distribution.

In *Salt of the Earth*, Biberman tells the true story of a strike that had been conducted against New Jersey Zinc in Bayard, New Mexico, by Local 890 of the Mine, Mill and Smelter Workers Union, a militant union that had been expelled from the Congress of Industrial Organizations (CIO) for alleged communist influence. *New York Times* film critic Bosley Crowther described it as

> . . . a strong pro-labor film with a particularly sympathetic interest in the Mexican-Americans with whom it deals. True, it frankly implies that the mine operators have taken advantage of the Mexican-born or descended laborers, have forced a "speed up" in their mining techniques and given them less respectable homes than provided the so-called "Anglo" laborers. It slaps at brutal police tactics in dealing with the strikers and it gets in some rough, sarcastic digs at the attitude of "the bosses" and the working of the Taft-Hartley Law.[12]

Crowther's attitude here reflects that of the mainstream studio establishment. Not only does his opening remark imply that pro-labor films are inherently not strong cinematically, but his next sentence, beginning with the qualifying "True," suggests that there is something wrong with the catalog of abuses the film presents. Finally, Crowther turns his sympathy away from the film by mentioning that it "gets in some rough, sarcastic digs" at the employers and federal labor law. Considering the rugged treatment the film, its cast, and directors received at the time, it is ironic that Crowther should have faulted the *film* for roughness.

One of the few clearly pro-labor films ever made, *Salt of the Earth* has to this day been seen by few Americans. Most of the film production unions, trying to be ultrapatriotic through this period, were led by Roy Brewer, then president of the stage employees union, who organized an effort to keep union labor from working on the film. And on the floor of Congress, Representative Donald Jackson of California attacked the film, while it was being filmed on location, as a "new weapon for Russia . . . deliberately designed to inflame racial hatreds and to depict the United States as the enemy of all colored peoples."[13] In many respects, therefore, the filming of this movie was as heroic a struggle as the strike it depicted. After its abbreviated release in 1954, the film was suppressed for over ten years.

In stark contrast to the suppression of Biberman's *Salt of the Earth*, the Kazan-Schulberg production of *On the Waterfront* has enjoyed wide release and frequent broadcast on network and cable television.

Originally a conception of Kazan and Arthur Miller, the idea for the film changed drastically after Kazan's cooperation with HUAC. Miller was incensed and went off to compose his play *The Crucible*. Kazan then teamed up with fellow HUAC witness Budd Schulberg to answer in cinema the charge of witch-hunting that Miller accused them of theatrically in *The Crucible*.

On the Waterfront tells the story of a young longshoreman named Terry Malloy (played by Marlon Brando), who begins as an ignorant dupe for a corrupt gang that controls the local union. When he falls in love with the beautiful Edie (played by Eva Marie Saint), he is slowly persuaded by her and the local Catholic priest to testify before the Waterfront Crime Commission against the corrupt leaders of the union: a variation on *Black Fury* with the addition of the mob-control theme.

It is no accident that the film revolves around testimony presented before a congressional committee. Certainly Kazan's and Schulberg's own experiences before HUAC formed the model for Terry Malloy's brave betrayal. It could be argued that the longshoremen and the priest are not anti-union, for they only want to clean the union up and give it back to the longshoremen. But the fact remains that the one film that portrayed a clean, worker-inspired union, *Salt of the Earth*, was viciously attacked, while a film that chose to look at the seamy side of the labor movement was given awards and the widest possible release.

Over the years, *On the Waterfront* would be copied and imitated with different places, names, and industries but always emphasizing union corruption, as if it were a new idea and as if the problem were endemic. The theme can even be found in popular comedy routines. A Bud Abbott and Lou Costello routine in which Abbott tells Costello he is "loafing" because he got a job at a bakery makes a joke out of the idea that Abbott would need a union card to "loaf."

In the same vein was the Columbia film *Inside Detroit* with Pat O'Brien and Dennis O'Keefe, released in January 1956, in which the mob tries to take over a local of the United Auto Workers. In true Hollywood style, *Inside Detroit* melodramatically describes the efforts of the union president (Dennis O'Keefe) to thwart the mobster's takeover by winning over the mobster's pretty daughter and his jaded moll. Though the union is ultimately successful in resisting the mob, the specter of criminal influence and association remains to haunt the auto industry's union movement just as it is hinted that the docks were only temporarily purged in *On the Waterfront*. This film also depicts the terroristic use of a bomb, reminiscent of the dynamite plot first seen in *Black Fury*, where Joe Radek threatens to blow up the mine and himself in a last-ditch gesture. Musmanno used the dynamite plot, no doubt, as a historical allusion to the Chicago Haymarket riot of 1886. But in *Inside Detroit* it is turned into the sinister and violently disruptive weapon of choice suggesting mob infiltration. The bomb plot soon becomes a Hollywood cliché of union portrayals.

Two more obvious heirs to *On the Waterfront* were the 1957 films *Edge of the City* and *Slaughter on Tenth Avenue*. In the MGM production, *Edge of the City*, whose title reveals the debt to Kazan and Schulberg, director Martin Ritt created virtually the same plot as in *On the Waterfront* with the added dimension of racial tension between a black and a white longshoreman, portrayed by Sidney Poitier and John Cassavetes. More typical of the *Waterfront* stereotype is Arnold Laven's depiction of labor "racketeers" in *Slaughter on Tenth Avenue*. Like *Inside Detroit*, the plot is set around a battle between a corrupt union leader and the honest but outgunned stevedores who want to take their union back. Richard Egan plays a green deputy prosecutor whose father was a union miner who "knew how to take care of goons like that." The scene at the end in which Egan joins the fistfight between the striking dockworkers is so derivative of *On the Waterfront* that the well-dressed union tough (Walter Matthau) even gets tossed in the drink.

Also in 1957, Columbia released Harry Kleiner's production of *The Garment Jungle*. Starring Lee J. Cobb as a militantly nonunion garment manufacturer, this film depicts the brutal beating and murder of a fiery union organizer. As sympathetic as that scenario seems, like *On the Waterfront* the film focuses on the mob's infiltration of the industry, and like the 1930s film *Racket Busters*, it is sympathetic to the martyred unionists but leaves the impression that these heroes are the exceptions and the mob represents the rule.

Yet another 1957 film, *The Pajama Game*, though avoiding the popular corruption theme, so subordinates the labor-management plot that it trivializes the workers' grievances. Based on the play, *7½ Cents*, originally produced by the International Ladies' Garment Workers' Union (ILGWU), *The Pajama Game* stars Doris Day as a union steward in a pajama factory. But in the screen version the sympathy is with the manager. The average filmgoer was likely to see the union more as a nuisance than as an advocate of oppressed workers, as was evident in the review of the *New York Times* critic, Bosley Crowther, who summarized the plot thus: "The new superintendent still has his troubles getting a unionized plant to work and getting Babe, of the grievance committee, to abandon her grievances."[14] No doubt many viewers of this film, like Crowther, came away with the feeling that unions encourage unproductive and unnecessary conflict.

By the end of the decade, the *Waterfront* corruption plot was so entrenched in Hollywood film idiom that Universal could produce a musical comedy about it. *Never Steal Anything Small* (1959) stars James Cagney as a stevedore who extorts money to run for the presidency of the longshoremen's union, merrily singing of his avarice, as the title suggests, and of his delight in subversive machinations.

The film is introduced with a prologue:

> This picture is sympathetically dedicated to labor and its problems in coping with a new and merry type of public enemy, the charming, well-dressed gentleman who cons his way to a union throne, and never needs to blow a safe again.

But the expression of sympathy is dubious in view of the connection it makes between criminality and accepted union activity. Cagney as Jake MacIllaney cheerfully admits that he is a gangster and racketeer, as if such were the expected credentials of a union leader. The underlying assumption of the film is that a union is a criminal syndicate, albeit more benign than the Mafia, but a racket even at its best and that its elections are shams and its funds at the free and easy disposal of the leaders for their personal pleasure and aggrandizement.

As before, the film industry's interest in labor came in spurts through the 1960s. World War II and the resulting boom economy may explain the long hiatus between *Black Fury* and *On the Waterfront*. Similarly, the absence of filmmakers' interest in labor in the 1960s may be explained by the presence of competing national issues.

The primary social issue dominating American liberalism in the 1960s was the battle for civil rights. Largely because of the expanding economy, labor issues were not high on media agendas. Even though the unions were in their busiest and most productive period of organizing, peaking in the early 1970s, their activities were not news or drama because the contract negotiations of the period were, in the main, smoothly and peacefully conducted.

Only as the economy began to bog down did the class consciousness at the heart of labor activism again emerge. In the first of a new series of labor films, director Martin Ritt, whose *Edge of the City* in 1957 had been the last of such films, was—paradoxically—to look back at one of the earliest labor struggles in the country. His 1970 production of *The Molly Maguires*, starring Sean Connery and Richard Harris, recalled the failed efforts of the immigrant Irish coal miners in Pennsylvania a hundred years before. Their struggle to organize was a violent and bloody one in which they engaged in guerrilla warfare with the company's hired goons and Pinkertons.

Although this film might be considered pro-union on its face, it paints such a violent picture of union organizing that most Americans are more likely to see the Maguires as terrorists than to be aware of the theme of betrayal or the inhuman treatment of the miners. Ultimately, the film only reinforces the old message of *On the Waterfront* that organized labor generally means organized violence.

One film that was almost pro-union but stopped short of exploring the issue was Hal Ashby's *Bound for Glory* (1976). The film is based on the autobiography of Woody Guthrie, the great American folk singer and composer of the Depression era, who wrote many of the most beloved union songs during his early years as a union organizer. David Carradine's role is reminiscent of that of the union leader played by John Carradine in *Grapes of Wrath*. But like its famous predecessor, *Bound for Glory* focuses more on the Depression itself than on the role of the union.

Unfortunately, just as Martin Ritt was beginning to develop some sympathy toward the plight of union organizers, two of the most scathing attacks on the labor movement ever filmed came out in 1978: Paul Schrader's *Blue Collar* and Norman Jewison's *F.I.S.T. Blue Collar* stars Richard Pryor, who with Yaphet Kotto and Harvey Keitel, plays a Detroit autoworker scrimping through the hard times of the mid–1970s. Like the 1930s film *Riffraff*, it starts as a breezy comedy. It is about three friends—one white, two black—who decide to rob the local union headquarters but are laughably incompetent. The humor lapses as their friendships are tested by a power play between the union leadership and the investigators from the crime commission. The film ends as another *On the Waterfront*. Yaphet Kotto has been murdered, and Harvey Keitel's character has decided to testify against the union. The movie leaves us with a grim picture of the autoworkers, their union, and the deep division between white and black workers.

A few months later, Jewison's *F.I.S.T.* gave the same basic message: unions are by nature violent and mired in corruption. In some respects, Jewison was trying to do for the Teamsters what Mario Puzzo and Francis Ford Coppola did for the Mafia in *The Godfather* (1972): show the human side of villainy in a nonjudgmental fashion. With Sylvester Stallone starring as the "union boss," and using material freely drawn from the Jimmy Hoffa story and the history of the United Mine Workers of America (UMWA), the film portrays thirty years in the life of the fictitious Federation of Inter-State Truckers, from its feeble beginnings to its emergence as an organization as powerful and corrupt as any of the industries it does business with.

F.I.S.T.'s screenwriters, Joe Eszterhas and Sylvester Stallone, tried to portray the main character sympathetically. The first half of the film shows the union's fierce struggle to survive and clearly demonstrates that the violence and criminality were started by the employers. It then puts the union organizer into the dilemma of losing the strike or working with the mob. After Stallone's character makes that hard choice, the dark consequences follow. One could view the movie as a lesson in the importance of ensuring labor's protection from harassment by employers so its leaders would not need to turn to the mob, but most viewers would get the same impression that was conveyed in *Blue Collar* and *On the Waterfront*—that there is no real difference between organized labor and organized crime.

On the Waterfront took on the International Longshoremen's Association, *Blue Collar* attacked the United Auto Workers, and *F.I.S.T.* went after the Teamsters. These were the principal non-AFL-CIO unions that had seen the greatest growth and therefore developed the most effective bargaining power in America since the 1930s.

Exceptions Taken

Finally, in 1979 Martin Ritt, at the age of sixty-five, directed a story about a union's efforts to organize workers in a small southern town that was dominated by and dependent on a cotton mill. Based on the true story of Crystal Lee Jordan, who struggled to organize the workers at a J. P. Stevens mill, this film is refreshingly devoid of the corrupt or power-mad labor "bosses," the workers who are ignorant dupes satisfying their need for recognition, and the intrepid investigators from the crime commission that had come to be clichés of labor movies over the past twenty-five years.

Instead, *Norma Rae* describes the personal commitment involved in union organizing. The two main characters, Sally Field in the title role and Ron Leibman as Reuben Marshasky, the young organizer sent from the international, struggle with the company and with their own mutual attraction. Though he's the pro, a glib, fast-talking Jew from New York, he is powerless to help the workers without Norma's local respect and identity. Sadly, *Norma Rae* stands nearly alone (except for the renegade *Salt of the Earth*) as Hollywood's token pro-labor film.

In the 1980s, one film picked up where *Norma Rae* left off. Mike Nichols's *Silkwood* (1983), like *Norma Rae*, featured a heroic woman struggling to assert her rights against a powerful industry. Starring Meryl Streep as Karen Silkwood, the film follows her career and personal life from the time when, working at a plutonium plant, she grows suspicious of policies and practices that may be cutting corners dangerously. On the sly, she snoops through company files looking for evidence. Publicly she joins the labor front, lobbying for safeguards. In the end, she meets with a suspicious accident, which points to the probable guilt of her employers.

But *Silkwood* is not so much about the protagonist's union activity as it is about her fears (and those of the audience) of the inherent dangers of nuclear energy. The film even suggests that Karen Silkwood was being used by the union officials, then left to the mercies of her employers. The union becomes just one more problem she has to deal with in her attempt to hold the company accountable for the health and safety of herself and her friends. A similar situation was depicted in the 1983 made-for-television movie *Kentucky Woman* starring Cheryl Ladd. The title character is the first female miner to gain some acceptance in the Appalachian coal mines but is unjustly fired when she tries to prevent a dangerous mine explosion. The union refuses to process her grievance until the catastrophic explosion she predicted proves she is right. The union depicted is not corrupt or inherently bad, but it reflects the chauvinism of the men who dominate it.

Nearly all the movies with pro-union sentiments follow this pattern. Commonly they deal with helpless workers who lack the power to demand the justice they seek; but these three exceptions feature women, who traditionally are stereotyped as helpless and powerless. A union of women is not seen as the threat to national or economic security that any union of men might be. Even in their rare efforts to favor unionized workers, filmmakers fall back on and therefore reinforce classic sexual stereotypes and do not challenge the fundamental portrayal of organized labor that has dominated the screen since *Black Fury*.

When unions of men are depicted, even in the 1980s, the theme is either the corruption or irrelevance of unions. In 1982, for instance, a made-for-television adaptation of Mark Twain's irreverent *Mysterious Stranger* deleted Twain's attack on religion (the paramount theme of his classic novella) and focused on a heavenly crusade led by an angel of God against the medieval guild that was about to go on an apparently foolish strike against a benevolent employer. Similarly, Ron Howard's *Gung Ho* (1986) glorifies the industrious autoworker, played by Michael Keaton, who leads his fellow workers to shed their union representation and work till they drop for their new and benevolent Japanese employers.

Trivialized and Traduced

As influential as films like *On the Waterfront, Blue Collar*, and *F.I.S.T.* have been in portraying the American union movement as corrupt and violent, greater impact by far has been made by the much larger number of films that, though not primarily about labor or unions, contain passing or peripheral references to unions or unionization.

In the early 1980s, for instance, the popular film *My Favorite Year* (1982) jokes about a corrupt "labor boss" whom the entire cast gallantly battles in the stirring conclusion. In *The River* (1984), Mel Gibson and Sissy Spacek, as the young farmers Tom and Mae Garvey, are beset with a series of tragic catastrophes. So Tom—without a second thought—becomes a scab laborer at a steel mill to pay off his debts.

Over and over again the heroes of movies are set against the unions they encounter. In *Teachers* (1984) Nick Nolte, as Alex Jurel, a popular public high school social studies teacher, tries to help his students despite the workings of a deeply entrenched "system." The steward of the teachers' union is portrayed as petty and out of touch, trying to make a big issue out of the union's negotiations for an extra three minutes off their starting time. In the end, when Alex is being fired on false charges, the steward—Larry Malloy (an echo of *On the Waterfront*'s Terry Malloy)—makes a deal with the school superintendent, trading Alex's job for the three minutes. In 1986 Columbia's comedy *Armed and Dangerous* had John Candy and Eugene Levy playing new security guards who rankle at being forced to join the International Alliance of Special Police and Guards, a corrupt union controlled by the mob. Not only are they forced to join the union, but when they try to file a grievance at the union meeting, their legitimate complaint is unfairly dismissed and the union president, a thieving mob boss, threatens to break their legs if they ever show their faces at another union meeting, whereupon they are reassigned to guard a toxic waste dump.

The portrayal of unions in these movies is unrelentingly negative. Whether this is purposeful or an outcome of an inherent institutional bias may never be known. Directors and producers are themselves, after all, employers or managers of union labor. Union bashing has become a cinematic cliché. Writers seem to go out of their way to include insulting remarks. Danny DeVito, directing and starring in his 1984 made-for-cable movie *The Ratings Game*, takes a swipe at unions in a scene of small talk on his first date with Rhea Perlman. In the movie *Innerspace* (1987), the major villain, who is a trader in stolen corporate technology, is made to appear more villainous by the addition to his résumé of the information that he is the administrator of the Teamsters' pension fund.

Another example of the sideswipe at labor in an otherwise unrelated production appears near the end of the film *Blazing Saddles* (1974), when the erratic Governor Lepetomane, played by Mel Brooks, asks if he can fire a man and is told he cannot because of "Local 32." He curses, "Damn unions!" and then has to stop the reporters from writing down the epithet, saying, "Are you crazy! I'll lose the blue-collar vote!" Certainly the politician's hypocrisy is the primary target of Brooks's barb, but underlying that obvious joke are the presumptions that unions protect bad workers and that union labor is unproductive.

There is another sideswipe in Twentieth Century-Fox's *Mannequin* (1987). Like the swipe in *Blazing Saddles*, the inference is made that unions protect bad workers. Here the fumbling store security guard Felix (G. W. Bailey) boldly threatens to call "the union" after being summarily fired. He is promptly reminded that there is no union representing him. Sympathy being against him is also subtly against unions or the possibility that a union would protect someone as egregiously incompetent as he is. The audience is made to breathe a collective sigh of relief that there is no union to defend his villainy.

Even the film *Breaking Away* (1979), which takes a much more sober look at the condition of working-class Americans, takes its swipe at unions. Ken Margolies observed that the scene outside the Indiana quarry in which two old-timers watch a man drive up in a Cadillac and comment, "It must be a safety inspector . . . or a union Organizer," uses the image of the corrupt union organizer to get a bitter laugh.[15]

Sideswipes at unions are most obvious in modern gangster movies such as Francis Ford Coppola's *The Godfather* (1972). Robert Duvall plays the mob counsel who attempts to extort a Hollywood producer with the veiled threat of instigating a dispute by his union workers. A few years later a series of films about Al Capone expanded the charge. Ben Gazarra, playing the lead in the 1975 *Capone* (Twentieth Century-Fox), brags to his lieutenants that he is going to infiltrate and take over "the unions." The same year, Tony Curtis depicted gangster Louis Buchalter in the film *Lepke* (Warner Brothers), which depicts unions in the 1920s extorting protection money from a poor garment manufacturer who is brutally murdered in the bargain. Similarly, and with even more detail, the new breed of made-for-television feature-length films seem to go out of their way to attack unions. In 1988, an ABC Sunday night movie, *Frank Nitti: The Enforcer*, portrays Capone's successor in the 1930s muscling in on "the stage-hands union," controlling its president, George Brown, and using him to extort payoffs from theater owners. Similar control is intimated over "the bartenders union." A year later Ray Sharkey, as Capone in *The Revenge of Al Capone* (1989), gleefully lists "the Milkman's Union" and "the Hod Carriers Union" (Laborers International) as being in his pocket.

In these scripts, "the union" is often controlled by the mobster-stars, rather than by a local, creating the impression that the entire national or international union is corrupt. All but one of the above-mentioned films were about a Northside Chicago mob, and whatever control the Capone gang may have had over the early unions, it could hardly have been more extensive than that city's local, but such a clarification is not considered necessary by the film writers.

But the real problem with Hollywood's portrayal of unions is its blatant inaccuracy. Most unions, particularly the well-established ones, are shown as being connected in some way to organized crime. In fact, a 1982 presidential commission on organized crime found that fewer than four hundred of the country's seventy thousand locals, less than 1 percent, had been suspected of such influence.[16] There is likely a parallel if not considerably higher incidence of crooked bankers, lawyers, doctors, and politicians as well. Yet no media portrayals of these professions would ever suggest endemic corruption.

Ron Howard's production of *Gung Ho*, in which Japanese carmakers are invited by the American workers in a small Pennsylvania town to reopen their auto plant and put them back to work, is based on the notion that the Japanese are successful because their workers are not unionized. According to statistics from the Japanese government, however, nearly 30 percent of the Japanese work force is organized, whereas that is true of less than 17 percent of American workers.[17]

In the late 1980s, filmmakers began to examine the excesses of corporate America and, as a result, somewhat relaxed their former bias against organized labor. On the one hand *Robocop* and *Robocop 2* lionized corporate America's creation of a high-tech scab, designed specifically to break the impending police union strike, yet some scenes suggest a strange sense of solidarity between the cyborg and his fellow officers. Still, the gruff but highly admired duty sergeant reminds the officers in the first *Robocop*, "We're not plumbers. Police officers don't strike!"

John Sayles's epic film *Matewan* and Oliver Stone's *Wall Street*, also released in 1987, both describe the villainy of corporate America when opposed by unions. In the former, Sayles pits an old-time pacifist, Wobbly organizer against a West Virginia coal company. The company fails to break the strike by bringing in blacks from the South and Italian immigrants from the East, and a full-scale war erupts when it finally sends its own private army in to quell the miners' uprising. As positive as *Matewan* is toward labor (and it was based closely on historic data) its ending in a gruesome shoot-out tends to reinforce the stereotypical image of labor violence as a part of union disputes. Furthermore, like *Salt of the Earth, Matewan* suffered very poor distribution. In Hawaii, for example, the film was shown for one week at the theater next to the state university, even though it showed to overflow crowds on the same premises as part of the famed East-West Center Film Festival. Whether the poor distribution of this high-quality pro-labor film was the result of deliberate suppression or the independent nature of Sayles's production, it was never accorded the access to American audiences enjoyed by the many other studio films that were much less flattering to unionization.

Fifty years after the character Jedidiah Leland first explained Hollywood's bias against unions, that bias is still prevalent in cinematic portrayals of the labor movement. In June 1991 American Playhouse aired a made-for-television bio-drama of the life of Clarence Darrow. Dorothy Rabinowitz, reviewing it for the *Wall Street Journal*, captures one aspect of its presentation of unions: "It is a remarkable visit back to the time when workers were at the utter mercy of management, when nine-year-olds labored in mines for 14 hours, when every right-thinking heart beat for the strikers and the unions stood for justice. The way things used to be."[18] One is not sure whether the writer is nostalgic for workers at the mercy of management or unions standing for justice. In any event, she misses the final scenes of the film, when Eugene Debs and the Industrial Workers of the World (IWW) leaders Darrow had defended appear to turn their backs on him in his hour of need. Again the theme is that once it has power labor is corrupt and unworthy.

Surprisingly, the most outstanding exception to the average cinematic portrayal of unions is the film *Wall Street*. Bearing an uncanny resemblance to the real life drama of Eastern Airlines and the International Association of Machinists, this film takes a much more realistic and, therefore, atypical view of unions. The machinists' union of a small airline that has been made the pawn in a stock war between two investors is small, like the majority of American unions. Instead of "big labor" pushing the workers around, we see "big Wall Street insiders" playing with people's lives and jobs as if they were so much pork belly on the commodities exchange. The three union negotiators are sincerely, even desperately, trying to save their members' jobs. In all, the film is a refreshing change from the ordinary treatment organized labor has come to expect at the hands of the moviemakers.

Jeremiah McGuire noted in his *Cinema and Value Philosophy* that

> . . . the film—as an arena of persuasion and felt-value experience, plus value ascription—is uniquely persuasive, primarily because of its ability to create an aura of impressions that easily create felt-value responses, plus the cinema's dependency in all its forms upon some type of value ascription for the film ever to be made. . . . They do not supply the audience with thoughts, as novels have always done; rather, they present man's conduct or behavior.[19]

As any union organizer knows, people's values are shaped mostly by experience and emotion and only a little by logical thought. For this reason, the portrayal of unions in the media, particularly in movies, plays a major role in shaping the attitudes of Americans toward labor unions. With few exceptions, that portrayal has been both unrepresentative and virulently negative.

2. Television News
Anchors Aweigh

In any age, information is power. And in this age, those who shape the electronic media will determine the character of our thought, the texture of our society, and the quality of our lives for years to come.
—Edwin Newman, *On Television*

Television is presumed to offer a more objective and unbiased approach to controversial or partisan topics than the other popular media. Unlike other media, radio and television are federally regulated and statutorily expected to honor a "public trust." Newspapers and films have been much freer to express their producers' opinions, whereas television and radio are expected to refrain from selling anything but consumer goods in clearly defined commercial segments. The rest of their programming should entertain comfortably and inform objectively.

When partisanship and controversy are permitted expression, the Federal Communications Commission, until 1987, required broadcasters to provide equal access to opposing viewpoints. Equal access, however, applied only to the most overt expressions of opinion and only to specific representatives of clearly defined and outspoken interest groups. Values and opinions expressed incidentally as part of noneditorial news or entertainment programs, being much harder to identify, generally escaped fair access regulation.

Television programming thus carries enormous potential for implanting and enforcing stereotypes and ideological agendas. Persuasion in a form and structure that viewers are prepared for can be met fairly and filtered through their conscious defenses. Persuasion cloaked in entertainment or news broadcasts enjoys a much greater potential for success.

Though television as a mass medium of communication and entertainment has been of major significance since the 1950s throughout the United States, its portrayal of labor did not come under scrutiny until the mid–1970s. Perhaps the best reason for labor's lack of attention to its broadcast coverage was expressed in Leila Sussman's concluding remarks to her 1945 study "Labor in the Radio News." After finding a marked bias against organized labor in radio reports, she predicted that "the presentation of labor in such an unfavorable way in the radio news can have two effects. It can foster an anti-labor psychology in the listening audience; and it can create a feeling in the ranks of labor that they simply do not have a chance for a fair hearing in the channels of mass communication."[1]

For these reasons, and probably also because labor did not generally distinguish broadcast media from the print media, in which it was accustomed to even more blatant bias, the labor movement ignored radio and television treatment until the 1970s. Then attention was primarily directed at television news reporting, with little consideration of labor's portrayal in televised entertainment programming. Both TV news and its dramatic series, however, regularly refer to organized labor or describe it to such an extent that each must be studied and critiqued separately.

Studies of Television Coverage of Labor

In 1975 a British team conducted the first detailed analysis of the television portrayal of labor in Great Britain. The Glasgow University Media Group was an eight-person research team, mostly sociologists, funded by Britain's Social Science Research Council and based at the University of Glasgow. John Eldridge, professor of sociology, was its senior member, though Greg Philo became the group's most active public spokesperson. The group's initial analysis of the way television reported on labor in the first five months of 1975 led to a series of studies that demonstrated that the television portrayal of trade unions was colored by the networks. Typically unions were blamed for national industrial and economic problems despite ample evidence to the contrary which was either ignored, smothered, or perverted.[2]

The Glasgow Group also found that television news consistently failed to provide viewers with the most basic and elementary information about labor disputes. The unions involved in disputes were often not identified; routine facts as to whether the disputes were official were not given; little or no effort was made to clarify the issues involved in the disputes; and the workers' view of a dispute was rarely if ever portrayed.[3]

As in Great Britain, American TV newscasters may be less likely to use overtly prejudicial labels in covering their stories than the other news media. With the notable exception of the 1988 episode of *The*

Reporters (Fox) entitled "Dying Teamster Boss," newscasters rarely express their personal views forthrightly. Instead, as seen in the Glasgow studies, labor is more likely to be the victim of what Cirino described as "bias through omission of news" and "the hidden editorial."[4]

A good example of these tactics was described by Klaus Bruhn Jensen in his detailed analysis of one week of American network news in September 1981. Of the eleven national stories he followed that week, one was the Solidarity March in Washington, D.C., organized by the AFL-CIO, and the other was a story about some North Carolina workers' attempt to attract industry to their area. Jensen discovered that coverage of the Solidarity March tended to "neutralize the protest." He quotes the following CBS summation of the Solidarity March as indicative: "If size and sound are the measures of success, the AFL-CIO can say tonight that it does represent the hearts and minds of American workers, and that with careful organization it may be able to re-cement the old Democratic civil rights–labor coalition into a strong anti-Reagan force." As Jensen notes, this report focuses strictly on labor as a political force, omitting any social or economic significance of the march. That omission, he remarks, is followed by an even greater one: "It is perhaps symptomatic of the news ideology that what is labeled 'the loudest, most organized opposition to Reagan's economic policies to date' is not covered again during the following week."[5] The quote also reveals a "hidden editorial" in the phrase "if size and sound are the measures of success." Whether or not the audience recognized the allusion to the Shakespearean tale of an idiot, "full of sound and fury, signifying nothing," common sense would tell almost anyone that "size and sound" are not valid measures of success. Finally, the quote implies that the network's interest in labor may be limited to the extent to which it is connected to the civil rights movement, a more clearly defined item on the liberal agenda.

Herbert Gans found that almost half of the television stories in the category of "protestors and rioters" in 1967 were about strikers. Gans also noted the basic reverence television journalists bear for our economic system. "Strikes," he found, "are frequently judged negatively, especially if they inconvenience 'the public,' contribute to inflation, or involve violence."[6]

Thirteen years later, the International Association of Machinists (IAM) conducted a similar national survey of news coverage that revealed little change. Their first study, which covered news reports and was aired in February 1980, concluded that corporate viewpoints rather than those of workers or unions were favored on all three networks: CBS by three to one, NBC by five to one, and ABC by as much as

Table 2.1. Percentage of total union coverage given to different subjects

	CBS	ABC	NBC
Strikes	26	31	25
Negotiations	16	17	24
Other	16	15	18
Meetings/Speeches	13	7	8
Political support	9	11	11
Crime	9	5	8
Individual members	6	2	3
Community service	6	2	3

Source: Jerry Rollings, "Mass Communications and the American Worker," in *Labor, the Working Class, and the Media*, eds. Vincent Mosco and Janet Wasko (Norwood, N.J.: Ablex Publishing, 1983), 144.

seven to one.[7] But the most dramatic finding of the Machinists' study was revealed in the pattern they observed of network reports on various union news subjects (see table 2.1).

Bias in Television News Programming

Though annual data from the Bureau of Labor Statistics consistently reveal a strike-incidence rate per contract negotiation of less than 2 percent, the media attention has just as consistently weighted its union news reports on strike coverage to suggest that strikes are a union's primary and ordinary activity and that negotiations are normally rather than exceptionally followed by strikes.

This error is perpetuated in a variety of ways. In a fairly typical example of what Cirino referred to as "bias in news images" and "bias in photographic selection," a Honolulu station (KITV, February 5, 1989, 10 P.M.) reported a contract ratification vote for nurses at Wilcox Hospital.[8] Though the contract was settled without a strike, as visual background to its report the station showed footage of nurses on a picket line originally filmed on September 6, 1987, two years earlier, instead of a current film of the negotiators actually hammering out a settlement at the bargaining table. Even though the footage was identified and accurately dated, it inaccurately implied that the current contract was also the result of a strike and reinforced the misconception that strikes are common.

Nor is this phenomenon observable only at the local level. According to the *CBS News Index* for 1986, that network broadcast 40 stories throughout the year on union contracts and 184 stories about strikes.[9]

Conversely, the scant attention paid to union community service projects (bias by omission) not only fails to encourage further union service, but encourages the general impression created by the focus on strikes that unions are public nuisances. In June 1988, for instance, the Maritime Trades Department of Honolulu's Port Council offered a special scholarship to a local boy scout, funding his travel and tuition for a two-week course in seamanship at the Lundeburg School in Piney Point, Maryland. Though all the media were alerted and invited to the presentation luncheon hosted by the Maritime unions, not one reporter accepted the invitation or covered the story.[10]

When a union's community service project is too large to ignore, the credit is often shifted to the employer. In May 1991 the National Association of Letter Carriers locals in Phoenix, Arizona, organized a food drive that became so popular that other locals in sixteen different cities throughout Arizona joined the campaign, and twenty-five tons of food were collected. Local television stations that reported on the collections never used the word *union* in describing the drive and spoke only of participating post offices and the carriers who were collecting the food. John Schwander, the lead union organizer of the drive, was interviewed but identified only as a Postal Service employee, as if the program had been organized and run by the Postal Service instead of the Letter Carriers union.

An example of what Cirino called "bias through placement" in broadcast media was seen in Honolulu (KITV, October 14, 1986, 6 P.M.), when the local station was covering the first day of a strike by housekeepers, clerical and maintenance workers, and licensed practical nurses at Kaiser Hospital.[11] Generally, on the first day of picketing in a strike the employees are in high spirits and unusually jubilant, mostly because the protracted period of unsuccessful negotiations has finally stopped and a considerable amount of stress and anxiety has been released in unambiguous, clear action. As a result, first-day pickets, with no prior experience to guide them, tend to be loud and joyful, with an almost picnic-like atmosphere that settles in to a more determined stance after a week or so.[12] The news report broadcast by KITV after the first day of picketing first featured the jubilant pickets dancing and singing on the line in front of the hospital, then switched to the reporter inside the hospital interviewing an elderly and infirm patient about the effect of the strikers' absence on their medical care. No additional commentary was needed in condemnation of the strike. And, as usual, no coverage was allotted to the workers' grievances that prompted the strike.

But probably the most common technique used against labor is what Cirino called "bias in the source of news."[13] An example is the following report in Honolulu (KHON-NBC, November 15, 1988, 10 P.M.):

JOE MOORE, news anchor: The state's public workers have high expectations for next year and the price could be high. Bruce Voss reports.

BRUCE VOSS, news reporter: The four-week-old strike at Molokai's Kaluakoi Resort is one of four walkouts that have marred an otherwise quiet year on the labor front. Employers' most costly battleground was at the hospitals where contracts covering registered nurses were reopened and substantially sweetened to attract more nurses. Elsewhere employers are warily watching wages creep up.

AL FRAGA, president of the Hawaii Employers' Council: Without the health care settlements the average wage the council negotiated this year is 4 percent, the first time since 1982 that settlements surpassed 3.5 percent.

VOSS: In his annual state of labor speech Hawaii Employers' Council president Al Fraga said that 1989 will be another light year for negotiations although there could be some tough contract talks at the bus company, newspapers, TV stations, supermarkets, and auto dealers.

FRAGA: We believe, however, that wage increases will remain below the inflation level.

VOSS: But the wild card private employers fear is next year's reopening of contracts covering some 45,000 employees in six state and county public workers' unions. In 1987, most settled for wage increases totaling 12 percent. With the state's economy booming and tax collections up, several public union negotiators have indicated that they'll be pushing for even higher wage increases next year.

FRAGA: Obviously the level of public sector settlements raises expectations of private employees. The politics of public sector bargaining must be balanced with economic realities in fairness to the taxpayers who foot the bill.

This report from start to finish was by, for, and to the state's employers. At no point was an attempt made to give the workers' perspective. From the opening remark of the reporter that "employers are warily watching wages creep up" it is clear that the reporter's sympathy is exclusively with the plight of the businesses and that wage increases are threatening to them. An employer who agreed to give wage increases to health care workers was described as "sweetening" the deal, while the union role was ignored.

But the real purpose of the report was clearly to prepare the public to oppose wage increases for state and county workers, despite the well-publicized surplus of state tax revenues. That the Employers' Council would take such a stand is understandable, but for the television reporters to accept and propagate the same agenda means that the local channel had taken an anti-labor, anti-union position in the upcoming bargaining.

These examples are not unusual—or extraordinarily offensive. They represent business as usual in local coverage of labor news. But it is not just in local news reporting that such a systematic bias is found.

Michael Robinson and Maura Clancey found in a 1985 study of network news for the Media Analysis Project at George Washington University that the liberalism of the "media elites" so adamantly decried by the Lichters and Rothman in the 1970s was not apparent fifteen years later. Their conclusion was rather that "network newsfolk may talk liberal, but that reflects an easy-listening liberalism that's far less leftist than surveys indicate."[14] Nowhere is this more apparent than in the network coverage of labor.

Yet another measure of network attention reveals the dominance of CBS in news and documentary programs featuring organized labor. A review of the programs described in Daniel Einstein's guide to network news and documentaries reveals that a total of thirty-six news specials on labor were broadcast on American television from the 1950s through the 1970s (see Appendix C). Of that number, eighteen were aired on CBS, ten on NBC, and eight on ABC. One-quarter of the programs in Einstein's guide that had to do with labor were on and about the Teamsters and their leaders, either Dave Beck or Jimmy Hoffa. Indeed, as Roberta Lynch observed in her article on media distortion, the Teamsters' notoriety "is such that for many people in this country the Teamsters Union is the labor movement."[15]

Even considering only CBS, which of the three networks is the most generous to labor as measured by the Machinists' survey as well as my analysis of Einstein's guide, the same patterns described in Britain by the Glasgow Group emerge in American television treatment of labor themes.

On the *CBS Evening News* for March 1, 1989, on the eve of the Eastern Airlines strike, the theme of corporate sympathy was immediately sounded in the opening remarks, which told of "a strike by the airline's 9,300 machinists, set for midnight Friday, which could ground the financially hobbled carrier forever." The theme is emphasized by the next speaker, Jordan Greene, identified as an airline analyst, who warns: "It's a battle to the end of Eastern. They won't yield, the company won't yield. The union says I'm going to take you and half of America down with me." This analyst is clearly invested by the reporter with the status of expert, but his last remark is a sweeping generalization. Instead of an insightful economic analysis, he gave an exaggerated and blatantly anti-union condemnation. The technique of calling on an "industry expert," whose interests and sympathies by training and personal investment are with the industrial management, is not uncommon. Such reporting is damaging because it conceals its true colors under the cloak of neutrality.

To measure these remarks more fairly, it is necessary to look at the complete report:

PETER VAN SANT, reporter: Eastern is demanding the powerful Machinist Union, which includes the airlines mechanics, accept $150 million in wage and benefit cuts. The Machinists have refused to yield a dime.

CHARLES BRYAN, Machinist Union leader: Our position right now is 100 percent. Absolutely 100 percent we will be striking at midnight Friday.

VAN SANT: Eastern's losses have been staggering, more than half a billion dollars in just the last two years. The airline has responded by shrinking, laying off thousands of employees, and cutting back hundreds of daily flights. Today Eastern employees begin receiving this videotape warning that support of a Machinists' strike could put them all on the unemployment line.

FRANK LORENZO, Texas Air chairman: If the pilots, flight attendants, non-contract employees support the picket line and don't come up or show up for work, Eastern cannot survive.

VAN SANT: The Machinists argue that Lorenzo, chairman of Eastern's parent company, has purposely wrecked Eastern's profits by selling off valuable assets. They claim Eastern wants a strike to destroy the Machinists union.

KAREN CEREMSAK, Eastern spokeswoman: We need a swift resolution to the difficulties to stop the financial hemorrhaging, plain and simple.

DAIL DULAMAGE, travel agent: Has he thought about what he's going to do if they go on strike?

VAN SANT: Travel agencies report that Eastern's problems are scaring away passengers by the thousands.

DULAMAGE: Even if they don't strike they have been tremendously damaged by the possibility of a strike.

VAN SANT: Some Machinists have already begun removing their tools from Eastern's maintenance hangars.

DAVID WACKERLING, Eastern machinist: People are ready to strike, that's all. They've had enough of it.

VAN SANT: Special security guards have been brought in to protect against employee vandalism or sabotage. Eastern says it will try to fly through a strike hiring mechanics with little or no experience.

REP. JAMES OBERSTAR, House Aviation Subcommittee: The FAA has the principal responsibility for assuring that the airlines live up to their obligation to the traveling public to maintain safe airlines, and FAA is going to do that.

VAN SANT: Machinist union leaders said today that if they strike other unions will help them disrupt air, ground, and sea transportation nationwide. But analysts say that the key to a successful Machinists' strike will be if Eastern's pilots honor the picket lines. That decision hasn't been made yet, leaving the airline's future up in the air. Peter Van Sant, CBS News, Atlanta.

DAN RATHER, anchor: Late today, Texas Air chairman Frank Lorenzo offered Eastern pilots a new contract in what's called "job security guarantees" in hopes they will cross Machinists' picket lines should a strike develop.

The report contains 450 words spoken by nine different people in seventeen exchanges. Two, Lorenzo and Ceremsak, are identified as management representatives, and two, Bryan and Wackerling, are union representatives. But this apparent balance hides the underlying bias reflected in the remarks of the reporter and the remaining "neutrals."

Industry analyst Jordan Greene speaks from the employer's perspective, and to a less blatant degree so does Dail Dulamage, the travel agent. Her remark that "they have been tremendously damaged by the possibility of a strike" is focused, as indeed is the whole report, on the economic harm to the employer rather than on the issues of the labor dispute. The viewer's sympathy, therefore, is directed entirely at the victimization of the employer by the union.

In his opening remark, Peter Van Sant labels the union rather than Lorenzo as "powerful," a subtle cue as to who is wrong. And the sentence "The Machinists have refused to yield a dime" leaves no doubt that the reporter believes the union is being unreasonable. Lorenzo's power in this conflict or his refusal to concede is not reported as such. The union's viewpoint is given short shrift by comparison (thirty-one words) and prefaced by the disclaimer "the Machinists argue." No disclaimer is attached to the airline's prediction of "employee vandalism or sabotage." Van Sant's report on the airline's preparation for such an eventuality is couched as an expectation of vandalism and sabotage. The union is thus convicted of a crime not committed, and the theme that the employer is being victimized is reinforced.

The role of the news reporter and anchor in this report cannot be underestimated. As Mark Crispin Miller noted in his analysis of prime-time television, "However trivial his questions, then, the newsman, just by virtue of his looks and placement, always comes across as the heroic representative of a rising generation."[16] By the time Dan Rather "wraps up" the story, saying the airline "hopes they [pilots] will cross the Machinists' picket lines," the average viewer has identified with the same "hopes" that this "powerful" union will be properly humbled.

In all this the union perspective was hardly mentioned and, to the extent that it was, it was portrayed as petty and unreasonable. CBS was not alone in this negative representation. The other network coverage was no better. And yet just a few weeks earlier, the Corporation for Public Broadcasting had produced a careful analysis of the dispute between Lorenzo and the Machinists.[17] Among others, Judy Woodruff on *Frontline* interviewed not just a generic "industry analyst" but Farrell Kupersmith, attorney for the pilots, who had previously represented Lorenzo in Continental's bankruptcy proceedings to void its former union contracts.

Kupersmith, of the firm Touche-Ross & Co., which could hardly be described as a union advocate, spoke with considerable credibility:

> Recognizing that we had been on the other side in the Continental matter, also recognizing that my firm, I would say proudly, is pro-business, we represent corporate America. I don't think we switched sides, 'cause I think we're still on the side of the system. And I think it's in the system's best interest to not allow it to be abused and used as a weapon, which is what we think is happening here at Eastern. It's a very clever corporate raid where the unionized airline is being dismantled for the benefit of the non-unionized carrier and for the interest of the holding company.

The *Frontline* episode described in some detail the ups and downs of the Machinists' relationship with Eastern's previous owners and revealed a pattern of union responsiveness to concessions when the owners made corresponding concessions.

Regrettably, the *Frontline* special, aired only on the Public Broadcasting System, had no effect on the network coverage of the dispute that followed. Although it may be argued that the network news did not have the luxury of time to treat the subject as thoroughly as the PBS special, the comparison is not unreasonable because the Eastern/Machinists conflict was not a sudden crisis that took reporters by surprise. *Frontline* did the story in January because the imminence of that labor-management dispute was apparent months earlier. And even if the networks were caught ill prepared, the comparison fairly shows how readily reporters accept employers' premises and values and how pervasively these attitudes imbue their coverage.

This penchant for the management view is not limited to the networks' harried coverage of fast-breaking stories. As CBS's *60 Minutes* demonstrated in its 1982 segment on the Coors boycott, muckraking, the traditional tool of progressivism, can be turned just as easily to the advantage of big corporations.

In a fifteen-minute report first aired in September 1982, Mike Wallace portrayed Coors Brewery as an all-American company, the victim of an unfair boycott by organized labor and misinformed minorities of Hispanics and homosexuals.[18] The program began with scenes of Burt Reynolds excerpted from the film *Smokey and the Bandit* and the cute alien from *E.T.* and referred to Paul Newman and Gerald Ford as "devotees" of the beer. If those four associations were not enough advertising for the quality of the product, the program included an inspiring account of the founding of the company by the owners' grandfather, a German immigrant, who built the company up from nothing. By contrast, the proponents of the boycott were shown to be homosexuals and labor unionists.

Most significantly, Wallace and the *60 Minutes* writers gave virtually no coverage to the background and issues of the labor dispute that prompted the boycott five years earlier. A subsequent analysis of the segment by a student reporter at Drake Law School revealed that Coors had forced a strike at the brewery not over wages but over its preemployment polygraph (lie detector) testing and its insistence on an open-shop clause, which would have allowed nonunion employees to participate in union benefits without paying dues or service fees.[19]

The issue of polygraph testing was considered in the program, but the company's history of union-busting was dismissed with the words that the workers had voted the union out "by a margin of 2-to-1" in 1978. No attempt was made to explain the importance of the open-shop issue and no mention was made of the fact that the strikers in 1978 were not permitted to vote in the election that expelled the union. Instead, Mike Wallace began his interview with Bill and Joe Coors, after listing some of the charges against them, with the sympathetic and encouraging question: "What lies are they telling, Joe Coors?"[20]

But the most damaging characteristic of Wallace's report was once again bias through omission of news. A. David Sickler, a former employee of Coors and the AFL-CIO boycott coordinator at the time, felt compelled to issue a five-page memo to the boycotters after the program first aired outlining the substantial evidence he had provided Wallace and producer Allan Marayanes that had never made it into the program.

The twenty-three items on Sickler's list included the names of seven former employees who offered to substantiate the boycotters' allegations regarding Coors's labor practices; a list of nine community and coalition leaders involved in the boycott who were willing to explain their allegations of employment discrimination; an unfair labor practice charge upheld by the National Labor Relations Board (NLRB) against the brewery in 1980; and information that the chapter president of the one Hispanic organization, the League of United Latin American Citizens (LULAC), cited on the program as praising Coors's employment practices, was initially hired by Coors in 1975 to change the company's image, and that the local chapter's award to Coors was opposed by the National LULAC.[21]

The coup de grace of the *60 Minutes* report, however, was the sequence filmed at the brewery in which Mike Wallace spoke with what was described as a random selection of employees at their lunch break. According to Wallace, "We wanted to know what Coors employees thought of all the accusations being leveled against their employers. Coors invited its employees to meet with us during their lunch hour, and we were surprised to find that hundreds of them were waiting to tell us a different story from the one we'd been hearing." Indeed, as the cameras revealed, the room was packed, and three different people, a Hispanic man and two women, stood up to praise the company to the unrestrained cheers and applause of the rest. This sequence was clearly the most convincing part of the report, and it is likely that few viewers noticed that each speaker also identified him or herself as a supervisor. As Sickler's memo reveals, it was impossible to tell that the entire assembly was not a random selection of employees, but rather the management and supervisory staff of the brewery assembled by Coors for a party in honor of Wallace and *60 Minutes*, a party which, according to Sickler, the producer, Allan Marayanes, said would not be filmed.[22]

Finally, the most destructive omission in this report was Wallace's failure to consider the positive effect the boycott had on Coors and even the supervisors who testified on Coors's behalf. Such omissions are all too common in news media treatment of labor campaigns. Wallace, for instance, clearly separated the 1977 allegations against the brewery from Coors's current reputation but failed to point out the effect of the boycott in achieving these improvements. The report emphasized the harm the boycott was doing to Coors but did not seem to find the victimization of the workers, particularly the 1977 workers who sacrificed their jobs for improvements in working conditions enjoyed by 1982 workers, relevant.

Similarly, the struggles of labor unions striking to raise their wages and improve working conditions is commonly approached by the media as both selfish in motivation and inflationary in effect. The media routinely fail to consider the positive effects that strikes, boycotts, and even failed organizing campaigns ordinarily have on industry standards that ultimately benefit the nonunion work force as well.

This blind spot reflects a narrowness of focus in ordinary news coverage that is concerned with the immediate at the expense of the long-term interpretation and reveals a class-biased economic perspective favoring the manager and the entrepreneur at the expense of the wage employee. Robert Miraldi, in an insightful study of the evolution of journalistic muckraking, tracked the series of network documentaries and exposés that focused on the plight of this country's migrant farm workers and found a similar pattern of disinterest and flagging sympathy for the victims of the American economic system. In the last of the series he studied, Morton Silverstein's 1980 NBC documentary, "What Harvest for the Reaper?" Miraldi found that "camera crews caught migrants in a job-action in an orchard, but the cameras shifted to the children who took the workers' places and ignored the worker grievances and the larger labor issues. One can only think that the cultural ambivalence toward labor and unions as a threatening form of organization, with their implied threat of strikes and disruptions, has caused the press to avoid the labor relations issue."[23] Unfortunately, as Miraldi observes, this ambivalence results in an avoidance of labor stories sympathetic to unionized workers. News stories about bad aspects of unions or stories that show unions in a negative light receive ample coverage.

The detailed critique of the Coors segment of the *60 Minutes* series would be unfair were it not representative of that program's portrayal of organized labor. According to the summaries in Daniel Einstein's network news guide, the five other *60 Minutes* segments on the labor movement all support the classic anti-union stereotypes. These segments were a report on George Meany and President Nixon, March 19, 1971; "Hoffa," a discussion with Mrs. Jimmy Hoffa and with former Hoffa associates regarding the former Teamster official's disappearance, April 11, 1976; "Unions, Money and Politics," an examination of the influence and power of U.S. labor unions, October 3, 1976; "Target: J. P. Stevens," as Mike Wallace calls it, "the story of big labor versus J. P. Stevens," March 13, 1977; and "Taking on the Teamsters," an examination of efforts to reform the giant union by rank-and-file members, December 3, 1978.[24] Power and corruption are the themes most commonly characterizing the television portrayals of organized labor, and the record of *60 Minutes* as well as the lion's share of overall network news attention has reinforced and propounded these stereotypes. Even when labor's foes are vastly more powerful or corrupt, the media's heavy thumb of denunciation almost always turns labor down.

Harvey Molotch, a sociology professor at the University of California at Santa Barbara, concluded (in a somewhat amusingly phrased metaphor) that "the reporter's 'nose for news' . . . includes as a critical component the sustenance of the ruling class."[25] As unpalatable as that conclusion might be to the news media, it is not unsupported. No less a figure than Walter Cronkite confessed to as much in his own *60 Minutes* interview: "What is objective reporting? . . . Well, we have our prejudices, we all have our biases, we have a structural problem in writing a news story and presenting it on television as to time and length, position in the paper, position on the news broadcast. These things are all going to be affected by our own beliefs; of course they are."[26]

The question seems not to be whether a bias exists but what is the nature of the bias. If the bias is indeed a liberal one, why is organized labor excluded from the liberal agenda? It is no coincidence that a 1989 report prepared by William Hoynes and David Croteau of Boston College revealed that viewpoints of labor leaders, next to "radical/ethnic leaders," were the least likely to be heard or seen on ABC's *Nightline*.[27] Not only did they find that labor representatives appeared only 1 percent of the time, but they also found that when a labor leader was featured, he or she was likely to be allotted a small number of lines as measured in the transcripts. The networks clearly do not consider labor to be representative of the public, as revealed in the Hoynes-Croteau study and in the 1984 and 1988 presidential election campaigns, when labor was regularly labeled a "special interest" outside the majority interests of the country.[28]

3. Television Dramas

Labor Snowed

> I feel we are like a group of people standing at the perimeter of a lake throwing pebbles into the water. The physicists tell us that each pebble makes the level of the water rise. We cannot see the water rising; we cannot hear it or feel it. Yet the physicists tell us that with each pebble that body of water is being affected. To carry the metaphor further, if the pebbles we have been throwing into the lake of social awareness have mattered at all, we don't see it. But we are happy to know that some people do.
> —Norman Lear, *All in the Family: A Critical Appraisal*

As Ralph Arthur Johnson correctly noted in 1981, dramas and situation comedies regularly aired on prime-time network television have an even greater ability to influence viewers' beliefs and values than do news programs or documentaries because they are "integrated less consciously, and thus engender little conscious refutation."[1]

Using the scripts held at the Television Script Archive at the University of Pennsylvania's Annenberg School of Communications in Philadelphia, together with reviews of other published indices of nationally produced prime-time TV dramas and situation comedies (sitcoms), I have surveyed the content of sixty-two televised episodes portraying labor unions or labor-management relations shown in the United States between 1974 and 1989 (see Appendix D). This list may not be definitive, but it is extensive enough to reveal the main themes of this medium's portrayal of labor over the past two decades.

For the most part, it has only been since the early 1970s that television series have dealt openly with labor unions as a possible subject of their plot or subplot development. A review of the plot synopses in Joel Eisner and David Krinsky's guide to TV sitcoms in syndication reveals virtually no presence of labor unions in any of the popular programs of the 1950s or 1960s. *The Life of Riley*, for example, which aired on NBC between October 1949 and August 1958 with 238 episodes syndicated, depicted the blue-collar existence of the character Chester A. Riley, played in the first season by Jackie Gleason and thereafter by William Bendix. Though several episodes were set in the aircraft plant where he and his

Table 3.1. Television dramatic programs dealing with labor relations, 1974–1989

Network	Number	Percent
CBS	29	47
NBC	21	34
ABC	12	19

friend Gillis worked, the plots seemed to go out of their way to avoid a reference to unions. Even in episodes in which he tried to get his pay raised or help a friend who had been fired, where a union would be most likely to be found, the plot synopses imply that the labor-management relationship was nonunion, even though such plants in that decade were largely unionized.[2]

With the possible exception of a lone episode of *The Untouchables*, which showed the mob infiltrating an honest local of a truckers' union, not until the landmark broadcast of the series *All in the Family* starring Carroll O'Connor as the infamous blue-collar bigot Archie Bunker, did network dramas or sitcoms take up questions of labor relations in a dramatic or comedic plot outside the traditional news or documentary framework. But ever since the third season of *All in the Family* and the four episodes that first aired between September 17 and October 5, 1974 (Appendix D, nos. 1–4), the network attention to the labor movement as a plot device for dramatic series has been constant and continuous. We may well wonder whether it is only a coincidence that, according to the statistics of union membership in the United States, 1975 marked the end of a thirty-year golden age of organized labor during which an average of 30 percent of the nation's work force was unionized. After 1975, the union share of the work force began slipping steadily to its current position of close to 17 percent of nonfarm labor.[3] Whether television has contributed to that decline or, as its defenders would no doubt maintain, is a candid reflector of the social forces responsible, may never be known. But a careful analysis of the themes common to television's fictional depictions of the labor movement will provide a guide to this discussion. Of the sixty-two programs considered in this analysis, all were produced for the three major networks and all were aired in prime-time viewing spots, giving them the widest possible audience exposure.

One might expect that these program episodes would be spread by chance evenly over the three major networks, but the networks differ in their attention to labor relations. CBS aired almost half of the episodes, followed by NBC, with ABC a distant third (see table 3.1).

Table 3.2. Overall portrayal of organized labor in surveyed episodes

	1974–1979	1980–1989	Total
Negative	28 (85%)	19 (66%)	47 (76%)
Positive	3 (9%)	6 (20%)	9 (14%)
Neutral	2 (6%)	4 (14%)	6 (10%)

As was true for the networks' news and documentary coverage, this uneven ratio reveals a probable purposefulness in the decision whether to portray labor themes. When the surveyed episodes are classified by season as well as network, over half of the sample (thirty-three) were presented in the first five seasons from the fall of 1974 through the spring of 1979. And ABC's distant third became even more distant in the 1980s, representing only four of its total of twelve in the last ten of the fifteen seasons surveyed. The other two networks reduced their coverage proportionately.

The quantity of coverage must, of course, be considered in relation to its content. In most cases it was relatively easy to determine whether the episode was making a positive or negative statement about the efficacy or general worth of labor unions. I therefore classified each of the surveyed episodes as either positive, negative, or neutral in its portrayal of organized labor and discovered that there was a clear difference between the first five seasons in the 1970s and the following ten seasons in the 1980s (see table 3.2).

In any given period of time, the overall portrayal of labor unions is likely to be negative, but it is interesting that the bias was at its peak at the same time the labor movement was at its peak in power and influence. Two sociological developments during that time period might explain this phenomenon. First, the mid- to late 1970s saw the demise of Jimmy Hoffa, and a considerable amount of other media attention was given to the Teamsters and the long history of federal investigations that had started with Robert Kennedy's probes in the late 1950s. Second, this period also saw the growth of an economic conservatism that, at least in the area of labor relations, appears to have been championed and encouraged by these television portrayals.

Power and Corruption Themes

Over and over again the twin themes of power and corruption characterize the depiction of organized labor in televised dramas. *Serpico* (Appendix D, no. 5), for instance, the first serious treatment of labor outside of the sitcom format since *The Untouchables*, established the most popular formula for depiction of organized labor. Set in Brooklyn, it shows the character John Maloney, a rough but big-hearted Irishman, running for president of his local truckers' union against Jock Powell. As the script instructs, Powell (a subliminal abbreviation of *powerful*) is cast in his "forties, a Jimmy Hoffa type, tough, rough, king of his mountain and not about to be dethroned."[4] The episode opens with the killing of Maloney's campaign worker and close friend Ed Demarest in a car-bomb explosion. Over the years, the car-bomb sequence becomes a TV cliché of labor union activity. No less than seven episodes of the total survey sample, more than 10 percent, depict an election contest that involves a car-bombing murder or attempted murder of the young reform candidate (Appendix D, nos. 5, 11, 21, 25, 27, 29, 56). Such episodes occur in nearly all the sample programs that depict a union election of officers, except for one or two sitcoms in which the union representative is hastily delegated spokesperson, usually against their will or better judgment. The theme that union politics are undemocratic occasions for terrorism and bullying is unrelenting in television depictions and is unfair to the labor movement at large in which the vast majority of union elections are conducted freely and democratically.

Another curious anomaly of the television picture of these union election campaigns is the reform candidate's accusation of "sweetheart deals." As Serpico's Maloney protests, "Do you want to go on putting up with violence and the sweetheart deals that Powell's been negotiating with management for six years?"[5] Similar allegations are voiced in at least three other scripts (Appendix D, nos. 12, 31, 60). A "sweetheart deal" is an older term for what in more recent times have been called— less critically—"concessions." The labor movement has been generally criticized for its power and resulting inflationary impact on the economy, yet the sweetheart deal critique implies that labor leaders have not been vigorous enough in their negotiations. This dichotomy is not usually worked out in the plots except to malign the motives of the existing union leadership. Significantly, for instance, the *Serpico* episode ends with Powell going to jail but Maloney losing the election anyway. Thus it is, as TV would have us believe, that our justice system is vindicated, but unions remain mired in their own institutionalized corruption.

In a 1977 episode of *Quincy* (Appendix D, no. 21) another veiled portrayal of the Hoffa look-alike is used to express the theme of bad union leadership in a form similar to that observed as typical of the feature-length films described in chapter 1. Here the character of Tony Gordon, president of a Philadelphia-based labor brotherhood, tells Quincy: "Well, lemme tell you a couple of things, Doctor. We did bust a few heads. That's how you run a labor union when you're getting started and you got a bunch of company goons to hassle with." The script describes his union hall as "a modern, impressive structure, as befits a labor organization as rich and powerful as the FWA [the rival Farm Workers union] is weak and struggling."[6] Gordon is unflatteringly contrasted to Roberto "Beto" Cruz, the charismatic leader of the fictitious Farm Workers' Alliance, whose honesty and goodness are beyond reproach but who is powerless and pitiable. The popular theme that weak union leaders are good and strong union leaders are bad flies in the face of the equally popular theme of sweetheart deals, but logical consistency seems to have very little to do with the care and feeding of such stereotypes.

Even the supposedly kinder treatment accorded unions in the 1980s subtly reinforces the same themes. A 1989 episode of the drama *Wiseguy* (Appendix D, no. 60) establishes sympathy for a poor local of New York's Chinese garment workers. But instead of blaming the abuse of these workers on the employers, it criticizes their national union leaders for being too weak and complacent and for signing sweetheart contracts.

Strike Portrayals

The most remarkable feature of the dramatic portrayal of labor in network programming is the high incidence of strikes and walkouts. Nearly 70 percent of the sample (forty-two episodes) described strikes, and another five programs depicted threatened strikes. All twelve of the ABC programs in the survey were about strikes. And of the fifteen episodes not about strikes or strike threats, seven were about corruption and infiltration of organized crime into union election campaigns, five more depicted the gulf between rank-and-file workers and their out-of-touch union leaders, and only three (Appendix D, nos. 6, 23, 48) showed the union in a positive light, advocating the legitimate rights of its members.

Although some of the strike depictions showed the union positively, particularly those episodes written shortly after the Hollywood writers' strike (Appendix D, nos. 59, 64), none of the positive depictions appeared in the first five seasons of the sample, and the other three were spread out equally, one on each of the major networks (Appendix D, nos. 34, 39, 51), suggesting tokenism.

The bulk of the television strike portrayals have reflected a negative image of them and a distorted sense of their purpose and frequency in industrial relations and collective bargaining. These dramas control viewers' perceptions in the way they present the point of view of the series' central character. The surveyed episodes can be classified ac-

Table 3.3. Position of main character in surveyed network dramatic programs

	First person	Second person	Third person
All episodes	12 (20%)	28 (45%)	22 (35%)
Strike episodes	11 (26%)	20 (48%)	11 (26%)

cording to the ways the central character might relate to the labor issue of the plot. Either the series' primary star is the laborer (first person) in the situation; is an employer or consumer (second person) directly affected by the issue but not a laborer; or is an outside observer, mediator, or catalyst (third person) not directly or personally affected by the dispute or the labor issue raised by the plot (see table 3.3).

The bulk of the episodes describe the labor issue from the point of view of the employer or consumer, showing a preference for that point of view over that of the first person in which the central character is the worker or laborer. This subtle placement of vantage surely must influence viewers' sympathies. Particularly when the plot depicts a strike or labor dispute, the themes will be influenced by the position of the series' central character.

Ralph Arthur Johnson's 1981 survey of prime-time television characters revealed a heavy weighting toward professional, white-collar, and managerial occupations.[7] No doubt this same class bias accounts for the dominance of the second person or employer in strike depictions. Yet when the occupations of the striking workers in my survey are tabulated, blue-collar occupations outnumber white-collar two to one. Twenty-eight of the forty-two episodes described blue-collar workers on strike, most commonly workers in some sort of plant. Only three of the blue-collar strike episodes described public employees, though half of the white-collar depictions (seven of fourteen) were public workers, either teachers or police officers.

The depiction of primarily blue-collar striking workers when the majority of regular prime-time characters are white-collar is clearly the result of the preference for a second person or employer's point of view. It relates to the larger issue of prevailing media values and reveals the pattern of liberalism most common to television dramatic series which Christopher Lasch first recognized in his study of Norman Lear's *All in the Family*. In the consistently condescending approach that series applied to its blue-collar anti-hero, Archie Bunker, Lasch discerned also a blatant class bias signaling a subtle shift in American liberalism: "*All in the Family* dramatizes experiences central to the formation of a new, liberal, managerial intelligentsia, which has turned on the ethic of ghettoes, developed a cosmopolitan outlook and cosmopolitan tastes through higher education, and now looks back on its origins with a mixture of superiority and sentimental regret."[8]

Indeed, in the popular sequel to *All in the Family* Archie has moved into the white-collar managerial world, where his notoriously blind conservatism is perhaps more consistent if not comfortable when, in one episode (Appendix D, no. 39), he is confronted with a labor movement emerging at his restaurant. Murray, Archie's partner, tries to persuade Archie to accept his employees' unionization, but Archie says, "Would you listen to the liberal here? Murray, don't you know nothin'? Once you start in with the unions, they take over. They're like a bad rash." But what is more interesting is Murray's abrupt change of heart when he hears what unionization may cost. Archie chides him: "Oh, listen to Mr. Big Union Man here. When it comes to spending your own money, you liberals are all the same: you gotta reach into your own pocket to find your heart."[9] This rare media scrutiny of its own pseudo-liberalism, however, had little effect on subsequent portrayals of labor.

A similar confrontation between liberal and conservative attitudes toward labor unions was the subject of a 1976 episode of the sitcom *All's Fair* (Appendix D, no. 9). Conservative Richard Barrington (Richard Crenna) and his liberal girl friend Charley (Bernadette Peters) find a picket line in front of Richard's condominium. While Charley grabs a picket sign and joins the line, saying, "These poor men have every right to better their working conditions by negotiating with their money-grubbing, labor-exploiting employers! The rotten tightwads," Richard argues, "Charley, it's a condominium. I own my own apartment. I'm one of the rotten tightwads." Significantly, Richard is accorded much more time to justify his opposition to the strikers than is Charley. Richard is asked what he has against unions and he answers: "I resent the way labor unions pose as the workingman's friend when actually they're nothing but elite clubs for the organized few. Most people out of work can't even get into a union. And not only that—if you clowns get what you want, the maintenance costs on my apartment will go right through the roof. The whole idea of *my* having to pay more money just because *you* join a union makes my blood boil."[10] No rebuttal or challenge is offered to the wisdom of these remarks, and the question is rendered moot when a hastily reached settlement is achieved and the strike is ended. The ultimate effect, though, is to discredit Charley's traditional liberal support for the laborer, which is portrayed as extremist, lacking deliberation or thoughtfulness, and naive, whereas Richard's anti-union diatribe is portrayed as fair-minded and well-informed.

Nor is this the worst of the TV treatment of labor portrayed in the survey sample. A set of themes, sometimes overlapping, sometimes featured alone, but most frequently unfriendly to organized labor, is readily discernible in the plots of these TV dramas, particularly the episodes depicting strikes. Daniel C. Hallin, media critic at Johns Hopkins University, discovered a "reformist conservatism" typical of television ideology. He notes that "the portrayal of conflict by no means always casts established institutions or authorities in a bad light. A great deal of television's conflict is good-against-evil conflict, evil being located outside the mainstream of society."[11] By this reckoning, it should come as no surprise that in labor-management disputes, labor is most often outside the mainstream.

A persistent theme that establishes the conviction that labor unions are no longer necessary is the portrayal of the collective bargaining process as simplistic or foolish. This theme is the popular sitcom variety of what Parenti observed as the portrayal of labor struggles as senseless, avoidable contests created by unions' unwillingness to negotiate in good faith.[12] It is apparent in a significant number of the television episodes surveyed (Appendix D, nos. 7, 20, 28, 33, 34, 36, 38, 52, 54, 55). For instance, a 1976 episode of *Phyllis* deliberately confused the bargaining between a city and its garbage workers' union with a personal spat Phyllis was having with Dan Valenti, the city official in charge of the mediation. Not only did the episode misrepresent the real role of mediators in such disputes, but it showed the union leader using the negotiations to coerce Dan into resolving his fight with Phyllis, a purpose obviously irrelevant to the issues of the labor dispute. Thus Phyllis's spat and the union contract proposals were assigned equal weight. This theme is also advanced in the abbreviated picture of a purported bargaining session. The script of *Hizzoner* (Appendix D, no. 28), for example, settles a long musicians' strike in a short page of amazingly simplistic dialogue. And an *Eight Is Enough* script (Appendix D, no. 38) settles a bitter strike when Bradford's son Nicholas simply explains to the labor and management negotiators, "If the other guy can't give what you want, then you've got to want something he can give."[13] These cursory portrayals of collective bargaining reduce and trivialize labor relations generally and the union role particularly.

The most derisive characterization of union bargaining was depicted in a 1984 episode of *Silver Spoons* (Appendix D, no. 55). Describing the union leader of the toy factory's employees as "an animal" who "keeps his toupee on with staples," the owner of the factory and star of the show evince only contempt for the union and the need to negotiate.[14] The owner's wife discovers that the union leader, who always wanted his own garden, is willing to accept concessions if he can get his garden, and the strike is settled by paying him off. In an episode of the popular program *Taxi* (Appendix D, no. 36), the union allows the personal degradation of Elaine Nardo (Marilu Henner), the shop steward, when she is forced to date Louis De Palma (Danny DeVito), their boss and a disgusting lecher, to settle a cab driver strike. More recently, in *St. Elsewhere* (Appendix D, no. 54), nurse Helen Rosenthal (Christina Pickles), who fanatically leads a nurses' strike, then a protest against the hospital's new mandatory drug testing policy, becomes a drug abuser and kills a patient in her care. In all of these programs, the theme that union bargaining is flawed, if not downright foolish, is unrelenting.

The depiction of strikes in the television dramas I surveyed definitely affirms Parenti's finding that the media place emphasis on the impact rather than the causes of strikes, laying the blame for them on the union and detailing the damage they do to the economy and the public weal.[15] A common theme running through some of the most popular television dramatic series that focuses on the damage caused by strikes is the conflict between professionalism and union loyalties (Appendix D, nos. 22, 32, 37, 47, 49, 54). Particularly in police, hospital, and teacher dramas there is a common resort to the strike as a plot device to test the characters' personal relationships and professional ethics.

This dramatic conflict between professionalism and union solidarity often pretends to an objectivity that is rarely equitable to the union. All too often the conflict revolves around the decision to respect or cross a picket line. And in almost every case that portrays this theme of professionalism versus solidarity, one or more of the star characters does cross the picket line and scab against the strikers (Appendix D, nos. 10, 19, 22, 32, 37, 38, 47, 49, 54, 58, 59, 61). The message that scabbing is or can be the right, even heroic, thing to do vilifies the striking pickets who must be endured by the scab in pursuit of his or her professional commitment.

In *Maude* (Appendix D, no. 22), for instance, Arthur Harmon, Maude's doctor, after brief attempts to honor the local doctors' strike, comes to his senses and realizes that he cannot resist his normal instincts to heal the sick. He and a fellow doctor laughingly admit at the end of the program that neither could resist seeing patients despite the strike. Even more devastating is the episode of *Chips* (Appendix D, no. 32) in which the series stars ride into a local city to take the place of that city's striking police force. The *Chips* officers not only cross the picket line, they insult and deride the strikers as incompetent fools, a characterization emphasized by the script's directions that the strikers look out of shape physically as well as professionally. By the end of the episode, the scabbing *Chips* team has solved the crime and shamed the striking officers for their lack of professionalism. The theme is particularly devastating because it tends to portray the scabbing worker as deeply involved in a moral dilemma and the striking workers as fanatics whose beliefs are not colored by shades of meaning. In the same episode of *St. Elsewhere* cited above (Appendix D, no. 54), Nurse Helen Rosenthal fanatically leads a nurses' strike against the hospital's kindly, long-suffering administrators Drs. Donald Westphall (Ed Flanders) and Auschlander, while the scabbing nurses are portrayed as caring, selfless professionals. *Bronx Zoo* (Appendix D, no. 58) and *Fame* (Appendix D, no. 47) ran similar series on teachers' strikes. Not unlike the film *Teachers*,[16] in which Nick Nolte stood up heroically as an individual siding neither with the teachers' union nor with the school's administrators, the strikebreaking (scab) teacher in *Bronx Zoo* is admired for his individuality and personal courage while the strikers are portrayed as mindless, uncaring, and selfish. And in *Fame* even the striking teachers find themselves unable to resist the need to work with their students outside of school to help them prepare their various performances.

The theme of professionalism dominates the white-collar strike portrayals, whereas in blue-collar depictions the theme is paternalism (Appendix D, nos. 14, 20, 26, 39, 44). The theme of professionalism emphasizes independence of thought and action, whereas that of paternalism encourages acquiescence and trust in the essential goodness of employers. In the popular series *Hill Street Blues* (Appendix D, nos. 45 and 46) an unusual appeal to these contradictory themes occurs when the police officers are on the verge of a strike. They must weigh their natural "cop instincts" to serve and protect against their union solidarity. And in several other episodes the Hispanic and black officers are drawn into coalitions that are vaguely construed as union subcommittees, protected by their contract. But these caucuses or coalitions are just as divisive as they are assertive of the minority officers' rights. The message is leave it to Captain Furillo. He knows best.

Daniel C. Hallin observed: "As entertainment, television is a consensual medium. It focuses on what people are presumed to share."[17] Unions often represent an institutional threat to that national consensus. An employee strike or slowdown is less threatening to the television image of this national consensus than the recognition of a union. A significant number of the strike depictions in the survey are nonunion strikes (Appendix D, nos. 20, 26, 39, 41, 49), in which no union is formed or recognized throughout the protest. In each case, the employers amazingly (or paternalistically) negotiate with their workers instead of firing them. And in each case the episode ends happily and order is resumed when the negotiations restore the "happy family" quality of the nonunion labor-management relationship.

Evidence of the networks' avoidance of union recognition may be seen, as Cirino posited, in their bias through omission as well.[18] In 1981, for instance, Saracen Productions and Rose and Asseyev Productions in association with Twentieth Century-Fox Television produced a sixty-minute pilot episode for a series based on the popular film *Norma Rae*, which described a bitter union organizing drive in a southern textile mill. As difficult as it may be to conceive of a plot for *Norma Rae* that omits the union themes, the script for that pilot refocused on a custody battle between Norma Rae and her ex-husband and featured the New York union organizer Reuben Marshasky almost as an afterthought, in a minor role supporting Norma Rae before her courtroom ordeal.[19] Yet even with the union themes so drastically reduced, the pilot was never aired.

The "sideswipe," a device described in chapter 1, is as devastating as any overt expression of bias. Like the cinema, television dramas, particularly comedies, regularly milk the labor union stereotype for an easy joke that reinforces the stereotype at the expense of a more accurate depiction of organized labor. The comedy program *D.C. Follies* (Fox, July 24, 1988) was interrupted by a mock commercial for a fictitious "Teamster Fund Insurance" that "holds you in their strong arms." Similarly, on the *St. Elsewhere* episode "Their Town" (NBC, March 13, 1989), three carpenters working on Dr. Westphall's new home in New Hampshire refuse a gracious offer to sit and eat with the doctor's wife, claiming that "union regulations require that we eat sitting on the floor."

The one bright note in these otherwise bleak portrayals of unions in television dramas appeared in a set of programs aired after the Hollywood writers' strike in March 1988. The popular prime-time program *Moonlighting* (ABC, March 22, 1988), aired during the strike, may inadvertently and with the best intentions have trivialized the plight of the striking writers when that show ended with a humorous dance routine through the offices of the striking writers. The program, written before the strike, fell about seven minutes short, according to the show's producer, Jay Daniel: "Normally we just turn to the writing staff and say we need another scene here."[20] Because that was impossible, Bruce Willis and Cybill Shepherd began singing "Wooly Bully" and danced through the offices of the show's five writers, who joined the silly skit carrying their picket signs.

After the strike, two well-known sitcoms consciously attempted to portray the plight of labor in a positive light. *Designing Women* (Appendix D, no. 59) featured the series stars, who operate a small interior decorating company, being picketed by employees of a drapery manufacturer that was supplying them. At first, the "designing women" cross the picket lines and try to work at the drapery factory to rush their job through. But they realize how sorry the working conditions and wages are for the striking workers, and they join the strikers to pressure the draper to settle. And in an episode of *Head of the Class* (Appendix D, no. 62), the teacher (Howard Hesseman) tells his class why he is committed to the teachers' union and the issues behind the existing teachers' strike. Building on his students' misconceptions (essentially the same as in this study's survey of high school students' attitudes, Appendix A), the teacher presents a lesson that is so convincing that, at the end of the episode, the class rejects the interference of a scab substitute.

Though not included in the survey, the ABC series *Homefront*, which nostalgically looks at life in the 1940s, ran a subplot through several episodes that aired in March and April 1992 depicting a small-town manufacturer who locked out all of his workers to stop a union organizing drive. In a climactic episode entitled "No Man Loyal and Neutral," the plant police beat up the union leadership, and, in apparent retaliation, the company representative's home is first vandalized, then showered with bullets. Tragically, his young wife is killed in the gunfire. The portrayal of the union is tainted by the many violent and bitter incidents of the lockout. Like the film *Matewan*, these episodes suggest that unions bring out the worst in human nature and are invariably the cause of bloody conflict, even though the series script is essentially sympathetic to the union workers and critical of the conniving employers.

But these positive portrayals are exceptional and they may reflect only a temporary change of attitude because of the writers' personal involvement in their own industry's strike. Even as an anomaly, however, they raise the question of where the responsibility lies for the labor union portrayals observed in this survey. Under normal circumstances, the authors or screenwriters would bear responsibility, but no pattern of assignments to particular writers is apparent. There are nearly as many writers represented in the survey as there are episodes. Patterns are apparent, for news as well as dramatic series, only in the network attention accorded labor plots or subjects. And for dramatic series, a significantly larger portion of the sample consisted of dramas produced by MTM (Mary Tyler Moore) studios. These findings suggest that the larger producers and the networks exercise enough control over the scripts to guide and determine the portrayals of organized labor. It would appear that the writers are responding to their own media clichés when they repeat and adapt the common themes described above. Accuracy in television depictions of the labor movement has not been a concern. Labor terminology is abused, and situations are often dramatized without respect for realism or the true plight of the union or nonunion labor depicted. The episode of *Designing Women* (Appendix D, no. 59) considered earlier does not mention that the union picket of the women's residence actually constituted a secondary boycott under the applicable federal law, and would have been illegal, subjecting the union to major fines, court injunction, and possible civil liability.

Though television programs and films often list in their credits consultants or special advisers for historical or professional accuracy when dealing with police, courtroom, or hospital dramas and documentaries, experienced labor leaders or business agents do not appear to have been consulted on any of the dramas surveyed. Labor portrayals, therefore, are left to what is assumed to be common knowledge. It is unfortunate that this common knowledge has been so riddled with misconceptions and ponderous stereotypes that the television image of organized labor has helped push the values and goals of the American labor movement off the liberal agenda.

4. Newspapers

The Labor Beat

In old days men had the rack. Now they have the press.
—Oscar Wilde, "The Soul of Men Under Socialism"

As Albert Zack, former director of public relations for the AFL-CIO, noted in his 1977 address to a conference on media relations, "The free trade union movement and the free press in this country share a common breeding ground—the first amendment to the Constitution."[1] Perhaps for this reason, the press and labor have over the years shared a love-hate relationship as either or both attempted to live up to those constitutional promises of freedom of speech and assembly, each in its own way asserting the preeminence of its role in bringing about social reform and the broader-based representation upon which democracy is founded.

Certainly there have been many times when the press and organized labor have worked together. In the early days of the labor movement, it was the muckraking press characterization of the "robber barons" and the "captains of industry" that provided workers with much of the rhetoric of their moral imperative to organize. More recent examples are harder to find, but occasionally, such as in the campaign of eight bank tellers in Willmar, Minnesota, to organize a union or the fight of shipyard workers at Pearl Harbor to stop the navy's use of toxic paints, the press has championed a labor union's cause.

For the most part, though, the treatment of labor in the press, and local newspapers in particular, has been and continues to be negative. The image of labor unions projected in the press, as in the other media, is one of corruption, greed, self-interest, and power. As Cirino and Parenti found, stories that support that stereotype are trumpeted while stories that are inconsistent with the stereotype are routinely quashed or run in such an unassuming context as to go unnoticed.[2]

In some cases this anti-labor bias is heavy-handed and deliberate. Local publishers and their editors are themselves employers dealing with their own workers—often unionized—in the less than happy circumstances that surround the process of collective bargaining. It is no surprise, then, that they should approach labor relations stories from a management perspective. And when these same publishers, as is often the case, are social companions with the very employers in their community likely to be embroiled in labor disputes, class loyalties can be expected to prevail.

From April 9 to April 18, 1972, for instance, the *Washington Post* ran a ten-part series of stories on America's labor unions reported by Haynes Johnson and Nick Kotz. The series, which later that year was compiled into a paperback book and distributed widely, was according to the cover blurb researched in three months. The ten headlines clearly reveal the stories' negative depictions: "Unrest Amid Rank and File," "Today's Worker: 'Idealism Gone'," "For Young Workers, Old Leaders," "Politics and Labor's 'Machine'," "Presidents Come and Go, but Labor's Might Stays," "Business Takes Aim at Labor's Power," "Building Trades Fueling Inflation," "Labor's Violent World: Big Money, Corruption," "The Dispute over Organizing: How Much Have Unions Lost?" "A Basic Problem: Work Attitudes Changing."[3] The publication of this series came the year after the *Post*'s publisher Katharine Graham took the company public and vowed to put an end to her workers' "archaic union practices."[4] It was no idle treat. In 1973 the printers were on strike, followed in 1974 by the Newspaper Guild, and in 1975, at the end of a bitter strike, the *Post* broke its pressmen's union by bringing in helicopters to fly printing plates to distant production facilities. Looking at the 1972 series by Johnson and Kotz in the light of the *Post*'s own labor relations history, the negative depiction of unions comes as no surprise.

Much of the time, the image of labor is colored by more subtle forms of bias that, because they may not be deliberate, have even greater potential for misinforming and stereotyping not only labor but any nonestablishment reform movement at odds with the known and familiar. A. J. Liebling, who framed some of the most telling criticisms of American yellow journalism, was among the first to notice the anti-labor bias in the early decades of the twentieth century. When Liebling entered Dartmouth College in 1920, he studied under John Moffatt Mecklin, a professor of sociology, who first called his attention to the untrustworthiness of the newspaper coverage of the great steel strike of 1919 and the newspaper bias against labor.[5] A sample of this coverage can be found in the following excerpt from the *Pittsburgh Chronicle-Telegraph*: "Yesterday the enemy of liberty was Prussianism. Today it is radicalism. Masquerading under the cloak of the American Federation of Labor a few radicals are striving for power. They hope to seize control of the industries and turn the company over to the 'red' rule of Syndicalism. . . . America is calling you. The steel strike will fail. Be a 100 percent American. Stand by America. . . . GO BACK TO WORK MONDAY."[6] This passage, which was typical of the treatment the strikers were receiving in papers throughout the country, was supplemented by editorial letters and advertisements provided by local churchmen, businessmen, and politicians who joined in portraying the unionists as communists and foreign insurgents bent on destroying the American way of life.

Another great critic of the media's labor coverage, Walter Lippmann, coined the term *stereotype* in 1922. Indeed, the portrayal of labor was commonly joined to the stereotype of the foreign-born communist agitator. But even when the bias was not as strident as it was against the steel strikers, Lippmann observed a systematic weakness in ordinary reportage that always seemed to work against labor: "A great deal, I think myself the crucial part, of what looks to the worker and the reformer as deliberate misrepresentation on the part of newspapers, is the direct outcome of a practical difficulty in uncovering the news, and the emotional difficulty of making distant facts interesting unless, as Emerson says, we can 'perceive [them] to be only a new version of our familiar experience' and can 'set about translating [them] at once into our own parallel facts.' "[7] More simply, the reporter must present news on the level of the public's self-interest and consciousness of the issue. Lippmann correctly observed that this usually results in labor stories that focus strictly on overt events or on how these events are likely to interfere with the readers' lives. Michael Parenti described the same problem as the fourth characteristic on his list of media misrepresentations: "Emphasis on the impact rather than the causes of strikes, laying the blame for the strike totally on the union and detailing the damage the strike does to the economy and the public weal."[8] When issues and causes are relegated to effects and consequences, media coverage focuses on strikes and boycotts rather than on the working conditions or wage inequities that may have occasioned them.

Antecedents of Modern Press Coverage

Although the period 1933 to 1941 has been said to be a time when the "Fourth Estate" was friendly to the house of labor,[9] that alliance was restricted to issues such as child labor and mine safety. When it came to strikes, newspapers fell back to their traditional defense of the major economic interests. During the 1934 waterfront strike on the West Coast, for example, John Francis Neylan, Hearst's man in San Francisco, called a meeting of all the major publishers in San Francisco and Oakland and told them: "We publishers have a responsibility to protect our community from Communism. What we need is a committee that can clear editorials and stories about the strike."[10] A similar attitude toward strike news was common throughout the 1930s, particularly in the case of CIO actions, because the papers found the smaller AFL craft unions less threatening than the CIO's goal of organizing the nation's industrial workers.

In Hawaii, however, in 1938, when a unique coalition of AFL and CIO unions was trying to organize the Inter-Island Steam Ship Company, the local press made no secret of its bias against an organizing strike that promised to bring the West Coast spirit of unionism to the islands. When a small army of local policemen opened fire on a sympathy demonstration of unarmed men and women sitting on the Hilo docks, the local papers described the demonstration as a "riot" that the police properly dispersed. This was not surprising inasmuch as the general manager of the local paper was a member of the chamber of commerce that had ordered the police to the docks.[11]

The problem has not diminished over the years but has, if anything, as the issues have grown more and more complex, worsened each decade since. In 1940 another journalist remarked:

> For some time there has been criticism of labor news in the American press. The New Deal insisted over and over again that it did not get a fair break in the newspapers. Radical groups denounce their treatment by the press. They denounce newspaper owners.
>
> There is some foundation for all these attacks. In the case of labor the difficulty has often been due to a lack of understanding.[12]

By 1940 the need for understanding had increased considerably. President Roosevelt had signed the Wagner Act into federal law, granting workers for the first time the legal right to organize unions and granting legal status to union agreements and the process by which they were negotiated. This, of course, was only the first of many federal and state laws that would eventually weave an increasingly complex web of labor relations issues considerably beyond the scope of the average local reporter and well beyond the ken of the general public's comfortable frame of reference.

The Labor Beat

For truly informed reporting on the subject, a paper had to be large enough to designate a labor beat and assign it to someone dedicated, if not educated, to a thorough, issue-based comprehension of that town's labor relations network. That requires a professional commitment from publisher, editor, and reporter alike that is the exception rather than the rule in the American press. Large, nationally syndicated papers tend to have the best, least-biased coverage. The *Wall Street Journal*, for example, though often guided by a conservative editorial policy, nevertheless has a reputation for high-quality, in-depth, informed labor reporting primarily because it has maintained a specialized complement of labor reporters. Sadly, the trend seems to be in the opposite direction. A New Jersey–based labor reporter noted:

> While business coverage is on the rise, labor journalism is declining in quantity and quality. "It has been declining for a long time, probably since the 1950s," says John Hoerr, an associate editor at *Business Week* who specializes in labor.
> The *San Francisco Chronicle*, which in the 1940s had two labor writers, has no one with that title now, though management says labor issues are handled by its three-person economics team.[13]

The practice in Hawaii is probably typical. A former labor reporter for the *Advertiser* came to that beat from the food section. One of the paper's more inquisitive reporters, she had, after a few years, developed considerable credibility in the labor community, at which point she was promoted to the economy and business beat. Her replacement had likewise to start from scratch and was identified as a labor reporter only when the article was about labor. His byline on a series on Japanese investment described him simply as a staff reporter, and within a year he too had moved off the labor beat into business reporting. Certainly these reporters tried their best to cover the news fairly and comprehensively, but the constant rotation of the labor beat is not designed to promote informed coverage. The same thing happens commonly at local papers throughout the country.

Describing the embarrassing inability of the local and national press to understand any of the developments in the 1981 coal strike, Curtis Seltzer revealed two primary failings in an article for the *Columbia Journalism Review*: the reporters had not developed any contacts among the rank-and-file members of the union, and they had no access to "independent coal observers."[14] In other words, the reporters covering the strike were not experienced enough to obtain any information except the official press releases of the coal companies and superficial, guarded comments from the union leadership.

Similarly, John Grimes, former labor writer for the *Wall Street Journal* recounted, "But when I used to go out into the field to report on labor, go to a union convention, or talk to some union leader, I would very often find that the local reporter assigned to the story was actually his newspaper's police reporter, who had been sent out to cover a strike or some other potentially dramatic development. He often had little perception of what the labor movement was, where it had come from, or what the important issues were."[15] The association of labor unions with crime reporting is probably the single most damaging form of bias affecting the labor movement. And though this bias may be less the result of any deliberate attempt to slur labor than the effect of the reporters' and editors' preconceptions or predispositions toward the subject, the effect is just as devastating. Reporters who come to the labor beat from the police beat naturally bring with them prejudices they may not be aware of. That they were assigned out of the police beat to labor indicates as well the connection between these two subjects in the mind of the city editor who made the assignment.

Clearly, writing is influenced as well. Stories about strikes and picket lines are preferred, and even when the news is about an election or ratification meeting, the tendency is to color it with the adjectives of crime. Jesse L. Carr's election was reported in the *Advertiser* in 1984, as follows: "Jesse L. Carr, 58, Alaska Teamsters boss who almost agreed to a merger of his fabulously rich union fiefdom with the Hawaii Teamsters seven years ago, is the new titular chief of all of the union's operations in 13 western states, including Hawaii."[16] This is an example of the press's aversion to using formal titles or proper names for labor leaders, giving the impression that they were elected to offices called "boss" or "chief." Reporters refer respectfully to the president or CEO of a business, but to them labor unions are led by chiefs or bosses, words that obviously suggest a lack of democratic selection. Yet business leadership is much less democratically selected than union leadership. Federal laws, like the Landrum-Griffin Act, require labor union democracy, while businesses are generally run by executive decree. Yet one would be hard-pressed to find a reporter referring to a large corporation as a "fabulously rich fiefdom." This story may be an extreme case of reporter bias, but the same tactics—in less concentrated form—are not uncommon throughout local labor coverage.

Labor unions themselves often fail to realize the full impact of the treatment they receive. As long as their own union is not being labeled or stereotyped, they feel safe. But to the general public, unions are unions. Fine distinctions between AFL-CIO and independent affiliates (such as the Teamsters and the ILWU until 1988) are not made. The ordinary reader is likely to lump all union coverage together and, for instance, confuse Carr's alleged "fiefdom" with the organization of unions in general.

The impact of this writing on the general public is difficult to assess. Even when the reporter has told the story fairly and evenly, the construction of the headline (which is controlled by an editor, not the reporter) or the size of the story and its proximity to the front page or other stories of a positive or negative nature may influence the final perception of that paper's readers.

Headlines and Placement of Labor Stories

In Leonard Doob's treatise on propaganda, the significance of headlines is given particular weight:

> Headlines are important as every newspaper man and almost every reader knows. Besides being readily perceived, they are almost always the first part of the story to be perceived and hence the responses they produce in the reader are likely to affect his subsequent perception of and reaction to the story itself. . . . Many individuals, moreover, read only the headlines and, therefore, their entire impression of a story is derived from this not necessarily adequate source.[17]

The average person reads through the headlines to find a story that seems interesting, so it can be assumed that many people read only the headlines and are most likely to read the labor headline together with the ones immediately before or after it.

Regular placement of labor stories next to police beat or other reports of criminal activity is bound to have an effect on readers. Hawaii's two major dailies, the *Honolulu Star-Bulletin* and the *Honolulu Advertiser* are generally believed to treat labor objectively,[18] but a study of the layout of their labor coverage reveals just such a pattern. In an example of Robert Cirino's bias in the headline and bias through "Coincidental" placement, these papers run their labor headlines next to unrelated but incriminating headlines telling of violent or repugnant criminal activity.[19] "Prince Kuhio Hotel Will Be Picketed" headlined a labor story that was printed just to the left of the headline "Rape, Robbery in Haleakala" in such a way that the casual reader might merge the stories. Similarly, the headline "HGEA Seeks Role in Police Union Dispute" was immediately followed by a story titled "Man, 60, Charged with Sex Abuse of Boy."[20]

The following stories appeared next to the regular "Police Beat" feature that summarizes the previous day's criminal arrests and investigations: "Sugar Labor Contract," "Foodland Employees Agree to Cut in Wages," and "Union, Pineapple Companies Reach Agreement."[21] But the effect is just as damaging when the labor story is next to a report about violent crime, even if it's not labeled *police beat*. This association of labor headlines with crime reports has not abated over the years. A log of labor coverage in the two Honolulu dailies reveals the regularity of the pattern.

In an average four-week period in which there would be about twenty-four labor stories, four to six stories were likely to be located next to a criminal report. The incidence increased in February and March. And the *Advertiser* tended to have a lower incidence than the *Star-Bulletin* primarily because the former carried more labor stories. From April 1 to May 10, 1988, for instance, the *Star-Bulletin* had a dozen labor stories, while the *Advertiser* carried two dozen. Each paper placed the labor report next to a criminal report four times. That represents 25 percent of the *Star-Bulletin*'s coverage and 12 percent of the *Advertiser*'s. Both papers do it as much as 30 percent of the time, and rarely as seldom as 10 percent of the time.

The question, of course, is, How much is too much? Most of the relevant scientific research is related to the general subject of subliminal perception, which, since Key's overestimation of the process in *Subliminal Seduction* (1973), has been discredited. Though psychologists and psychiatrists have attacked the idea, advertisers and public relations professionals have continued to explore its possibilities, and recent research supports the idea that "supraliminal" advertising aimed at image creation is effective.[22] Such research usually involves a film format in which a brief message is inserted about five times at one-sixtieth of a second over a two-minute period. These findings suggest that even a 10 percent occurrence of labor headlines next to criminal reports would have the potential—particularly over time—of creating a public image of labor tainted by criminal association.

But the other question that should be considered involves editorial layout decision making. Why is it not more appropriate to carry labor stories, especially those about major local industries' labor contract settlements or contract ratifications, in the business section? What reason is there for placing contract or even peaceful strike news in or around the police beat, where it is bound to color public perception and contribute to the stereotyped image of corruption and vice in the labor movement?

Labor Treatment Compared to Business Treatment

To be fair to the editors and press "gatekeepers" who organize these stories, one may conclude that they probably are not maliciously or even deliberately trying to tar labor. Stories are laid out the way they are because labor news is classified by the editors, as Lippmann theorized, as "a new version of familiar experience."

This editorial pigeon-holing of labor stories associates labor not only with criminality, but with many other elements of the stereotype as well. David Ignatius, a former reporter for the *Wall Street Journal*, studied the way his colleagues unanimously championed Edward Sadlowski in his 1977 campaign for the presidency of the United Steel Workers against the older, less colorful Lloyd McBride. Though McBride won the election, Ignatius concluded that the lopsided partisan coverage, which supported Sadlowski while portraying McBride as a tool of the labor establishment, constituted a class bias: "Older, conservative labor leaders like George Meany of the A.F.L.-C.I.O. and I. W. Abel of the Steelworkers tend to be treated by the press with considerable suspicion. Meany, for example, is often characterized as 'cigar-smoking,' which would be a trivial detail were it not a sort of shorthand for 'boss.' Similarly, Abel's name is often preceded by phrases like '$75,000-a-year steelworkers chief,' which is presumably intended to mean 'overpaid.'"[23] There is a certain journalistic nostalgia that harkens back to the young, rabble-rousing union organizer of the 1920s and 1930s. As the labor movement has matured and leadership has passed into the hands of more experienced and professional negotiators wearing suits and ties, the press has not been comfortable with this transition and continuously degrades the image of such leaders.

Each summer, for instance, the local papers report on the salaries earned by Hawaii's labor leadership. This is "news" because federal law requires unions to report their expenses and the union's financial status annually, so the data are conveniently available as public information. But the story is always written in such a way as to suggest, as Ignatius noted, that the leaders are overpaid. Normally a calculation is provided to indicate how much more the leader makes than an average member. Yet, as Michael Parenti noted as his third feature of press bias, the paper rarely runs a similar column disclosing the salaries of top management leaders or, when it does, no calculation of its ratio to the salaries of employees is considered relevant.[24]

The figures provided in the unions' federal reports tend to be skewed somewhat because the government requires that the financial disclosure include as salary such items as travel expenses and meal allowances for legitimate union business. The result is that inexperienced reporters erroneously inflate the salaries of union leaders who have been actively organizing out of town or attending training at the George Meany Center in Maryland. The net effect is that the more effort union leaders expend trying to organize or improve their representational skills in any year, the more likely they are to be portrayed as overpaid union bosses milking the membership.

Another example of the double standard in the reporting of business versus labor stories can be seen in the different presentations of positive stories. Unions, for instance, have been very active in a variety of community service projects, and yet stories featuring these projects rarely credit the union in the headline, rarely are accompanied by a photograph, and rarely are printed in the A section.

In 1987 and 1988 the Carpenters union in Hawaii sponsored an islandwide car wash to raise money for Boy Scouts and Girl Scouts in some of the poorer school districts so they could go to summer camp. In each case well over $10,000 was raised and the union provided all the expenses and adult labor. The item in the Sunday paper in 1987 read "Car Wash Raises Funds for Scouts" and in 1988, "Scouts Fund-Raising Carwash Tomorrow."[25] Neither headline mentioned the union. Yet, when in June 1987 the *Advertiser* donated a sum half as large to the American Red Cross, that story was run over the width of the entire page, with a three-by-five photo showing the parties exchanging the bank check.[26]

Business donations are extolled; labor's are ignored or given short shrift. The *Advertiser* published a five-by-five photograph of R. J. Pfeiffer, "chairman and chief executive officer of Alexander & Baldwin Inc.," as he handed a check over to children representing the YMCA. But when the Honolulu Port Council, a coalition of several maritime unions, awarded a scholarship to a Hawaii Boy Scout to attend a summer program at the Harry Lundeberg School of Seamanship in Maryland, not one member of the local press responded to an invitation to attend the awards luncheon. In response to the council's press release, a story was published under the headline, "Tanabe Selected Scout of the Year." Though a picture of the scout accompanied the story, the paper declined to print a photo of the scout receiving his award though such a photo was offered by the council. The same month Hawaiian Cement Company awarded a series of scholarships (open only to children of its employees) but the *Star-Bulletin* ran it with the company's name prominent in the headline and three photographs of the recipients.[27]

In 1987 the *Honolulu Star-Bulletin* started two special features to acknowledge a range of local figures in business and public affairs. Titled "Executive Profile" and "NewsMaker," the series presents positive image-builders for those fortunate enough to be featured. Though similar in many respects to a *Wall Street Journal* series called "Who's News?" which regularly features union presidents and directors as well as major financiers and CEOs, the *Star-Bulletin* columns have a different application. In the year following their inception, only one column was given to a labor leader,[28] and she was not the primary or most visible executive officer of that union.

The media control the visibility of labor by controlling and filtering its images. It is by choice that one story is reported over another; it is by conviction that one story or one angle of coverage is apparent in a situation while another is not. The word *grievance*, for instance, is much misunderstood in the public mind. The average American has been led to perceive grievances negatively as the method by which unions prevent employers from discharging unproductive, arrogant, and insubordinate workers. It is a headline when a teachers' union defends a teacher accused of child abuse or when a transport workers' union grieves the drug testing of its members. But in January 1986, after the Challenger space shuttle explosion, when a postal worker on Maui was reprimanded for lowering the flag to half-staff without his supervisor's approval, almost no mention was made in the press of the Postal Workers Union grievance that eventually was responsible for removing the improper discipline.

The principle appears to be that news that is bad for labor is big news; when the news is good, it is not news at all or is hardly worth mentioning. In 1986, for example, Walter Kupau, the business manager of the Carpenters Local 745, was embroiled in a highly publicized dispute with a Maui contractor the union was trying to organize. At about the same time he was accused of attacking a Mililani construction foreman, and the two stories were intertwined in the press. In the Maui case, Kupau was convicted of perjury before the grand jury because he insisted that the union picket was informational rather than recognitional. For this he was found guilty and sentenced to a two-year term in federal prison. The headline reporting the dismissal of his appeal to the federal court was a banner running across the whole of the front page proclaiming: "Kupau's Perjury Sentence Upheld," while the news that felony assault charges, improperly brought against him, were subsequently dropped was reported two days earlier over a single column on page 6, with less than half the headline space.[29]

Press Coverage of Strikes

Nowhere is the image of labor more damaging than in the coverage and reporting of strikes. It is said that harmony seldom makes a headline, but it should not be expecting too much for the press to give a balanced view of labor disputes. According to the Bureau of Labor Statistics, less then 2 percent of contracts negotiated in any year result in a strike.[30] Put another way, better than 98 percent of the time collective bargaining is successful in reaching agreement without recourse to strike. And yet the public perception of unions is dominated by images of the picketline and the strike. Organized employer councils and chambers of commerce annually furnish statistics to the press on the lost man-hours and wages, which reporters, for the most part, scoop up and serve out without ever realizing that far more hours and wages are lost annually to unemployment and industrial injuries.

Again, when the news is bad for labor, it is big. News of strikes or even of threatened strikes commonly receives banner headlines, whether or not the union or the industry involved represents a significant portion of the local economy. But when settlement is reached, particularly if there was little or no threat of a strike, the news is small and printed far from the front page. The impact of this reporting can be seen in the results of this study's survey (Appendix A) in which more than half of the high school juniors and seniors responding indicated their belief that the incidence of strikes was 12 percent or higher. This misconception makes it harder for unions to organize new workers, who are easily convinced by employers' arguments that unionization will inevitably lead to a financially disastrous strike.

Furthermore, the quality as well as the quantity of strike coverage is often prejudicial. Many years ago Lippmann remarked: "If you study the way many a strike is reported in the press, you will find, very often, that the issues are rarely in the headlines, barely in the leading paragraphs, and sometimes not even mentioned anywhere."[31] As Lippmann noted, the press tends to concentrate reporting on the strike's intrusion on the reader's comfort or convenience, often characterizing the public as the innocent victim of a conflict that should have been confined to the parties involved. Culpability for this rude interruption is generally ascribed only to the union, even in cases of lockouts when the employer is the immediate cause of the interruption. In such cases, reporters usually rush out to the company spokesperson, who has a prepared statement demeaning the union's position and supporting the public feeling that the union is totally to blame for the disruption of their services. As Zack noted: "Every union proposal is called a 'demand' and every management proposal is called an 'offer.' Every strike is calculated in lost wages, never in the lost self-esteem that would result if the workers had caved in to management demands and tolerated unfettered management domination of their lives. Every strike is a strike against the public interest, or inflationary, or pigheaded, in the opinion of the press."[32]

The following article, which appeared on the front page, described a recent California teachers' strike. Note the dominance of the employer point of view:

> L.A. teachers strike for more pay
> LOS ANGELES—Teachers in the nation's second-largest school district went on strike today, threatening to create chaos for nearly 600,000 students in the final weeks of school.
> United Teachers–Los Angeles, representing 22,000 teachers, is demanding a 21 percent pay hike over two years and more control over classrooms. District administrators said they planned to keep the schools open by using substitute teachers.
> Board of Education President Roberta Weintraud, speaking for the majority on a deeply divided school board, said the district would not budge from what she termed one of the best contract offers for teachers in the nation.[33]

The headline asserts that the only motive of the teachers is "more pay," that is, greed, despite the information in the second paragraph that classroom control is also an outstanding issue. In the first paragraph, the report characterizes the goal of the strike as a threat to create chaos for the students. This description is blatantly biased. The word *threat* implies a sinister if not malicious intent, and the hidden editorial message is that the strike is wrong. Furthermore, the teachers' "demand" is given precisely, while the employer's position is described subjectively as "one of the best contract offers for teachers in the nation." Inclusion of the response of the school administrators and the Board of Education official allots twice as much space to the employer's views as to the union's. The teachers' viewpoint regarding classroom control or the justification of their wage package is not explained. In all likelihood, the information about the teachers' "demands" was obtained directly from the employer.

It is a rare journalist who is capable of breaking through this clichéd coverage or who ever manages to report the union's perspective fairly or with comprehension. Part of the fault lies with the press, but in some cases the union point of view is less accessible than that of the employer. Michael Hoyt, a former reporter for the *Record* in Bergen County, New Jersey, related his early efforts to cover both sides of a labor dispute:

> It was at lunch, I think, that I learned that the long-running strike at an electrical-parts plant outside town was coming to a head. Soon the workers would vote on whether to keep the union and continue the strike, or de-certify and go back to work. They had been out for months.
>
> The plant owner's message, when I called, was that if the strike continued he would shut the plant permanently. This was a region of high unem-ployment, and the factory was one of the few new industries the town had been able to attract. The town fathers felt that gaining a reputation for having a militant work force would be disastrous.
>
> All that remained for my story was the perspective from the picket line, but no one would talk. The picketers stared at me like a tree full of owls. A woman picketer finally explained: nothing from the strikers' point of view, she said, had been printed in the newspaper since the strike had begun, some months before I'd been hired. More than once the publisher had insulted the strikers in her column.
>
> Earlier that summer, when members of the publisher's favorite church youth choir were arrested at a marijuana picnic, she had tried to kill the story. But the editor, a fair-minded man, had stood up to her. With the sincerity of a believer, I assured the strikers that my story would get printed and that it would be balanced—and, finally, the picket line talked. But their skepticism was justified. The publisher ordered the story killed; the editor complied. Church choirs are one thing; labor is serious.[34]

Another disturbing outcome of the press's habits of getting its news primarily from the employer and of focusing on the way the strike affects the general public is the tendency to accent the strike's ineffectiveness. In the spring of 1985, the Transport Workers Union conducted a very effective strike against Pan American World Airways. The *Star-Bulletin* headline read, "Pan Am Hawaii Flights Continue Despite Strike." A few days later, after the already effective strike became even tighter, the *Star-Bulletin* headlined, "Pan American Flight Arrives Here from Tokyo." In much smaller type it grudgingly admitted, "But Strike Grounds Others."[35] Similarly, in 1986, the headline describing the In-land Boatmen's Union picket of Dillingham Tug and Barge read, "Isle Produce Moves Despite Strike by IBU."

For the sake of accuracy, one might have expected the Pan Am head-line to have read: "Pan Am Flights Grounded by Strike" with the low-ercase note appended, "lone Tokyo flight arrives." The real question, though, is why the reports should so commonly stress the strike's in-effectiveness. Clearly, it is to the advantage of the struck employer to make would-be customers believe the strike is not adversely affecting its services. Worse, however, is the disheartening effect such coverage has on the striking employees. Such headlines reveal the overriding influence attached by the reporter to the employer's public relations release.

Everett Martin, writing in the 1920s, drew the following useful distinction between education and propaganda: "Education aims at independence of judgment. Propaganda offers ready-made opinions for the unthinking herd. Education and propaganda are directly opposed both in aim and method. . . . The educator fails unless he achieves an open mind; the propagandist unless he achieves a closed mind."[36] The most common examples of the press treatment of organized labor read like anti-union propaganda, whereas the primary social function of the news media should be to inform and educate.

In April 1988, the chairman of the Honolulu City Council excoriated the press at a speech before the Honolulu Community-Media Council for bias in misrepresentative headlines and what he called selective storytelling. A. A. Smyser, former editor of the *Honolulu Star-Bulletin*, replied in the paper the following week by pleading "nolo contendere" or no contest.

> My own strong conviction after half a century as a newspaperman is that there is no such thing as an "unbiased" account of anything, and that we all will be able to understand each other a little better if we can agree on this. . . . My own bias is that we will always have bias and always have subjectivity. There's no way out of it. But we still can—and should—demand accuracy of our print and video media. Also balance. And fairness. And a chance to talk back.[37]

This defense is too facile and leaves the perpetrator free to sin again. Recognizing that there is no such thing as a totally unbiased viewpoint is good only if it helps to caution the media about expressing their bias in fact. When we look to the press for news, we are or we should be looking for new information and, whenever possible, for a new way to understand what has happened. Article V of the "Canons of Journalism" first developed in 1922 by the American Society of Newspaper Editors proclaims: "Impartiality—Sound practice makes clear distinction between news reports and expression of opinion. News reports should be free from opinion or bias of any kind."[38] Labor has a right to expect a more conscientious effort by the press to live up to this ethical code.

5. Cartoons

Drawn and Quartered

I'm not bad. I'm just drawn that way.
—Jessica Rabbit in *Who Framed Roger Rabbit*

The old saw that a picture is worth a thousand words cannot be more accurately applied than in calculating the impact of editorial cartoons and popular syndicated cartoon strips on the labor movement. Studies show that twenty to thirty times more adults read newspaper comic strips than editorials.[1] In the print media cartoons come closest to fulfilling the entertainment function that television provides in its prime-time programming. Because cartoons take up a small proportion of newspaper space compared to news and advertising, the focus of attention on them is proportionately greater than on the much more diffuse programming of the video media. Yet in both cases, comedy, satire, drama, and melodrama are allowed the free reign of artistic expression that encourages the portrayal of issues in the light of simple, uncomplicated, often unchallenged values.

To the cartoonist, the labor movement and its leadership have traditionally held the same unprotected, unsympathetic status reserved for politics and corrupt politicians. To some extent, of course, ridicule is the essence of the cartoonist's craft, and it is wrong to expect generous treatment from pens dedicated professionally to lampooning all institutions, great and small. We can reasonably expect, however, a commitment to challenge common, undeliberated attitudes. But to the extent that cartoonists simply distill and exaggerate existing popular stereotypes, the medium fails to stir our thinking and presumes only to confirm the prevailing cultural hegemony.

The Birth of Editorial Cartoons about Labor

Historically, the ideological framework that cartoonists have attached to the image of labor can be traced back to the work of Thomas Nast, who from 1862 to 1885 was the political cartoonist for *Harper's Weekly*. Expressing a Radical Republican political philosophy, Nast and the editors of *Harper's Weekly* sought to focus national attention on government corruption, the end of government land grants to railroads and private corporations, and the need for a civil service system.[2] Radical Republicanism and its more conservative offshoot, Liberal Republicanism, were espoused by a large number of postbellum newspapers in addition to *Harper's Weekly*. This first "liberal" alliance of politicians, journalists, and intellectuals belonged to the Republican party and was decidedly anti-union in character.

Nast is best remembered for his scathing attack on the corruption of New York's Tweed Ring, which ruled Tammany Hall and the city government from 1866 to 1871. Less well remembered is his deep prejudice against the Irish, Catholicism, and Democrats that is evident throughout his cartoons. And Nast's influence on the development of the Liberal Republican agenda was considerable.

In addition to popularizing the famous donkey and elephant symbols for the Democratic and Republican parties, he defined what would become the standard graphic image of the American laborer. Later supplanted by the hard hat and lunch box of the twentieth century, Nast's white male laborer sported a white, flat-topped, four cornered, paper machinists' cap and carried a cylindrical dinner pail.[3] The most typical theme Nast and his contemporaries illustrated with this image was the danger of labor's seduction by outside union organizers. To Nast, union meant only the Union of the United States. Labor union organizers were simply anarchists and communists hoping to destroy capitalism. His cartoon in the March 16, 1878, *Harper's Weekly*, "Always Killing the Goose That Lays the Golden Egg," enunciates the theme most clearly (figure 5.1). The laborer, with the golden egg of his wages in his pocket, has been duped by the onlooking communist into destroying the prolific goose of capitalism. On the wall behind the two are the inflammatory labor slogans of the day, "Labor Is Capital" next to the more offensive and threatening "Up with the Red Flag." Seventy-five years before the notorious red-baiting of Senator Joesph McCarthy after World War II, Nast launched the first media attempt at labeling the nation's fledgling union movement as a communist conspiracy.

After the Haymarket riot in May 1886, Nast published a cartoon

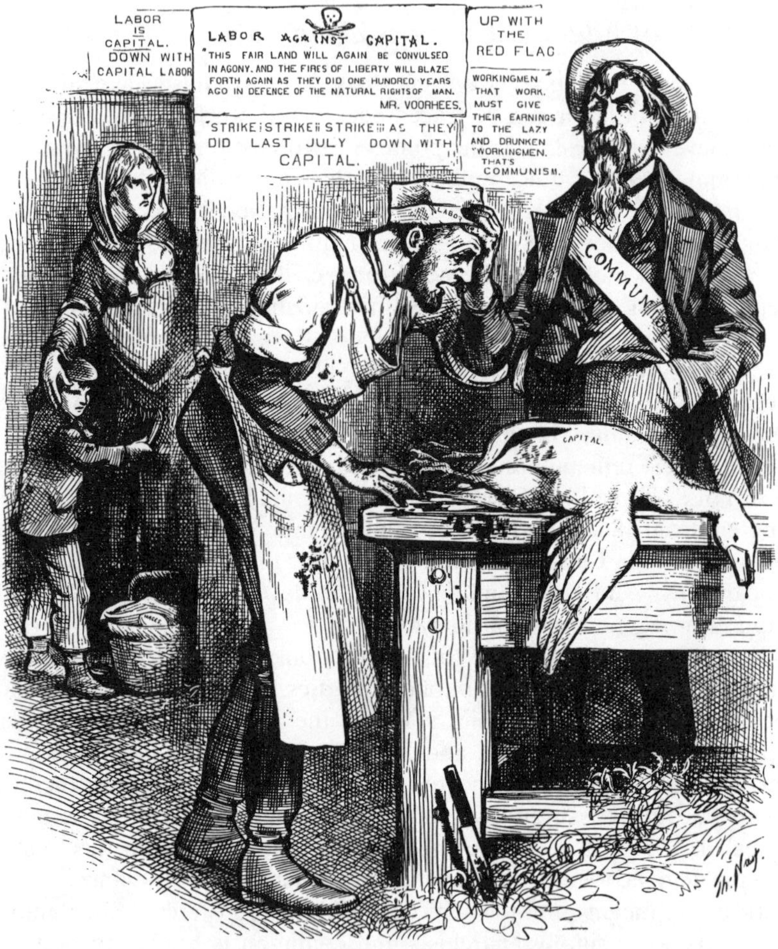

Always Killing the Goose That Lays the Golden Egg.

COMMUNISTIC STATESMAN (*without responsibility*). "Nothing in it, after all; it's too
bad; now I thought he was just full of them."

Figure 5.1. Thomas Nast, *Harper's Weekly*, March 16, 1878, vol. 22, p. 205.

showing Miss Liberty clutching in one hand the Haymarket conspirators
and in the other the great sword of justice and wearing a wedding ring
with the word "Union" engraved on it.[4] Nast, much like members of
the contemporary media described by Parenti, was setting "emphasis
on the impact rather than the causes of strikes, laying the blame for the
strike totally on the union and detailing the damage the strike does to

the economy and the public weal." To Nast and to the great majority of his contemporaries and his latter-day disciples, the grievances that cause labor disputes are apparently not relevant or worthy of attention. These great media clarions of the national conscience have tended to believe that labor should know its place and accept its lot humbly and quietly.

Nast's biographer Morton Keller astutely observed: "Nast's sensitivity to social reform co-existed with a quick sympathy for postwar American business enterprise. . . . It might seem that there is a failure of sensitivity here; that an artistic conscience quick to react to political and social injustice somehow went blank when it confronted the issues posed by the economy."[5] To Nast and the others, the workingman was less deserving of pity than the businessman. Joseph Keppler, for example, who illustrated the New York weekly *Puck*, picked up the Nastian symbols as well as sentiment toward labor. Like Nast, Keppler, though an immigrant, was a Republican who saw questions of economic morality only in terms of the contest between big and small business. The workers' view and plight were of no interest except as they might threaten the entrepreneurial promise that constituted the American dream of independent wealth and personal fortune. From this perspective, the dependence of the laborer was held in contempt. As the black slave was considered the "white man's burden," the common laborer has been the businessman's burden throughout the history of his media portrayal.

Keppler's drawing in the August 13, 1879, issue of *Puck* bears the caption "Has Capital Any Rights That Labor Is Bound To Respect?" (figure 5.2). It depicts the symbolic workingman perched atop five other men, each personifying a burden that the poor, bent businessman at the bottom must endure. While the businessman groans under the weight of his taxes and debts, the laborer sitting on his back gleefully waves a picket sign calling for the eight-hour day.

The labor movement grew and became stronger in the 1880s, and cartoonists became even less sympathetic to it. Fearful of the unions' growing control of the work force, cartoonists abandoned the humble cap and dinner pail and began to describe unions as a "Labor Trust." In 1886 a *Puck* cartoon showed a well-dressed, arrogant man, fat and sassy, carried on a palanquin by a throng of striking workers with a banner over his head proclaiming: "I was discharged, and I will be reinstated if all my fellow-workman have to suffer."[6] The cartoon reflects the view held by employers and their media that the unions' struggle to achieve job-security protections (which, in fact, require only that the employer have "just cause" for termination) unreasonably prevent employers from firing bad workers.

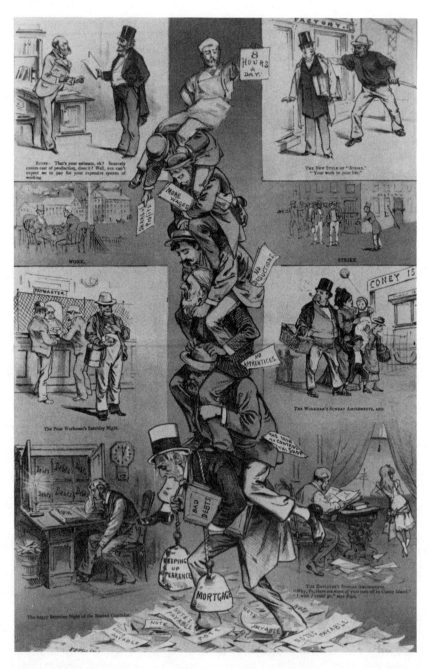

Figure 5.2. Joseph Keppler. "HAS CAPITAL ANY RIGHTS THAT LABOR IS BOUND TO RESPECT?" *Puck*, vol. 5, no. 127 (August 13, 1879): 360–61.

Figure 5.3. Reprinted by permission from M. B. Schnapper, *American Labor: A Pictorial Social History* (Washington, D.C.: Public Affairs Press, 1972), 410.

By the early twentieth century, union interest began to mount in spreading the labor movement's reach from the older trade and craft unions into the larger realm of the nation's unskilled industrial workers. The newly organized Industrial Workers of the World (IWW) or Wobblies, as they were soon known, quickly grew in size and influence, immediately attracting the unfriendly notice of the press. With even greater effect than the fear generated by the organization of the various craft unions, the Wobblies' cries of "One Big Union" stirred memories of the Haymarket and Pullman strikes that threatened to mobilize workers by class rather than just occupation. The media reaction was reminiscent of Nast's attack: these were not unionists but anarchists. The victim was no longer a poor businessman, but the entire country. The threat of union organization, encouraged by the waves of immigrants that were swelling the ranks of the workers, was imagined as a threat to the nation. The anti-Wobbly cartoons usually pictured Uncle Sam, symbol of America, being threatened by an anarchist, clad in the familiar garb of the immigrant and carrying the lighted bomb of industrial terrorism (figure 5.3). The theme that unions are un-American in their values, strategies, and membership runs deep and long through the history of media treatment.

In Hawaii, for instance, at about the same time the Wobblies were being vilified as anarchists, the *Pacific Commercial Advertiser* printed a

Figure 5.4. From the *Pacific Commercial Advertiser* (Honolulu, Hawaii), February 1, 1920, p. 4 (author's collection).

cartoon of a kimono-clad, immigrant Japanese plantation worker throwing a brick with the note "strike" tied to it (figure 5.4). Missing the figure of the plantation owner, the brick strikes instead Uncle Sam squarely in the head. Though the Hawaiian plantation strikes of that day were not organized by the IWW, the media weapon and its ultimate target were clearly the same.

A basic incongruity of the media's attitude toward labor is the ambivalence that seems to characterize the cartoonists' conception of labor and the status quo. On one hand, most of these graphic journalists feel they are honor bound to attack the complacent and the mighty. On the other, in every contest between the prevailing economic system and the rights of labor, they regard unionists as dangerous anarchists, threatening the fabric of national unity.

The Cartoon Stereotype of Labor

This dilemma was soon resolved by the adoption of the theme that labor was too mighty, complacent, and entrenched. This theme can be traced back to the 1880s when *Puck* and the other weeklies were running cartoons like the one that depicts Sam Gompers, first president of the American Federation of Labor, as "The Labor Pope" with Terence Powderly, founder of the AFL's predecessor, the Knights of Labor, seated at his right and Whitelaw Reid, owner of the *New York Tribune*, kissing Gompers's feet (figure 5.5). When Powderly set up the Knights' headquarters in an expensive Philadelphia residence in 1887, the *Puck*

Figure 5.5. Reprinted by permission from Schnapper, *American Labor*, 227.

illustrators caricatured him as a pampered labor boss enjoying "the pleasures of Byzantine ease and grandeur" while a butler held back the plain-clothed workmen and their families.[7]

More recently, editorial cartoonists have concentrated on the themes of money, greed, and power when they are being generous and on images of corruption and violence at their most self-righteous. To represent all of these themes most effectively, cartoonists have indulged in the now accepted image of slovenly obesity to represent laborers and their leaders. In our century the fat, cigar-chomping brute has replaced the kinder image of the worker carrying a dinner pail and wearing a cap popularized by Thomas Nast in the 1870s and 1880s.

Labor leaders are not represented as worker advocates. Rather they are shown as feeding on the hard labor of poor, benighted workers who have been somehow duped into contributing their limited wealth to the personal aggrandizement of the union leadership at no benefit to themselves. The cartoon of rival labor leaders John L. Lewis and William Green (figure 5.6), for instance, which dates back to the rift between the CIO and the AFL in the 1930s and 1940s, portrays them suppressing an innocent worker with the weight of their combined obese bodies.

Similarly, George Meany, president of the AFL-CIO from the mid-1950s through the 1970s, was typically portrayed feasting at the expense of the public weal (figure 5.7). By then, however, the focus was on the victimization of the general public instead of the common laborer, who had been idealized in Nast's time.

Not only have the popular caricatures of John L. Lewis in the 1930s

Figure 5.6. Reprinted by permission from Schnapper, *American Labor*, 512.

and 1940s and George Meany in the 1950s and 1960s hammered this image deep into the consciousness of the average American, but more often than not the workers themselves suffer the same portrayal. Despite the increased number of women in the American work force, the figure of the American laborer cartoonists have continued to favor is male,

Figure 5.7. Reprinted by permission of Gib Crockett, courtesy of the George Meany Memorial Archives.

Ugly customer

Figure 5.8. Reprinted by permission from the *Honolulu Advertiser*, November 11, 1971.

muscle-bound but overweight, unkempt, and violent by nature. *Honolulu Advertiser* cartoonist Harry Lyons expressed the image grotesquely in his drawing of a dispute at the Pearl City Tavern in a suburb of Honolulu (figure 5.8). This "ugly customer" was immediately recognizable as the union workers hoping to organize the tavern, not because the drawing resembled any single disputant but because the public has come to accept the image as a depiction of working-class people. Like Archie Bunker as portrayed by Carroll O'Connor, this image is a class-biased projection of ignorance and vulgarity.

One of the most revealing examples of the inconsistency of this stereotype may be seen by contrasting two expressions of the genre penned by the *Honolulu Advertiser* cartoonist Dick Adair in the mid–1980s (figures 5.9 and 5.10). In the first, the overweight, complacent, seemingly unproductive laborer is shown shifting his position without relieving the burden of his oppressive weight on the poor employer, who must pay for the workers' compensation policy that would cover his employees in the event of an industrial injury. The second depicts an overweight construction worker, complete with hard hat and rude behavior, not only blocking the tourists' view but obviously preparing to erect a build-

Figure 5.9. Reprinted by permission from the *Honolulu Advertiser*, March 5, 1985.

ing that will destroy the beauty of the beach. The first cartoon, reminiscent of Keppler's drawing of the living pyramid burdening the employer in 1879 (figure 5.2), depicts the workers' interests—insofar as they are bad for business—as self-serving and burdensome to the public weal; the second depicts the workers' interests—even when they are supportive of employers—as again self-serving and burdensome to the public weal. In each case the cartoonist lambastes labor for attempting to protect its welfare but neither attacks nor ridicules the self-serving interests of labor's opposition. More often, as Adair's antidevelopment cartoon (figure 5.10) illustrates, the common laborer becomes a convenient scapegoat for a white-collar power interest who remains invisible and therefore invulnerable to the editorial attack, while the laborer suffers the misdirected rage of the public.

Another inconsistency inherent in the popular cartoon stereotype of labor emerges in depictions of its strength. Artists are fond of representing labor as fat and unproductive, and yet, when they depict bargaining or negotiations, they show labor as muscle-bound and powerful. A pair of cartoons published in the *Honolulu Star-Bulletin* less than two months apart depict powerful unions arm-wrestling with the employer and squeezing the innocent public or the striking airline employees in their grip (figures 5.11 and 5.12). The second of these is particularly ironic, because the union described is the University of Hawaii Professional Assembly (UHPA), which represents the state university faculty and has never enjoyed a powerful negotiating posture. Obviously the point of both cartoons is to criticize the ability of labor when it is able to bargain on an equal footing with management. In this medium, labor is depicted as strong only when it is disruptive; otherwise, the cartoonists revert to flabby, lazy caricatures.

In a review of the editorial cartoons in the two Honolulu dailies in the last three and a half years of the 1980s, twenty-nine cartoons were compared, each depicting organized labor in conflict with some business or economic interest. Since editorial cartoons generally leave no doubt as to their sympathy or antipathy, it was possible to designate each cartoon as either positive or negative in its portrayal of labor versus management. By this measure, only seven of the twenty-nine were found to present a positive representation of labor, and of those seven, three were nationally syndicated cartoons republished by the local papers, two were about strikes or strike threats that were settled amicably, and the sixth was about the Polish union *Solidarność*. The only local editorial cartoon in the group that indicated a preference for labor rather than management was a March 1989 *Star-Bulletin* drawing that described the U.S. Supreme Court as unfriendly to labor.[8]

Most of the twenty-two cartoons negative to labor were related to the national stories of a recent Department of Justice probe of the Teamsters. Because the average newspaper reader, who has only a peripheral awareness of unions, is not likely to distinguish the Teamsters from

Figure 5.10. Reprinted by permission from the *Honolulu Advertiser*, April 14, 1987.

other national or local unions, media attention to any one union's or one local's corruption tends to tar the whole labor movement with the same brush. The average high school student, for instance, when asked to name a labor leader, is most likely to name Jimmy Hoffa or Jackie

Figure 5.11. Corky Trinidad. Reprinted by permission of the *Honolulu Star-Bulletin*, March 7, 1989.

Presser and is least likely to have heard of Lane Kirkland, president of the AFL-CIO, or Mary Hartwood Futrell, when she was president of the National Education Association, though these two unions represent equally large constituencies of the American labor movement.

No fewer than ten of the twenty-two negative cartoons, or one-third of the total editorial cartoons and 45 percent of all the negative depictions, focused on the Teamsters and the theme of union corruption. The vast majority of these cartoons did not give any indication of the nature of the corruption or criminal charges. Rather, the cartoonists typically considered the union's corruption as a premise upon which their joke might be based. In May 1986, for instance, the *Advertiser* published a nationally syndicated cartoon without a caption, showing the high walls of a state prison bearing the sign "Welcome Teamsters Convention" (figure 5.13). No editorial cartoons in the sample considered the long-standing political connection and mutual support of the Teamsters with the Republican party. Though the sample included cartoons published during the national elections in 1988 and the media attacks on the Teamsters continued apace, the media association between political parties and unions was deftly focused away from the Republicans.

The second most prevalent labor topic of the editorial cartoonists was the two nationally significant strikes that occurred during the sample

No way out.

Figure 5.12. Henry Yuen. Reprinted by permission of the *Honolulu Star-Bulletin*, April 28, 1989.

period. Seventeen percent of the total and 23 percent of the negative cartoons concerned either the writers' strike of 1988 or the Eastern Airlines strike of 1989. The three cartoons on the writers' strike were variations on the theme that the quality of television scripts was so poor to begin with that the strike only revealed how valueless these union writers are.[9] The Eastern Airlines cartoons followed the pattern of the television coverage noted earlier. One (figure 5.14), for instance, depicted in two frames a representative from each of the three striking unions first threatening the airline owner, Frank Lorenzo, then pointing their guns at their own heads. Not only are all three unions made to look foolish, but the strike as a strategy is compared to a weapon of ultimate violence, which, it may be inferred, is as outdated and bankrupt as is the myth of the Old West in the modern world. Furthermore, each of the unionists is drawn with a huge pear-shaped body and tiny head, as if incapable of human intellect, and the machinist, the one blue-collar unionist, is drawn with a noticeable paunch consistent with the media stereotype of the overweight, unproductive laborer.

Considering how the union movement has shrunk in recent years and how often employers have brought the full force of unsympathetic leg-

Figure 5.13. Paul Conrad. Copyright, 1986, *Los Angeles Times*. Reprinted by permission.

islation to bear on workers who have attempted to organize or obtain representation in the workplace, it is surprising that there have not been an equal number of cartoons expressing the workers' perspective. One notable exception, however, is Dan Wasserman of the *Boston Globe*, a rare champion of labor issues whose work is often syndicated nationally. But beyond Wasserman, one has to look at the union newsletters and the work of artists like Huck and Konopacki, who compose primarily for union newsletter distribution, to find sympathetic depictions of unions or issues of worker protection.

Figure 5.14. From the *Honolulu Advertiser*, March 15, 1989. Reprinted by permission of Don Wright, *The Palm Beach Post*.

Comic Strips

Heywood Broun, noted journalist and founding president of the Newspaper Guild, once dubbed the comics the "proletarian novels of America."[10] One might expect them to show a more generous attitude toward labor and trade unions than is typical of editorial cartoons and caricatures, which are more closely guided and directly controlled by owners and editors. In fact, the portrayal of the labor movement in comic strips is less proletarian than bourgeois.

To understand this phenomenon it is necessary to consider the basic differences between these two forms of newspaper cartoons. Comic strips are marketed and popularized nationally in a much different form than editorial cartoons. The general tendency throughout the media toward merger and conglomeration is equally evident in the marketing of comics. The Metro-Puck organization, which was formed by the merger of the Metro Comics Network and Hearst's *Puck, the Comic Weekly*, in 1988 represented 267 of the more than 500 newspapers that carry comics.[11] This does not mean that local editors have no choices. At the American Society of Newspaper Editors' meeting in the spring of 1989 one workshop concerned the problems and promises of syndicated comic strips.[12] Syndicates currently offer more than 300 strips, which they calculate are read by 75 percent of the newspaper-reading audience.[13] Yet once a paper has selected a strip, considerable reader loyalty develops, making it difficult for editors to cancel strips that contradict the paper's editorial views or policies. Marty Claus, managing editor of the *Detroit Free Press*, remarked, "Pulling a strip draws so much attention to it and to you as a censor, that you're reluctant to do it."[14] As a result, comic strip artists, when seeking an audience early in their careers, tend to take a conservative position, hoping not to appear to threaten the diverse editorial positions of the nation's newspapers. Once syndicated, however, comic strip artists operate with considerably more autonomy than do editorial cartoonists, and the opinions expressed in comic strips are less likely to coincide with those of the newspapers they occupy than practically any other feature. The question is the extent to which this caution in expressing either liberal or conservative values in their formative stages affects syndicated artists once they are in a position to express themselves.

In general, newspaper editors tend to be more conservative on political and social issues, and comic strip artists that take any position tend to be more liberal. In the fall of 1988, for instance, a character in the popular strip "Cathy" endorsed liberal Democrat Michael Dukakis for president, and thirty papers across the country pulled the strip until the campaign was over.[15] Similar threats followed the controversial positions reflected more subtly in Garry Trudeau's "Doonesbury."

But, once again, when portraying labor unions, the comics' otherwise liberal agenda reverts to the same stereotyping common to the other entertainment media. On July 6, 1990, the "Cathy" strip showed her two yuppie friends suffering a contractor's disruption of their home because "the drywall suppliers are on strike and it'd be 10 weeks before we could repair any holes!"

My survey of nationally syndicated comic strips appearing in the two Honolulu dailies over a four-year period from the fall of 1985 through the summer of 1989 located forty-six comic strips that described or alluded to organized labor or union activities. Over half appeared in Berke Breathed's strip "Bloom County," which ran a series on a supposed comic-strip character strike in the fall of 1987. The remaining twenty were "Doonesbury," "Wizard of Id," "B.C.," "Shoe," "Mother Goose & Grimm," and "Cathy" in that order.

Unlike the editorial cartoons, it is not easy to categorize the strips by their negative or positive portrayals of labor unions. Typically a comic strip ridicules all the participants and all their views. Seldom is anyone spared, and there is no right side to a dispute. This strategy has protected most of the artists from charges of bias. They pretend to be "equal

BLOOM COUNTY   **by Berke Breathed**

Figure 5.15. "Bloom County" © 1987 Washington Post Writers Group. Reprinted with permission.

BLOOM COUNTY   **by Berke Breathed**

Figure 5.16. "Bloom County" © 1987 Washington Post Writers Group. Reprinted with permission.

opportunity satirists" and are considered unbiased when they disparage everything. So the comic strips' ridicule of labor is less important than the nature of the ridicule and the extent to which these strips accept and perpetuate the standard media stereotypes.

"Bloom County" had more sequences on labor than any other strip in the survey. The strip began in the early 1980s and quickly developed a huge national audience. It was syndicated by the Washington Post Writers Group to about eight hundred newspapers, including nearly all of the major metropolitan newspapers in the country.[16] From October 19 to November 13, 1987, the strip's artist, Berke Breathed, partially as a protest over an imminent change in newspaper formats reducing the space allotted to his cartoon, created an imaginary strike against the management of "Bloom County, Inc.," over the striking characters' grievance that their strip was now too small.

While this strip was running, the nations' papers were following the National Football League Players' Association (NFL) strike. Breathed's creation of the cartoon character strike clearly satirized the NFL strike and raised the question of the appropriateness of union representation

Figure 5.17. "Bloom County" © 1987 Washington Post Writers Group. Reprinted with permission.

Figure 5.18. "Bloom County" © 1987 Washington Post Writers Group. Reprinted with permission.

and collective bargaining in the nonindustrial and traditionally nonunion private sector.

The demand of these cartoon characters for a larger strip is made to seem ridiculous and suggests that real union strike issues are similarly petty. The fictitious CEO of Bloom, Inc., W. A. Thornhump, is also made to appear ridiculous in his reactions to the strikers, but the humor of the situation lies in the reader's distance and consequent ability to see the folly of the dispute. While editorial cartoonists tend to exaggerate defects and vices, comic strip artists prefer to trivialize and reduce the significance of beliefs and accomplishments.

Four examples from the "Bloom County" series (figures 5.15–5.18) show the typical media stereotypes of labor unions. In the first example, from October 22 (figure 5.15), young Milo, now a picket captain, orders one of his imaginary monsters out of his anxiety closet to participate in the strike and pay his dues, both against the creature's will. The previous day, when Milo rousted Opus against similar resistance, Opus argued, "Think of the readers! The poor, joyless, innocent."[17]

The second example (figure 5.16), from the following week (October

Doonesbury

BY GARRY TRUDEAU

Figure 5.19. "Doonesbury" copyright 1987 G. B. Trudeau. Reprinted with permission of Universal Press Syndicate. All rights reserved.

27, 1987), shows W. A. Thornhump, management chairman, labeling the strikers "gangsters and philistines" united in an "Evil Connection" to communism, sin, hemorrhoids, and Khadafy. By ridiculing management, Breathed appears to be supporting the strikers, but as the strike drags on, even the lovable Opus resorts to violence and attacks scab Steve Dallas (November 2, 1987, figure 5.17). That day's strip opens with the provocative headline from the fictitious *Bloom Picayune* proclaiming, "Strike Tensions Near Hysteria." Breathed's imaginary strike is, after all, lost when the union "caves," and the characters are left in a worse condition than before the strike (see last box of figure 5.18, published on November 9).

In the final analysis, the two major themes of the "Bloom County" strike are anti-labor. The sequence showed that for some workers unionization and concerted activity, though legally permissible, are ludicrous: unions are not for everyone. Workers not traditionally represented by unions probably should not be. The other message is that strikes are wasteful, hazardous, and easily broken by management.

The treatment accorded labor in the other comic strips is no better. Five strips of Garry Trudeau's "Doonesbury," for example, appeared in the survey, all of which portrayed organized labor badly. The first, in 1987, showed three arbitragers at a computer terminal selling off trusts and rolling over investment funds in astronomical amounts as if they were playing a video game (figure 5.19). The last block shows a loser, who just dropped $4 million in one bad exchange, being warned, "Steady, kid. That's the Teamster account." The threat of violence implied in the punch line relies on and reinforces the popular image of the "evil connection" Breathed satirized later that year. Three of the other four in the "Doonesbury" set are "sideswipes" in which a non-union or management character disdainfully dismisses union interference.[18] And one chastises a fictitious authors' guild for failing more aggressively to support the work of blacklisted or hit-listed writers such

WIZARD OF ID   **BY BRANT PARKER & JOHNNY HART**

Figure 5.20. "Wizard of Id" by Brant Parker and Johnny Hart, April 17, 1986. © 1986 North American Syndicate, Inc. Reprinted by permission of Johnny Hart and NAS, Inc.

as Salman Rushdie, who was suffering for his controversial book *Satanic Verses*.[19] In each case, the union is attacked for its weakness and perceived irrelevance. "Bloom County" and "Doonesbury" were among the most numerous comic strips in the survey, and they gave the kindest portrayals of labor, ridiculing the management perspective. Most of the popular strips never even broach labor relations themes.

Johnny Hart's "B.C.," a cross between "Peanuts" and the "Flintstones," is a more common example of the reduction of labor to the absurd in comic-strip portrayals. In a late 1985 strip, one of Hart's cavemen, leaning over a rock labeled "Union Headquarters," is approached by a snake who wants to join because "Striking is my 'Biz'."[20] And in a Sunday eight-block cartoon in 1988, father and son ants, discussing careers, say, "When I grow up, I want to be an umpire or a union boss," because "I love to call strikes."[21] To this cartoonist, strikes are clearly the sole business of labor unions, which are led by "bosses" rather than presidents, agents, or stewards. The related theme that not everyone should have the right to strike is expressed in "B.C." in January 1989 when Hart's prehistoric fisherman is forced to quit because his bait has walked off the job.[22]

The worst treatment of labor in all the strips surveyed is found in Brant Parker and Johnny Hart's "Wizard of Id." They consistently pursue the theme that unions are foolish organizations that improperly elevate the status of unskilled labor and allow workers unproductive employment. In one example from 1986 (figure 5.20), the promotion of a stable hand who makes neater piles is the occasion for the coworker to quip, "Of such things are trade unions made." "Such things" are, of course, piles of manure, which leaves no doubt as to the cartoonist's view of labor unions.

Similarly, in a 1987 strip, they stab at the pretentiousness of unionization when they show an immigrant at the customs desk declaring

Figure 5.21. "Wizard of Id" by Brant Parker and Johnny Hart, July 3, 1987. © 1987 North American Syndicate, Inc. Reprinted by permission of Johnny Hart and NAS, Inc.

"Agricultural Harvest Specialist" as his occupation, to which the Wizard comments, "The migratory workers finally got a union."[23] This might well be the first time in the history of media that the much-abused migrant farm workers have suffered criticism for their efforts to unionize. Though this attack on the farm workers may be unusual, in most other respects their treatment of unions is typical. An earlier 1987 installment, for instance, revealed a discussion between Sir Rodney and the King in which the difference between a "work slow-down," then being applied by the King's guard force, and a strike is given by Rodney: "In a strike you don't get paid."[24] This acerbic remark leaves the reader with the impression that unions are not only greedy and selfish but cowardly as well. The implicit notion is that the guard force union was using the slowdown because it did not have the courage to strike openly and accept the consequences.

Finally, Parker and Hart point to the single most infuriating wound unions have inflicted on employers, the coffee break. The idea that ordinary workers should have the right to take coffee breaks or in any way limit the right of their overseers to intimidate them seems to excite the most virulent anti-union condemnations. One of their July 1987 strips is typical of such attacks. In it (figure 5.21), the soldiers are apparently unionized and both sides have stopped the battle to take their coffee breaks. Once again the themes are that unions are not for everybody, that unions impair productivity, and that unions are nuisances and leave managers powerless to manage.

The treatment of labor has not improved since the survey. In January 1990 another "Wizard of Id" takes up the stereotype of criminal activity. Rodney reports to the King that the prisoners have gone on strike, and the King responds, "I didn't know they had a union." Rodney explains in the last box, "That's where they all came from."[25] This allegation is not directed at the Teamsters or any other specific union; it is a generalization that is a full-blown stereotype.

GEECH®

by Jerry Bittle

Figure 5.22. "Geech" copyright 1990 Universal Press Syndicate. Reprinted with permission. All rights reserved.

Greg Howard, author of the relatively new strip "Sally Forth," decided in the first few months of syndication to take up the stereotype that union labor is unproductive by staging a mother-daughter talk in which the daughter muses about taking vacation from school early so she can lie around the house and relax. When her mother reminds her that as a student she does not get sick leave or vacation days, she answers in the last box, "Didn't I tell you? We joined the AFL-CIO."[26] Not only does this punch line express the old theme that unions protect bad workers, but the daughter's smug attitude conveys the idea that unions encourage laziness and that workers generally want to join unions because they are lazy.

This same theme, in a more exaggerated form, was the subject of Jerry Bittle's October 30, 1990, "Geech" (figure 5.22). Rivaling the Johnny Hart-Brant Parker strips for anti-union animus, this strip depicts two unkempt deliverymen carrying a box marked "Fragile" and "This end up" upside down into a man's home. The homeowner's admonition to be careful is answered with, "Not to worry. We're union." Once in the house, they drop it with a huge "Crash!" and an ominous "Tinkle,"

Mother Goose & Grimm

Figure 5.23. "Mother Goose and Grimm" © 1991 Grimmy Inc. Reprinted by permission.

Off the Leash

"Guess what—we went on strike today, and I
got the foreman in his right boot!"

Figure 5.24. "Off the Leash" © 1990 United Feature Syndicate, Inc. Reprinted by
permission of UFS, Inc.

whereupon the homeowner complains, "I thought you said not to
worry!?" The smug reply in the last box is the punch line, "We're not.
We're union."

The other major stereotype is that union workers, particularly construction workers, are strike-happy. The "Cathy" strip cited above promoted that image, and it continues to be the most popular image when
unions are mentioned at all. The April 15, 1991, "Mother Goose and
Grimm" strip is a good example (figure 5.23). In a single large rectan-
gular box the dog, Grimmy, is confronted by a horde of tiny insects
carrying three large picket signs that read, "More Pay!" "Strike," and
"Unfair!" Grimmy's bubble reveals his conclusion: "Carpenter ants."
The assumption is not only that carpenters frequently strike but that
the probable goal of the strike is "more pay," when, in fact, in the 1980s
and early 1990s workers more commonly sought to prevent pay and
benefit cuts rather than to increase wages.

Likewise, W. B. Park's popular "Off the Leash," in which the artist
often uses animals to lampoon human foibles, suggested in a set of 1990
cartoons that violence and brutality are common to strikes and labor
relations. On April 10 (figure 5.24), a scene in the living room of a

snake family is depicted. The blue-collar husband, complete with lunch pail and hard hat, boasts to his wife, "Guess what—we went on strike today, and I got the foreman in his right boot." And in a cartoon the following month, a wolf pack stands menacingly before the desk of their pig employer. The caption reads, "Shoot, Boss, you don't have to worry about us—we're non-union."[27]

These examples show that a class bias lies behind the generally negative treatment accorded labor unions in the comic strips. A study of comic strips in the 1940s and 1950s revealed that the preferred occupations of cartoon characters were professional and managerial and that lower-status occupations were much less likely to be assigned to major characters.[28] If recent surveys of racial depictions are any indicator, there has been little change in occupational preferences. In 1988 the *Detroit Free Press*, after a month-long study of its comic page, found that it featured 5,250 white characters and 31 black characters.[29] Because the media are staffed and regulated largely by white male professionals, it is little wonder that the dominant portrayal of the labor movement is essentially managerial in its sympathies.

6. *Labor Tarred and Feathered*

Walter Kupau

Nor has the plutocracy ever fostered an inquiring spirit among its intellectual valets and footmen, which is to say, among the gentlemen who
compose headlines and leading articles for its newspapers. . . . [the press]
is, in the true sense, never well informed. It is seldom intelligent, save
in the arts of the mob-master.
—H. L. Mencken, *The National Letters, Prejudices*

From May 1983 to December 1986 three of Hawaii's newspapers in
Honolulu and on Maui reported a long and complicated series of events
and legal contests arising out of a labor dispute between Carpenters
Union Local 745 and a Maui construction contractor. This chapter analyzes the range and content of the press coverage accorded the union
and Hawaiian labor leader Walter Kupau, the key union figure in this
coverage, as an example of the media portrayal of organized labor.

This study reveals how a local press can single out a union or its leader
for special adverse treatment beyond that merited by the facts of the
case. In such instances, the initial editorial opinion of the paper toward
the union tends to inhibit fair consideration or fresh interpretations of
ensuing developments. Editorial policy thus biases public opinion
against the union and its leadership in a way that not only tarnishes the
reputation of the union but negatively affects the overall image of organized labor in that community.

Article V of the "Canons of Journalism" defined impartiality by pointing out the important distinction between news reports and the expression of editorial opinion. According to that code, "News reports should
be free from opinion or bias of any kind."[1] More recently Everette
Dennis, executive director of the Gannett Center for Media Studies,
described press objectivity as the "crown jewel in American journalism,
as our reporting, unlike that of European papers, moved away from
party politics and heavy-breathing ideology and established a functional
difference between news columns and editorial columns."[2] Subjects of

press coverage, whether they are labor leaders or not, have a right to expect the press to make a conscientious effort to live up to this ethical code.

The press coverage of the case of *C & W Construction v. the International Brotherhood of Carpenters and Joiners of America, Local 745*, and of the local's business representative and financial secretary, Walter Kupau, is significant for at least three reasons. First, the local papers, to varying degrees, early and consistently adopted an anti-union, anti-Kupau perspective that permeated their news reporting and editorial columns. This "lynch-mob" mentality prevented the papers from seriously considering alternate interpretations of the subsequent events. Second, coverage of the central issue of the dispute intimated that the union defendant was guilty of egregious criminal violence instead of a relatively common form of nonviolent organizational picketing. And third, there is evidence in the pattern of coverage of what has been called "pack journalism" in the way two of the papers appear to have followed the attack, not independently but at the heels of the lead paper.[3]

The Papers

The history of all three papers goes back to the nineteenth century to the days of the "Big 5," when five large, plantation-based companies owned almost every financial enterprise in Hawaii. Since 1971 the *Star-Bulletin* has been owned by the Gannett Pacific Corporation, and the *Advertiser* and *Maui News* remain locally owned. Though the *Advertiser* and the *Star-Bulletin* are separately owned, under a state-approved joint operating agreement in effect since 1962, they share production facilities and combine to produce a single Sunday edition.

The two Honolulu papers, the *Advertiser* and the *Star-Bulletin*, circulate throughout the state of Hawaii, while the readership of the *Maui News* is confined for the most part to Maui County's three islands, Maui, Molokai, and Lanai. Collectively, therefore, they are the newspapers most likely to cover this story, and their combined readership is well over 208,000 people.[4]

The newspapers studied here do not all habitually express archconservative or anti-labor editorial perspectives. Indeed, Hawaii is generally acknowledged to have a much more favorable attitude toward labor unions than may be found in the rest of the country. A higher percentage of Hawaii's work force is unionized, including most of the newspaper reporters and production staff.[5] Certainly all three papers would disclaim any partisan affiliation or intentional bias. Nevertheless, in this case, the newspapers violated generally accepted canons of journalistic ethics and created a negative picture of organized labor.

Walter Kupau

Though the incidents on which the case and the ensuing press coverage are based date back only to 1980, it is important to know something of the background of the principal union figure, Walter Kupau. The son of an army officer, he was born in Kalihi in 1937. Kupau grew up in that poor and notoriously roughneck part of Honolulu and is one of an ever decreasing minority of indigenous Hawaiians who have been struggling without much success for cultural identity in the state's American institutions.[6] Though his family was able to send him to a local parochial high school for a time, like many native Hawaiians he had difficulty adjusting to formal education. Eventually his family sent him to live with relatives in San Francisco.[7] He graduated from high school there and spent three years in the Army Corps of Engineers. After that, he returned to Hawaii and started working as a construction laborer. In the early 1960s, he worked his way through the union apprenticeship program and began work as a union carpenter.

In 1965 he was elected job steward for the workers at the Lagoon Towers at the Hilton Hawaiian Village and began a rapid rise through the union's leadership. By 1969 he was elected president of the Hawaii State AFL-CIO. At the same time he served as the administrative assistant to the former financial secretary of the Carpenters' local, Stanley Yanagi. He ran against Yanagi in 1975 for that position and lost, though he won reelection as president of the state AFL-CIO. In 1977 Kupau launched a campaign to stop what he believed was organized crime's attempt to gain control of the state's key construction unions, naming Henry Huihui and Wilfred "Nappy" Pulawa as the two most notorious criminal figures in that effort.[8] In 1978, almost a year after Stanley Yanagi died, Walter Kupau won election in a hotly contested race against Yanagi's handpicked successor. In a rare example of intervention, the president of the union's international office in Washington, D.C., moved to disqualify Kupau. A federal judge finally ordered his installation over the objections of the mainland officers. The international's role in this dispute, of course, left a deep breach between Walter Kupau and the mainland officials.

By the time of his clash with the Mungovans, the owners of a nonunion construction company, and the ensuing legal dispute, Walter Kupau had earned a reputation as a colorful but aggressive union activist, unafraid to speak up for labor or to express his opinions in a local style of oratory that, in the 1960s, the press found refreshing and entertaining if not sympathetic copy. More significant, by this time, Kupau had made for himself a long list of powerful adversaries.[9]

His avowed goal in both the 1975 and 1978 union elections was to double the union's membership and increase unionization of the state's building contractors. In 1980 his leadership was put to the test when he led the Carpenters on a four-week general strike that succeeded in winning an unprecedented 58 percent increase in their wage package.[10] At the same time, the strike drove a bitter wedge between the Carpenters and some of the more conservative unions in the Building Trades Council that resulted in three of the major unions crossing the Carpenters' picket lines during the latter half of the strike.[11]

Nor was Kupau reluctant to speak out in the political arena. An early backer of the state's first Democratic governor, John Burns, Kupau also became an outspoken critic of Honolulu's mayor, Frank Fasi. By the 1980s, though, his political alliances had changed. He had become a critic of Democratic Governor George Ariyoshi and a staunch supporter and defender of Fasi, who by then was a Republican.

Indeed, by 1981, Walter Kupau's relentless pursuit of the leadership goals he had set in 1975 had created for him a strong support base in his union at the expense of an ever-growing list of enemies among the outside interests he had either bruised or ignored in the process.[12]

The Issues in the Legal Dispute

Of all of Kupau's various campaigns, his organizing agenda would prove to be the most controversial. Following a national trend based on a recession economy and a growing series of legal decisions unfavorable to union organizing, by 1982 the union share of the state's construction labor was down to about 30 percent and dropping.[13] Organizing in the construction industry is one of the most difficult and legally complex operations under American labor law. Though the original purpose of the New Deal's Wagner Act was to give workers the right to join unions and require employers to recognize workers' unions and bargain with them in good faith, unionization of construction workers never seemed to fit the pattern cut for it by the framers of the National Labor Relations Act. Instead, the law provides a process designed for more conventional industrial workers which presumes a stable work force that is not normal to the construction industry. Federal law, for instance, encourages workers and their employers to wage union election campaigns, and, if the union is successful, the parties are expected to bargain until a contract settlement is reached. The problem is that a construction contractor does not generally maintain a permanent work force but hires masons, electricians, carpenters, and plumbers in sequence and only for as many days as the work requires.

In the construction industry, then, the practice is for the craft unions to train workers and maintain the work force through the union hiring hall to which contractors may apply for workers as needed. To use the union hiring hall, a contractor must sign a master agreement to pay wages that are negotiated with the local contractors' association. Consequently, the methods of organizing or expanding the union's membership are entirely different in the construction industry than in other industries.

Labor law generally forbids unions from exerting influence on the employer when they are trying to organize workers. For example, the law forbids union picketing of an employer's premises if the purpose of the picket is to urge the employer to subscribe to a master agreement with the union. Though this policy makes sense for workers in an auto or garment factory, in the construction industry, it prevents the union or any interested workers from conducting a legal campaign among the workers during the few days or even weeks that the contractor is using a given craft's services. And even if it were possible to achieve recognition before a contract could reasonably be bargained, which regularly consumes months of effort, the job would be long done, and the workers would futilely be attempting the whole process again with a new contractor.

In practice, then, construction unions have to try to persuade contractors to use trained union craftsmen from their respective halls. To persuade nonunion contractors, the unions may legally conduct a picket that is strictly "informational" and is therefore protected by the First Amendment. Construction unions across the country conduct such informational picketing using picket signs that inform the public that "this contractor is not paying area standard wages," for instance. Of course, everyone realizes the real aim of such picketing is to convince the contractor to use union labor.[14]

This distinction between legal, informational picketing and illegal organizational picketing was the key issue in the dispute between the Carpenters' Union and the Maui construction company. The dispute eventually resulted in the conviction of Walter Kupau and two of the union's Maui agents for perjury, that is, for describing their union's picket as informational when other evidence suggested its purpose was organizational.

Facts of the Case

1979 *Walter Mungovan,* a former union carpenter, and his wife, Cher, started business as C&W Construction on Maui.

1980 *In December* the Carpenters Union began informational picketing of "C&W Construction" work sites.

1981 *February 3:* Walter Mungovan secretly taped conversations with the local Maui union agents suggesting that the purpose of the union pickets was organizational.

February 27: Walter Mungovan secretly taped a phone conversation with Walter Kupau, who assured him that the pickets would come down if he signed an acceptable agreement.

June: Mungovan filed unfair labor practice charges with the NLRB against the Carpenters for conducting an organizational picket of his company.

1981 *June:* Carpenters filed a civil suit in circuit court charging Mungovan and Honolulu attorney Barry Marr with violating Hawaii's electronic eavesdropping law. Mungovan filed a countersuit in circuit court accusing Walter Kupau and the Carpenters Union of causing him "severe emotional distress, loss of business income and loss of earnings."

1982 *NLRB charges* against the Carpenters Union were dropped because they had been improperly filed by the NLRB attorney.

1983 *The Federal Bureau of Investigation* (FBI) and the U.S. Attorney's Office charged the two Carpenters agents on Maui and Walter Kupau with perjury made on the affidavits filed in response to Mungovan's 1981 NLRB complaint, on the basis that the union had claimed that its pickets were informational although Mungovan had made audiotapes that indicated the purpose of the picket was organizational.

May 13: Mungovan reported that two unidentified men tried to abduct him from his apartment at the Hilton Hawaiian Village.

May 18: The FBI placed Walter Mungovan in the federal witness protection program, without his wife or her son.

May 21: The two Maui agents of the Carpenters, William Nishibayashi and Ralph Torres, were found guilty of perjury and each was sentenced to six months in jail.

August 18: A federal grand jury indicted Walter Kupau on seven counts of perjury.

November 17: Walter Kupau was found guilty of six counts of perjury.

December 27: Federal Judge Harold Fong denied Kupau's appeal to overturn the verdict.

1984 *May 14:* Nishibayashi and Torres lost their appeal before the Ninth Circuit to overturn their convictions.

November 5: During a Carpenters' strike, an Oahu construction foreman, Thomas Murchison, was allegedly assaulted by three union agents.

November 10: Walter Kupau was charged with hindering prosecution (a misdemeanor) because he drove the van that brought the three agents back from Mililani.

1985 *February 20:* Kupau was indicted on felony charges of hindering prosecution in the Mililani assault case.

November 4: A circuit court jury acquitted one of the agents and reduced to petty misdemeanor the charges against the two other agents in the Mililani assault case.

1986 *January 28:* The Ninth Circuit Court of Appeals rejected Kupau's motion to overturn his perjury conviction.

January 31: The felony charge against Kupau in the Mililani assault case was dismissed by the state's circuit court.

June 12: Walter Kupau was taken to Lompoc Federal Prison in California, where he served six months of his two-year sentence before being furloughed to a halfway house in Hawaii.

Analysis of Coverage

Though three papers reported the events of this case to the state's residents, the *Honolulu Advertiser* led the way and the other papers generally reacted to the *Advertiser* coverage or followed suit. A review of the 1983 headlines of the three papers reveals the *Advertiser*'s dominance.[15] During these first eight months of the story's life, the *Advertiser* ran fifty-two articles, the *Star-Bulletin* twenty-five, and the *Maui News* twenty-eight.

The *Advertiser*'s coverage was distinctive in another respect as well. Most newspapers designate one or more reporters to the so-called labor beat. The *Advertiser* had so designated Charles Turner and Sandy Oshiro and the *Star-Bulletin*, Phil Mayer. Labor stories typically went to these beat reporters unless there was some reason why their objectivity might be called into question. Phil Mayer, for example, disqualified himself because he had once worked for Kupau.[16] The *Advertiser*, from the time it broke the story in 1983 through 1986, pulled the story from its labor reporters and turned it over to Walter Wright, a specially designated investigative reporter, who was directed to deal exclusively with all aspects of the Kupau-Mungovan dispute.

It is not clear why Wright was assigned to this story, but it meant that the *Advertiser* gave it more coverage than either of the other papers found appropriate. Indeed, Walter Kupau raised the issue of a "media attack" even as the events of the case were beginning to unfold.[17] Though three *Advertiser* reporters wrote on the case from time to time, Walter Wright carried the lead. All but eight of the credited bylines during the first eight months were attributed to Wright.

Headlines are significant both in their content and their placement. Even when a reporter has portrayed a story fairly and evenly, the construction of the headline can indicate a bias. The layout of the story can also affect the way it is perceived. The size of the headline and the proximity of the story to the front page or to other stories of a positive or negative nature influence the readers' perception. These decisions are almost entirely out of the control of the beat reporter and are made by a separate editor.

Leonard Doob, writing on propaganda, noted that headlines have a pronounced influence on the way stories are perceived by readers. Not only are they the first exposure readers have to a story, but many people read only the headlines and, therefore, their entire impression of an issue comes from these terse messages.[18]

The *Advertiser* first broke the Kupau-Mungovan story in 1981, when Charles Turner picked it up from the circuit court suits filed. The headline read, "Suit, Countersuit in Bugging Accusation."[19] This headline is atypical in that it did not implicate, accuse, or unfairly associate either litigant. The body of the article was also objective and carefully constructed to express both disputants' cases in an understandable and forthright manner.

When the story was next taken up, in May 1983, a new perspective was immediately apparent from the headline, "FBI probing Carpenters, Kupau Says."[20] What Kupau actually said, as was revealed in the second paragraph of the text, was that the FBI was "harassing" the union. This two-page story, over fourteen hundred words, was the first of Walter Wright's articles. It details the background of the perjury charges that were pending against the two Maui agents, Torres and Nishibayashi. But the headline suggests the prospect of future discoveries of union malfeasance, when in fact the case was already being tried with as much evidence as was ever presented in court.

Wright's next two articles on May 15 and 17 were more overt in their bias. The first, headlined "Tape Technology—Last Word in Crime Fighting," appeared in the *Sunday Star-Bulletin and Advertiser* and so enjoyed the combined circulation of both dailies. As the title suggests, the lengthy article defended the Maui contractor's technique of secretly taping his conversations. It also compared Mungovan's labor dispute with the FBI's campaign against organized crime. Furthermore, Wright's article argued against the union's suit, based on Hawaii's 1978 law prohibiting electronic eavesdropping. Without mentioning the suit specifically, Wright was asserting that people who are protected by a law that has protected criminals must also be criminals.

In the May 17 article, the connection is made more obvious. Titled "Contractor: Taped Union 'Threats,' " this piece throws objectivity to the wind in its reference to "threats" that in the sixth paragraph the article concedes were not taped: "But Mungovan acknowledged he failed to lure Nishibayashi into repeating that threat while Nishibayashi was being recorded in a later conversation."[21] The *alleged* threat was that Mungovan's home would be "torched" if he refused to sign up with the union. That no recording existed to corroborate this allegation, despite both sides' concession that the tape was made without Nishibayashi's knowledge, was interpreted only to mean that Mungovan was not lucky enough to tape the threat the first time. No consideration was given to the equally plausible interpretation that there was no threat in the first place and that Mungovan was hoping to lure Nishibayashi into making such a threat so that the NLRB would enjoin the Carpenters' organizing efforts. Clearly, the reporter had already determined what the crime was, who was guilty, and who was the victim. In fact, the issue of the trial was perjury, not "terroristic threatening." None of the agents was ever tried or found guilty (except in the media) of threats. But the tactic of guilt by association, begun in the headlines and carried into the construction and argument of these early stories, had established a negative attitude toward Walter Kupau and the Carpenters Union. This attitude was evident as early as May 1983 while the first of the two trials was still in progress and before the *Star-Bulletin* had even begun its coverage.

The image of labor is also affected by the placement, or environment, of a headline. As Doob noted, most people who scan the newspaper read only the headlines and read them in tandem with the headlines of neighboring stories on the same page, creating—where there is an environmental pattern—a subliminal association or link between the stories. For years, labor stories had suffered from the common editorial penchant for placing the labor beat and police beat on the same page. Though this practice has declined in recent years, a survey of *Advertiser* and *Star-Bulletin* labor stories revealed that each paper still tended to place the labor report next to a crime report.

In the first month of the *Advertiser*'s coverage of the Carpenters' perjury trial there was a high incidence of environmental guilt by association. On May 20 the headline "Didn't Lie, 2 Carpenter Unionists Testify" appears under a story whose headline was "Cellblock Suicide Case Goes to Jury." On May 25 the story of the federal investigation of a house fire on the island of Oahu (which the FBI hoped to link to Walter Kupau and the Carpenters) was printed next to a large photo of a fireworks display over the Brooklyn Bridge curiously unrelated to any of the other stories on that page, but easily mistaken for a picture of a burning house. Similarly, on June 1, the headline that first disclosed that Mungovan had been placed in the witness protection program, "Contractor Put under Protection," appeared on the front page over a special obituary for boxing great Jack Dempsey and the headline "Dempsey Dies" and an old photo of Dempsey with his fists up in a threatening stance. At first glance, the Dempsey photo looks as though it belongs to the Mungovan story rather than to the obituary.

The assumption of guilt by association is even more blatant in the text of another of the May 1983 articles by Walter Wright. On May 25, Wright reported on the denial of documents requested by the Carpenters under the Freedom of Information Act (FOIA). According to the article, such requests under the FOIA are typical of the way Russia, the Mafia, and big corporations try to find out "what the government knows about them" as if seeking such information were inherently un-American. Case after case of Detroit organized crime families and Cosa Nostra informants are cited to defend the denial of documents to the Carpenters Union as though they were logically related, as though the Carpenters Union was a public enemy just as Russia and the Mafia were perceived to be. Not unlike George Bush's attack on the American Civil Liberties Union during the 1988 presidential campaign, a legitimate and even laudable institution (in this case the FOIA) is made to appear subversive in a form of yellow journalism.

This same article illustrates another shortcoming that often contributes to imbalance and distortion in press coverage. In dealing with labor disputes, reporters usually prefer management sources and informants. The majority of the May 25 article on the Carpenters' FOIA request consists of a virtual transcription of the response of the government agent, William Ervin, to the denial of the requests. Of the five hundred words in that article, only fifty-six are devoted to the union's position and that passage consists solely of the text of the union's written request filed with the government: "The Carpenters' Union said in the request letter it revealed yesterday that it wanted any information the government had about the 17 union officials or employees, and had or would submit authorization forms from each of those individuals."[22] Beyond the issue of the legal status of this request or the government's denial, it is difficult to understand why the request should be characterized as subversive. Bias in the source of news, as Cirino called it, commonly results, as it does here, in advocacy reporting.

Other examples of the press's preference for interviewing those on the nonunion side of a labor dispute can be seen in the frequency with which the reporters asked Cher Mungovan to comment on developments. The preference is particularly curious because it was Cher's husband, Walter Mungovan, who was both plaintiff and principal witness. Though she was part-owner of the company, as the court proceedings revealed, Cher was not a direct witness to any of the alleged threats or organizing interviews that were heard by the court. And yet it was Cher, not Walter, who went to Washington, D.C., to testify before Senate hearings to amend federal labor law, and it was Cher who became the focus of the press coverage.

The *Advertiser* was not the only paper that allowed itself to be directed by the Mungovan press releases or inclined to accept unquestioningly and uncritically Cher Mungovan's version of events she never witnessed. All three papers ran stories that were virtual panegyrics in praise of the heroic young couple's valiant struggle against the unionists.

The *Advertiser* began the series on the Mungovans with Walter Wright's story on July 25, 1983, under the headline "The Trials for Viet Vet, Wife Just Beginning." Not only does this article exaggerate Walter Mungovan's military career, which was in any event irrelevant to the case, but it attempts again to establish the un-American nature of unionism:

> "This is America," Cher told her husband when he said the union wanted to organize him. "No one can force you to sign."
> It was America, but, Mungovan would say later, it became worse than Vietnam.[23]

Although the trial was not about violence, threats, or the brutality that these and other press descriptions of imagined mayhem suggested, the continual onslaught of press insinuations to the contrary clearly went beyond the scope of reporting and smacked of an editorial crusade. In the eyes of the law, the union agents were tried and convicted of perjury for saying their picket line was informational; in the eyes of the media and its public, the union was guilty, without a trial, of criminal threats, extortion, arson, and assault.

These articles were very damaging not only to Walter Kupau but to the union movement in general. The headlines of most of the articles that followed this first *Advertiser* attack feature the word *union* instead of *carpenters* or the names of the defendants, thereby tarring all unions with the same tainted brush:

Advertiser
July 25, 1983:   "The Trials for Viet Vet, Wife Just Beginning"
February 7, 1984: "Mrs. Mungovan Hopes to Join Husband"
April 30, 1984:   "Senators Due to Hear Mungovan Today; Step-son, 12, Also Will Tell of Tribulations"

Star-Bulletin
October 26, 1983:   "Maui Woman Testifies on Union Harassment"
November 5, 1983:   "Union Ruined Firm, Mungovan Testifies"
February 8, 1984:   "Cher Mungovan Raps Isle Unions"
October 30, 1987:   "Mungovan Wages Long, Hard Fight in Union Dispute"

Maui News
November 24, 1983: "Battle Site Over Unions Returns to Washington"
January 6, 1984:   "Hard Line Made Dispute Inevitable"
January 6, 1984:   "Mungovan Dispute Brings Ills of Union Excesses into Focus"
January 26, 1984:   "Mungovan Anger Not with Unions Alone"
May 1, 1984:   "Once Happy Family Tells How Union Ruined Lives"

Formal editorial opinion of all three papers, even when it expressed opposition to Kupau's actions in this case, attempted to distinguish the rest of the union movement from censure. And yet the persistent reference to unions generically in the headlines listed above was bound to accomplish the opposite impression.

"Pack journalism," in this case the apparent connection between the coverage of the *Advertiser* and the other papers, is a phenomenon first noted during the Watergate era.[24] After the *Washington Post* finally succeeded in exposing the cover-up, many of the country's previously pro-administration papers suddenly turned on Nixon with a vengeance, hastening his resignation and creating the misleading impression that the press was exercising a liberal bias. Actually the press was exercising the much less admirable practice of ganging up on fallen prey. The same thing happened to Gary Hart and vice-presidential candidate Dan Quayle. A similar phenomenon is evident in the Hawaii press coverage of the Kupau-Mungovan dispute.

After the *Advertiser* drew first blood in its attack, it was not long before the other papers followed. Once Walter Wright's articles had begun to attract public notice, particularly after the perjury convictions of Nishibayashi and Torres, first the *Maui News* and then the *Star-Bulletin* were quick to join the attack. The *Maui News* began its coverage by simply borrowing the story from the *Advertiser*. Of the twenty-four stories it printed in an eight-month period in 1983, nineteen credited Honolulu (UPI) with the byline. United Press International (UPI) is a wire service that picks up the lead stories from one paper and transmits them nationally for the benefit of its subscribers. Since the *Advertiser* had introduced and was leading the coverage of this story, the UPI material was largely drawn from its coverage. To some extent the *Maui News*'s reliance on the wire stories may be understandable because, though the disputants were primarily Maui residents, the trial was in Honolulu. But more background information could have been available had the *Maui News* been interested in the story earlier.

Once the *Maui News* did become interested, its coverage quickly took on the character of a crusade. During the eight months of its initial coverage, the *Maui News* featured four editorial attacks on the Carpenters or Walter Kupau personally. That was twice as many editorials as appeared in the two Honolulu papers and represents one-seventh of their entire coverage.

The remaining articles published in the *Maui News* reveal, particularly throughout 1983, the growing editorial hostility toward Walter Kupau. The first stories were excerpts from the *Advertiser* picked up through the UPI. By June, however, about a week after the first editorial condemnation of Kupau's defense, the headline featuring the report about Kupau's offer for information on Walter Mungovan's two alleged abductors read "Carpenters Boss Offers Reward." The term *boss* instead of *leader*, *agent*, or *head* is always unfavorable, suggesting he was not elected democratically and maintains his power by force and coercion. It is a loaded label that dredges up a loathsome stereotype and reveals the user's bias.

Though the *Star-Bulletin*'s coverage was, by comparison, considerably less pointed in its attack, its treatment of Kupau's trial and the Mungovan family seemed to follow the *Advertiser*'s lead. The bulk of the stories were written by the paper's court reporter Charles Memminger, whose coverage does not reveal as much sympathy for Mungovan as Walter Wright's. Yet the headlines, which were not written by the reporter but by a desk editor, consistently pick up the anti-union features of the story. Over Memminger's article on November 5, for instance, the headline was "Union Ruined Firm, Mungovan Testifies."[25] The selection of that nugget from all the testimony, instead of "Mungovan Planned to

Sign up with Union," which was also reported in that article, or instead of any of Walter Kupau's comments, reveals an editorial policy decision that had already determined which side of the story should be emphasized.

Unlike the *Advertiser*, whose coverage pattern was largely the product of its local reporter, Walter Wright, the *Star-Bulletin*, a Gannett paper, often carried stories by out-of-state reporters and commentators. In October 1983, the story "Maui Woman Testifies on Union Harassment" was taken from the Associated Press (AP); in February 1984 the story "Cher Mungovan Raps Isle Unions" was written by Jessica Lee, of Gannett's News Service; and in April 1984 the story "Mungovan's Son Testifies in Senate" was written by John Teare of Gannett.[26] Near the end of the story's life in 1987, *Star-Bulletin* writer Ann Murakami wrote a "report" that told only the Mungovan side of the story. Under the headline, "Mungovan Wages a Long, Hard Fight in Union Dispute," the story makes no pretense to objectivity or balance. The article is an accurate "report" only of Cher Mungovan's diatribe against the Carpenters Union: "In the meantime, Mungovan said, it's been 'very emotionally and financially draining' for her family. She said she must fight alone, and it's like fighting a 'mighty conglomerate corporation.'"[27] This portrayal of the Mungovans as the victims of a large and powerful conspiracy was only one possible interpretation of the facts. Just as likely was Kupau's belief that the large and powerful federal government had conspired to crush the union's efforts to survive the incursion of nonunion construction.

The press bias against Walter Kupau in the handling of the Mungovan case is just as apparent in its omissions as in its commission. As reporters began to identify with Cher Mungovan, they gave less attention to details that did not support their negative opinion of Walter Kupau. From the beginning, Kupau had insisted that this case was engineered by the federal government to stop the spread of union organizing in Hawaii's construction industry.[28] Without question, Walter Kupau's administration of the Carpenters local had made it the most active and aggressive union organizer in the labor community. Yet at no time did any of the Hawaii press give serious consideration to Kupau's charges.

Walter Kupau also raised the question of racial prejudice throughout the campaign. Not only did the papers fail to credit the validity of such charges, but the *Maui News* editorialized on the ridiculousness of the allegation.[29] It is true, however, that the Mungovans, recent residents of Hawaii, like the federal investigators and prosecutors as well as the overwhelming majority of the jury, were Caucasian and that the key issue in the union defense dealt with the intended meaning of English spoken in the local "pidgin" patois. It is also true that the case was taken out of the hands of the local police and local NLRB office and handled exclusively by mainland, primarily Caucasian, officials. Finally, it is true that the case almost immediately became a platform for a legislative attack on the entire labor movement staged by the National Right-to-Work Committee in Washington, D.C., before a special Republican-controlled Senate committee.

Though none of the papers at the time elected to deal with the discriminatory impact of this racially "stacked deck," it is no coincidence that not long after Walter Kupau's conviction, the federal jury pools were restructured to avoid just such imbalances as Kupau decried.

The coverage also failed to consider a growing body of evidence that called the credibility of the Mungovans' testimony into question. It is hard, for example, to reconcile the image of them as poor, hopeless, and downtrodden with the deft management of their frequent press releases and the wide circulation accorded their version of the story. Starting with two columns by Jack Anderson in September 1983, which were syndicated throughout the country,[30] a barrage of national articles in *Reader's Digest*, the *Wall Street Journal*, the *Washington Times*, the *New York Times*, the *Washington Post* and even London's *Daily Mail* revealed a media handling of the Mungovan dispute that was professionally conceived and indicative of a political agenda that appears to validate Kupau's expressed suspicions.[31]

The pattern throughout the coverage was for the press to accept unquestioningly any information attested to by either of the Mungovans and to dismiss or ridicule everything proffered by Walter Kupau. A fair report would have considered the possible flaws in both sides of the case. Why, for example, did Mungovan not place his wife and stepson in the witness protection program with or instead of himself? A threat, if one ever existed, would be even more effectively made against a witness's loved ones than against his own person. The papers were content with Cher's response that she needed to stay out to pursue the civil suits against the union, but this answer ignores the question of the alleged danger to her or her husband. And if Walter Mungovan was able to be a witness in court from the federal program, why wouldn't Cher Mungovan have been able to maintain the suits just as well from the program? None of the three reporters ever pursued these questions to a satisfactory conclusion.

Though the reporters were quick to accept any information released by the Mungovans or their government informants, information Walter and Cher Mungovan expressed in their trial depositions, which should have been more reliable, was virtually ignored as a source. The depositions, which were available to the reporters, reveal a range of improprieties and improbabilities that are inconsistent with the image of heroic victim the press projected.[32] Walter Mungovan, a high school dropout, had himself been a union carpenter and served as a union steward and member of the negotiating committee. He started his construction company with funds Cher's family provided together with a worker's compensation settlement he received from a former employer (which would ordinarily mean he was disabled and unable to continue working).[33]

Conclusions

There is certainly enough evidence in the record to cast some doubt on the government's case against Kupau and to justify a serious inquiry into his charges of government union-busting. That no connection was ever made between Mungovan's alleged abductors and the Carpenters Union or Walter Kupau has not mitigated the effect of the press coverage in just such an insinuation. Walter Kupau was tried in the press and found guilty of crimes he was never accused of in court. Although the press reports did not make overt accusations, the implications they suggested were just as damaging and virtually impossible to contest.

It is common for news editors to defend occasional instances of bias, the labeling headline, the tactic of guilt by association, or even the more subtle preference for anti-union sources by dismissing these negative portrayals as lapses in otherwise objective coverage. But fair coverage will never result from a pattern of objectivity so disturbed, for objectivity is not just a pattern of gyroscopic fluctuations between opposite poles. A slanted word, paragraph, or headline is not compensated or excused by the following day's fairness. The final orbit of such treatment is bound to be skewed.

Nor is it a defense to claim that bias was unintended or that, being unintended, it was not bias at all. When black civil rights groups and feminists first called attention to the deeply prejudicial impact of such words as *nigra* or *girl*, the issue of intentionality was shown to be irrelevant. Labor's resentment of the tactics illustrated in this study has generally been ignored or dismissed by the press, as were the frequent complaints raised by Walter Kupau throughout his trial. Press bias should be regarded in the same light as scandal, slander, and rumor because it cannot be recalled or mitigated. The responsibility of the press is, therefore, enormous and should never be limited only to the harm it has consciously and willfully caused. In the words of feminist writer Joanna Russ:

> The boys throw stones at the frogs in jest,
> But the frogs die in earnest.[34]

It is hoped that such studies as this one will help establish a new sensitivity in the press and throughout the media to the negative impact of their traditional patterns of labor coverage and establish a heightened awareness among reporters and editors of the need to curb unconscious tendencies that might influence their portrayals of organized labor.

7. *Labor Buried Alive*

The Mine Workers' Pittston Strike

Twenty-five years ago the great interests, in their war upon labor, had not yet completed their united front, and an occasional voice of protest could be heard through a gap here and there in the iron ring. This has all been changed.
—Big Bill Haywood, *Bill Haywood's Book*

From April 1989 to February 1990, nearly two thousand mine workers represented by the United Mine Workers of America (UMWA) struck the Pittston Coal Group, a subsidiary of the Pittston Company, in the coalfields of Virginia, West Virginia, and Kentucky. In what may be regarded as one of the most important labor disputes of the twentieth century, the Mine Workers' strike attracted a variety of national and international attention, and the resultant media coverage spanned the range from local newspaper reports to network television specials. An analysis of this coverage reveals many basic patterns underlying the press treatment commonly afforded unions on strike. In comparison to other highly visible labor disputes in the same period, such as the machinists', pilots', and flight attendants' strike against Eastern Airlines or the Amalgamated Transit Union strike of Greyhound Lines, coverage of the Pittston strike may seem benign, but a closer examination of this ostensibly tame portrayal reveals the classic anti-union bias that has plagued labor unions throughout this century.

Although the issues in the mine workers' dispute were seen by many labor relations professionals as pivotal to the future of collective bargaining, these strike issues were never considered newsworthy. The future of negotiated health care and retiree benefit plans, a staple of the majority of union contracts, and the innovative tactics attempted by the newly reorganized and revitalized union leadership were repeatedly relegated in the local and national press to the timeworn stereotypes of strike violence; greedy and mindless unionists were victimizing strike-breakers, who were glorified as latter-day industrial pioneers.

The Key Issues in the Dispute

Largely as a result of reverses suffered by the labor movement over the previous eight years, the United Mine Workers at Pittston were positioned either to defend or abandon forever some of the most basic benefits of unionization. Between 1980 and 1988 appointments of conservatives to the National Labor Relations Board and the Supreme Court by President Ronald Reagan had so altered the balance of power between labor and management that the straightforward and fundamental rights to organize and engage in concerted activity, thought to be inalienable rights of labor since the passage of the Wagner Act in 1935, were one by one being revoked or so convoluted by the courts that a union steward would need a law degree to know what to do.

Over the course of the 1980s the American economic base changed from industrial production to service and communications industries. American workers, largely untrained and unprepared for these changes, suffered the brunt of this reorganization. Gone were the days when Americans pointed with pride to the high standard of living available to the average blue-collar worker. Inexplicably, these same workers were now being pointed at as overpaid, unproductive, and spoiled for achieving the same benefits that once made the United States the envy of the world.

Mining in America, like steel and auto production before it, was changing from a national industry to a global swap meet, in which the already victimized workers and their unions were blamed for trying to hold on to their hard-won benefits. Pittston Coal Group had challenged the United Mine Workers in four basic areas: In a threat to job security, the company sought the power to subcontract nearly every UMWA job to a nonunion subsidiary (a subversion of labor law commonly called double-breasting) and remove a successorship clause that would have protected union benefits in the event mines or mining operations are sold off. The company was challenging seniority preference to miners in assigning overtime, regular eight-hour work shifts, or both. It was denying them the right to refuse work on Sundays and holidays, while at the same time it laid off more than 4,000 miners, for whom it claimed there was no work. Pensions and health care for retirees were threatened when Pittston unilaterally withdrew from the multiemployer pension plan and discontinued coverage for 130,000 retirees, widows, and disabled miners. This last issue had, perhaps, the broadest and farthest-reaching implications. The rising costs of health care had clearly become a national dilemma by 1988, and the Pittston stand against the United Mine Workers was widely regarded as the first major battle that would likely set the precedent for management negotiations on this issue throughout the country. Much was riding on this dispute, and the mine workers found themselves on the front line of a battle that was almost certain to redefine what benefits unions might expect through the next decade and beyond.

Analysis of Coverage

A chronology of the key events from the prestrike negotiations to the settlement reached, spanning the period of one year between the closing months of 1988 and New Year's Eve 1989, is provided on pages 136–39.

Two main themes typified the media coverage of these events. First, the union's largely successful efforts to employ peaceful means and the tactics of civil disobedience were considered unnewsworthy because they were inconsistent with the media stereotype of violent and power-mad union thugs. Second, the issues of the dispute were either not treated or were expressed from an employer's perspective so that the dispute appeared senseless to the general public, and the union was made to appear outdated and irrelevant in a contemporary labor relations environment.

In early August 1989, when the UMWA strike was in its fifth month and a Soviet miners' strike was in its second month, Joel Swartz, a union sympathizer, decided to conduct an informal public opinion poll of the citizens of St. Paul and Minneapolis to test his theory that the local press had systematically neglected the workers' strike at Pittston while extensively covering that of the Soviet miners. He asked people to pick from a list of four countries, in two of which major coal strikes were going on. He asked the people who picked the United States as one of the countries to name one or more of the issues in the dispute. He expected his results to be skewed upward because 25 percent of the people he polled were delegates to a St. Paul union council meeting. Yet, as Alexander Cockburn reported in the *Nation*, Swartz found that only 28 percent of the people he polled knew there was a coal strike in the United States while 83 percent knew of the Soviet strike.[1] Of the nondelegates he polled, only 16 percent knew of the Pittston strike, and virtually no one was able to name any of the major strike issues.

Similarly, on September 21, 1989, just after ninety-eight miners and a local Protestant minister took over Pittston's Moss 3 plant, a review of television coverage conducted by *People's Daily World* showed that neither ABC, CBS, nor NBC had covered the event although the miners sent each network a videotape of their action.[2] The first national media attention accorded the event did not appear until September 19, forty hours after it happened, in an Associated Press story picked up by the *Washington Post* and *USA Today*. As Jonathan Tasini pointed out in his report published by Fairness and Accuracy in Reporting (FAIR), it was virtually ignored by the national media even though it was the first major takeover of a plant by striking American workers since the 1937 sitdown strike by autoworkers at the General Motors plant in Flint, Michigan.[3]

The patterns of media portrayals of the Pittston strikers will be best understood by considering the press and television news coverage separately.

Newspaper Coverage

Legions of reporters covered the events of this strike. In general attitude and depth of coverage, most of the newspapers fall into one of three major categories: the local coalfield community and township papers that were completely immersed in the strike on a day-to-day basis; the surrounding nearby metropolitan dailies; and the large but distant national press, linked to papers in the first two categories by the news services, predominantly the AP and UPI. Like concentric waves emanating from a disturbance on the surface of a pond, these three groups were distinct and very much determined in character by their relative proximity to the strike and its personal impact.

The local coalfield papers like the *Dickenson Star*, the *Bristol Herald-Courier*, the *Coalfield Progress*, the *Clinch Valley Times*, the *Lebanon Banner*, and the *Tazewell Free Press*, to name a few, were so close to the news and the communities affected that their coverage reflected as nearly as possible the feelings of the people living in the strikebound areas. Because an overwhelming number of the people in these communities were striking miners or their families, the local papers not surprisingly provided the most sympathetic coverage of the strike.

In the second level of press coverage, however, the character of the coverage was dramatically different. Five papers in three major nearby metropolitan areas constituted the second level: in Charleston, West Virginia, the *Daily Mail* and the *Gazette*; in Roanoke, Virginia, the *Times*; and in Richmond, Virginia, the *Times-Dispatch* and the *News Leader*. Charleston is about 150 miles from the struck coalfields, Roanoke just over 200 miles, and Richmond over 400 miles away. Why their relative geographic proximity should have affected their coverage is difficult to fathom, yet it is possible to classify each paper's official position to the strikers in direct relationship to its distance from the epicenter of strike activity.

Among these papers the *Richmond Times-Dispatch* was the most outspoken critic of the union, running a string of editorials throughout the strike condemning the union's goals, leadership, and tactics. The opening paragraph of Edward Grimsley's October 18 editorial reveals the tenor of this onslaught, "United Mine Workers President Richard Trumka must be feeling pretty good these days. He and his fellow union bosses have begun to reap the rewards of an aggressive disinformation campaign about the union's 6-month-old strike against Pittston Coal Group." Back in July the paper had run a letter to the editor from strike supporter Shirley R. Salyer, but it was placed around an editorial cartoon containing the following dialogue between two overweight pickets:

FIRST PICKET: This is what America is about, Simmons. In some countries strikes are met with brute violence.

SIMMONS: What if our strike does not work?

FIRST PICKET: Then we start shooting and setting trucks on fire.[4]

In October, the other Richmond paper, the *News Leader*, ran an extensive interview with Paul Douglas, Pittston's chairman, extolling the company's position complete with photographs of alleged union violence, all provided by Pittston. In an accompanying editorial the *News Leader* likened the UMWA leadership to the North Vietnamese and accused the union of "heartlessness and widespread terror." Yet other accounts indicated that property destruction had been relatively minor and even the state police spoke favorably of the strikers' behavior.[5]

The union was, in fact, highly successful in its concerted effort to avoid violence in spite of the long history of bloody encounters hanging in the minds of generations of Appalachian miners. For nearly a hundred years, coal companies had waged all-out campaigns to break the mine workers' union. From Matewan to Harlan County the stories of these battles were legend. That the union was able to convince so many of the Pittston strikers to put that history aside and have faith in the unfamiliar tactics of nonviolence and civil disobedience was no small accomplishment. Instead of crediting the union or its leaders for this unprecedented restraint and self-discipline, the Richmond press and the others in the second-wave category of papers elected to see only what they anticipated. Reports of rock-throwing and flattened tires were ex-

Figure 7.1. Pittston Strike Coverage

1989	*Times*	*WSJ*
April	0	0
May	4	0
June	9	1
July	13	6
August	2	3
September	1	0
October	4	0
November	2	3
December	4	0
Total	39	13

aggerated, while incidents of picket-line violence in which the strikers were attacked by armed drivers and company security forces were ignored, as were many other stories that should have been regarded as vital to the public trust. For instance, the father of the judge who was levying all the fines on the union for its civil disobedience of the court injunctions was Donald McGlothlin, Sr., a delegate to the statehouse. In October and November, Jackie Stump, a member of the union's International District Board, conducted a write-in campaign for the same statehouse seat and successfully unseated McGlothlin by a two-to-one margin. Despite this personal relationship and even though the judge's cousins owned nonunion coal mines in the region, at no time, in spite of the union's repeated motions, would Judge McGlothlin recuse himself in the case. This conflict of interest and the subsequent union support that Stump's election represented were not considered newsworthy by the second-wave papers or the wire services.

The third wave of newspapers, though primarily influenced by the second wave, received reports through the buffer of the news services. For the purposes of this brief review, the *New York Times* and the *Wall Street Journal*, identified by Jude Wanniski's *Media Guide* as the "pace-setters," will be used as representative examples of the national coverage.[6]

Throughout the nine months of the strike the *New York Times* ran a total of thirty-nine stories, the vast majority of which came from the Associated Press wire service. The coverage did not begin until the second month of the strike, and then only—it appears—because of the visit of Jesse Jackson. The relative significance accorded the story may be construed by its placement. Though this first story was not placed near the police report, over 25 percent of all the Pittston strike stories were immediately adjacent to a crime report. Instead, in what looks like a cruel joke, the Jesse Jackson story on May 2 was run on page A–

14 next to a photo of a cow and the second half of an article on rural homelessness.

A closer look at the thirty-nine headlines appearing in the *New York Times*, when compared to the overall strike chronology provided on pages 136–39, reveals a common pattern of editorial selection:

May
"Jackson Exhorts Striking Miners in Virginia"
"U.S. Mediation Is Accepted in 28-Day Coal Strike"
"Unusual Proxy Fight at Pittston" (with photo of arrest)
"Pittston Dividend First in 6 Years"

June
"Thousand Walk Off Mining Jobs and Threaten a Wider Coal Strike"
"Wildcat Coal Strike Being Linked to Union"
"Coal Strike Extends to 3 Mines in Kentucky"
"Federal Judge Frees Leaders of Mine Workers' Campaign"
"3 Freed Union Leaders Vow to Continue with Coal Strike"
"Coal Strike Spreads, but Years Have Blunted the Weapon"
"A Shrunken but Defiant Union: Labor Takes Heart in the Miners' Walkout"
"Governor Invites Coal Strike Leaders to Talk"
"Judge Orders End to Strike Actions"

July
"Moving a Strike from Coal Pits to Suburbia"
"UMW Fined Again in Virginia Coal Fight"
"Miners' Union Calls Holiday as Thousands Strike"
"A Voice from Coal Country: 'It Was Old Men Made This Union' "
"Miners Union Cooling-Off Period Starts with Gunfire and Explosion"
"Ruling Says Acts of Coal Company Caused Strike"
"Union Leader Urges Miners to End Walkout"
"Most Union Miners to Return to Coal Fields in Appalachia"
"Thousands Back in Coal Mines: West Virginia Pickets March On"
"Talks to Resume in Coal Walkout"
"Coal Talks on Again, off Again"
"Coal Strike Disturbs Supply of Lower-Priced Electricity"
"U.M.W. Is Fined Again"

August
"Coal Strike: Armageddon for U.M.W. and Leader?"
"Labor Leaders Arrested at Rally Backing Union Workers on Strike"

September
"Violence in Coal Strike Is Increasing"

October
"Mine Workers Request Ties with AFL-CIO"
"Greenwich Politely Bored at Miners"
"Labor Secretary Gets 2 Sides to Meet in Long Coal Strike"
"New Plan Offered in Miners' Strike"

November
"Tension Easing, but Miners' Strike Against Pittston Goes On"
"Judge Says Pittston Co. Violated Securities Rules"

December
"Bitter Coal Strike May Be at an End, but Ripples from Dispute Are Widely Felt"
"Talks Are Recessed in Coal Strike"
"Coal Strike Talks Off; Mediator Predicting a Settlement Friday"
"Pittston Resumes Mine Strike Talks"

As Tasini's study correctly observes, stories of court fines against the union were regularly reported in the *Times*, but the connection of the fines to the passive, civil-disobedience strategies of the union was not mentioned. Even more partial coverage is accorded the company in the absence of corresponding stories of the repeated NLRB charges against Pittston. Not only does American labor law provide less punitive remedies against employers who violate the law than it does against unions, the press is equally reverential in coverage of employers' violations. The July 12 headline after Pittston was charged by the NLRB with an unfair labor practice (ULP) tamely remarks at the bottom of page A–10, "Ruling Says Acts of Coal Company Caused Strike." Not only is the word *ruling* ambiguous, but the sentence is so general that it suggests less a legal finding of guilt than an obvious statement of the company's participation in the negotiations that resulted in the dispute, and it does not identify Pittston by name.

The issue of newsworthiness raises serious questions about the editorial slant of a paper. Although it is difficult to compare the relative weight of stories like the Soviet versus the Pittston mine workers' strikes, editorial decisions that result in stories that make the union look bad while avoiding or muting stories that make the company look bad eventually come to appear as an anti-union bias. For instance, what merits a story's placement on the front page? The Pittston stories in the *New York Times*, rare though they were, never ran on the front page, even when the sympathy walkout idled mines in virtually all the surrounding states. Yet, unaccountably, a July 28 story that autoworkers in Tennessee voted against union representation made the front page, with photo, and was continued on page A-6.

The *Times* and other national third-wave papers neglected to cover the mine workers' establishment of two solidarity camps in the coalfields that became relief and support centers for striking miners as well as rallying centers for visiting unionists from around the country and the world. Nor was there a follow-up story to the report of a U.S. House subcommittee issued on August 4 which concluded that the legal system had failed to treat Pittston and the UMWA equally in their labor dispute.

To be fair, in the case of the third-wave papers particularly, the selection or failure to select labor stories may not be entirely the paper's fault. Most national and other distant newspapers rely heavily on the wire services. The Associated Press, United Press International, and Reuters maintain news-gathering bureaus that cull local stories and make preliminary determinations not only about their newsworthiness but also about whether to send them out in a local or national distribution pattern. Patricia Edwards of the UMWA national office recalls that the union repeatedly ran into a stone wall in attempting to convince the Associated Press office to make more of its stories available to the national papers. The AP had classified the majority of the stories on the strike as "regional," thereby limiting their access to other national papers.[7]

But editors on both sides of the wire can easily kill a good labor story if they wish to do so. Kenneth Gagala, labor and urban affairs director at the University of Minnesota, ran into a similar wall when he called the labor reporter at the *Minneapolis Star-Tribune* to set up an interview with the UMWA regional director, Brad Burton, who was in town to talk about the Pittston strike. Though the month before the same paper covered the visit of Marty Levitt, a former union-busting consultant, a section editor flatly ordered the labor reporter not to interview Burton.[8]

The major event that was covered was the June 12 wildcat sympathy strikes that stopped mining across nine more states when forty-five thousand miners (one-third of the nation's mine workers) walked out to show support for the sixteen hundred strikers at Pittston. The headlines covering this walkout commonly denigrated the significance of the widespread support. On June 25, just after the walkout began, the *Times* ran a sympathetic article under the headline, "Labor Takes Heart in the Miners' Walkout," but that sympathy was not so subtly undercut by the prefatory lead title, "A Shrunken but Defiant Union." This story, like the June 22 story by B. Drummond Ayres, "Coal Strike Spreads, but Years Have Blunted the Weapon," pressed the theme that the miners are to be pitied for their hopeless gesture because the union as an institution is no longer relevant.

A second major event receiving attention in the *Times* was the demonstration by mine worker pickets and the proxy fight conducted by the union at Pittston's corporate headquarters in Greenwich, Connecticut. The two stories by Nick Ravo illustrate an underlying class bias that has infected much of the labor coverage by stereotyping union workers as uncouth, blue-collar Archie Bunker types. Ravo concluded that the proxy campaign was discredited: "It's a public relations ploy, no doubt about it. The same miners who scream obscenities in Carbo, Va., become cross-carrying missionaries in Greenwich, one of the nations wealthiest towns."[9] Without actually using the word *hicks*, Ravo's two articles, on July 5 and October 7, stereotype the Pittston strikers as ignorant and undignified louts who do not belong in New England. Alexander Cockburn of the *Nation* traced this condescending attitude through a string of articles on the mine workers: "*Newsweek* in 1978 described the miners as 'a breed apart from the rest of the populace— clannish and fatalistic, wary and independent, hell-raising and violent, promiscuous and enduring.' *Time* called them 'independent, outspoken, and not addicted to regular work.' In 1981 the *Wall Street Journal* noted that the miners may have been motivated to strike by the onset of fishing season; this was also considered plausible by *Newsweek*."[10] These blatant class and anti-southern prejudices are regularly permitted by the media and go unchecked and unchallenged although similarly virulent racial or sexual remarks would create a furor of public outrage. It is particularly to his credit that Jesse Jackson, of all the national figures, was able to see through these century-old prejudices and stereotypes and champion the miners' cause.

Joe Corcoran, the UMWA director of public relations during the strike, observed that, at least in the case of the Pittston strike, "the best labor coverage is at the extremes," citing the well-known conservative publications *Business Week* and the *Wall Street Journal* as examples.[11] But the *Wall Street Journal* ran only thirteen stories on the mine workers during the nine months of the strike, with the balance devoted to the sympathy wildcat strikes that began in mid-June.

Labor coverage in the business journals tends to be better than average newspaper reporting because the staff reporters have relatively greater expertise. Nevertheless, knowing the ins and outs of business writing does not always translate to well-informed labor reporting, which is often ensnarled in complicated legal issues. The UMWA public relations staff was continually frustrated with the inability of reporters to understand or care about the legal issues that were as important to the dispute as were the economic issues. The mine workers expressed particular frustration at the failure of the *Wall Street Journal* reporter to identify the strike properly. There is a significant legal distinction between an ordinary "contract dispute" or economic strike and an unfair labor practice strike, which the Pittston strike was.[12] Just as frustrating to the union was the lack of coverage of the issue of double-breasting, whereby Pittston, following a national trend in union-busting, had created a nonunion subsidiary and slowly set about transferring operations and accounts to the so-called nonunion breast while downsizing the union operation under the pretense of reduced business.

As the following list suggests, reports of violence and union arrests dominated the *Journal*'s coverage:

June 22: "Coal-Mine Strike Divides a Family and a Community," A1
July 10: "UMW Plans Work Stoppage in Nine States," A3
July 11: "Coal Mines Still Hampered by Violence and Picketing," C12
July 12: "UMW Proposes to Resume Negotiations with Pittston," A5
July 17: "Coalfield Crisis: Proliferating Strikes Threaten Many Mines—And Mine Union Too . . . Union's Future Is at Stake as It Strives to Impose Discipline on Its Members," A1, A4
July 18: "Wildcat Strikes Resume at Mines in West Virginia," A4
July 19: "Pittston and Mine Workers to Resume Contract Talks," C16
August 8: "Labor of Love: How a Mine in Arizona Wooed Workers Away from Union Loyalties," A1
August 22: "Pittston Chief Digs in Against UMW," B5
August 25: "Labor Leaders Kirkland, Trumka Arrested in Protest," A14
October 5: "United Mine Workers Union Applies to Rejoin AFL-CIO after Long Absence," B10
November 7: "Man Admits Planting Bomb at Pittston Mine," A4
November 20: "Pittston: Rebirth of the Unions?" A14
November 30: "Judge Rules Pittston Denied Holders Vote On Union Resolutions," C6

The most common theme of the *Journal*'s coverage, aside from the random incidents of violence, was the aspersion that union president Richard Trumka lacked support from the rank and file and was losing control of the union. Reporter Alecia Swasy, whose byline ran over five of the thirteen stories, repeatedly raised this issue, implying that the strike issues were related to Trumka's internal political problems. On July 11, for instance, she wrote, "He [Trumka] also may be seeking to gain control over an increasingly divided rank-and-file." In the next sentence, she concluded: "While one group of miners wants to return to work, others have used violent tactics to keep the mines closed." In other words, there are only scabs or terrorists left, and no one is supporting Trumka's strategy of civil disobedience. In view of the thousands of miners and their family members who were arrested throughout that period, this conclusion lacks foundation and incorrectly suggests that violence on the picket line was more the rule than the exception. The following week, in an even longer article, Swasy picked up the same themes, as the opening sentence reveals: "After nearly a decade of labor peace, a wave of violence in the nation's coalfields is threatening leadership of the United Mine Workers and the union's very existence."[13]

At the heart of the *Journal* coverage, as one might expect, was a clear preference for management sources and points of view to the exclusion of the union perspective. In Swasy's July 18 article, for instance, only one source is quoted and that is a management negotiator commenting on the erratic nature of the mine worker leadership. And on October 5 the same reporter, writing about the reaffiliation of the UMWA with the AFL-CIO, quotes a management consultant whose analysis was predictably disparaging: "It won't improve the image of the UMW. . . . Their attitude about labor relations is a thing of the past."[14] Labor-management consultants, more commonly known as union busters, would hardly seem to be an unbiased source of opinion on union affiliation.

The ultimate example of this preference for the management point of view was the *Journal*'s August 22 article in the "Who's News" column. Written by Alecia Swasy under the title "Pittston Chief Digs in Against UMW," it was a virtual panegyric in praise of Pittston's CEO, Paul Douglas. In a box next to one of the *Journal*'s distinctive "dot drawings" of Douglas's determined visage are his vital statistics in large type, including the entry, "CHALLENGE: To wrest concessions from the United Mine Workers and settle strike."

Perhaps because of the obvious tilt this article implied in its coverage, a few months later the *Journal* published nearly as large an article reflecting a union perspective. It was, however, not a *Journal* reporter's interview as the Douglas piece was but an essay by Greg Tarpinian, who was pointedly identified as the "director of the Labor Research Association in New York, a union-funded group." Not only does this outside authorship with appropriate disclaimer detract from the credibility of the article, but the interrogatory nature of the headline, "Pittston: Rebirth of the Unions?," implies either disagreement or ambivalence but definitely not the contents of Tarpinian's essay.[15]

Finally, in the same nine-month period of the strike, two related articles, though not about Pittston, contributed to the theme that unions are no longer relevant. On August 8, *Journal* reporter Marj Charlier did a feature that ran on the front page and beyond about Cyprus copper mines in Arizona, entitled "Labor of Love: How a Mine in Arizona Wooed Workers Away From Union Loyalties." Like the Douglas interview, this piece heaped praise on the company management and the new employee attitudes that permitted a union-free workplace. But even more radically conservative than any of the *Journal*'s own reports was the essay by Spiro Agnew that appeared on August 10. The title, "Democracy Doesn't Need Picketers," well reflected Agnew's argument. To be consistent, one might have expected the *Journal* editors to title the piece with a question such as the one that headed the Tarpinian piece: "Does Democracy Need Picketers?" Though Agnew directed his remarks at activists in general and made no specific reference to the mine workers, the article was an attack on the strategy of civil disobedience for any purpose, and the timing with respect to the Pittston strike could hardly be a coincidence.[16]

Television Coverage

As Tasini noted, the miners' strike at Pittston was virtually ignored by the major television news programs. By his accounting, over the nine months of the strike the three networks' combined coverage amounted to just twenty-two minutes and forty seconds of news, and the first story was not broadcast until April 30, twenty-five days after it began.[17]

On Thursday, June 15, 1989, CBS aired a one-hour documentary on the mine workers' Pittston strike that was based on the reports of four newsmen who had conducted interviews the previous month in Dickenson County, Virginia. In many respects this program, aired in the middle of the strike, became a part of the strike and had considerable influence on the events that unfolded thereafter. The title, *48 Hours*: "On Strike!," suggests that the Pittston strike was emblematic of strikes in general or that the program would explore this strike as an example of the meaning of strikes in general. Whatever its larger purpose, the program constituted the majority of the national media coverage the strike received on television that year.

The CBS team, presumably under the direction of Dan Rather, who hosted the program, appears to have attempted to take a neutral position. The program was divided into eight segments, the titles of which suggest that four reflected the union perspective and the other four reflected management. In fact, the appearance of neutrality was deceptive. Not only was the union perspective subtly undercut and distorted, but the anti-union interviews were so arranged as to direct the sympathy of the viewer away from the strikers' issues and toward Pittston's.

The program established its bias through the structural framework of the eight segments and the nature of the reporters' questions, which often presumed union impropriety and/or unreasonableness. Structurally, the eight program segments appeared to offer a deliberately balanced presentation. The segment titles and reporters were as follows:

1. Union Family, by Eric Engberg
2. Company Man, by Robert Krulwich
3. "King Scab," by Bob Faw
4. Strike Duty, by Ron Allen
5. Crossing the Line, by Robert Krulwich
6. Coal Miner's Daughter, by Bob Faw
7. Union Spirit, by Robert Krulwich
8. Holding the Line, by Eric Engberg

At first glance it would seem that the segments were meant to be divided as follows:

Union side:

1.	Union Family, by Eric Engberg	3:21
6.	Coal Miner's Daughter, by Bob Faw	5:30
7.	Union Spirit, by Robert Krulwich	5:40
8.	Holding the Line, by Eric Engberg	6:00
		20:31 minutes

Company side:

2.	Company Man, by Robert Krulwich	8:00
3.	"King Scab," by Bob Faw	6:03
4.	Strike Duty, by Ron Allen	5:09
5.	Crossing the Line, by Robert Krulwich	3:26
		22:38 minutes

But a description of the segments' perspectives reveals significantly different weighting:

1.	Union Family	=	typical miners' family
2.	Company Man	=	the company president
3.	"King Scab"	=	scab leader
4.	Strike Duty	=	state troopers/police
5.	Crossing the Line	=	scab miners & company foremen
6.	Coal Miner's Daughter	=	miners' children
7.	Union Spirit	=	Matewan retirees
8.	Holding the Line	=	strike leadership & miners

Therefore, through its interview framework, the program subtly creates the impression that there are four sides in the dispute: the striking miners, the company, the scabs, and the police. No matter how much time or how many segments are dedicated to the union, the sense that the official union position represents a minority of interests is bound to result once the conflict is framed in this quadrilateral matrix. This erroneous impression is all the more likely to prevail because the program did not consider the relevance of the popularity of the strike in proportion to the overall number of miners. Despite their personal interviews with striking miners' families, this failure to report accurately on the widespread support for the strike throughout the tristate Appalachian coal country in effect proved the CBS reporters guilty of Parenti's sixth characteristic of labor dispute reporting by which union solidarity and mutual support stories are discounted. The inordinate amount of time given to scabs and strikebreakers implied that nearly as many miners opposed the strike as supported it, when in fact the miners' solidarity in the Pittston strike was remarkable by any standard.

Perhaps the most telling mark of the program's bias, however, could be seen in what Cirino referred to as the "art of interviewing." Division of the program into union and management segments might be fair if each subject were given an equal opportunity to express his or her position. But the interview format places considerable power in the hands of the reporter, who selects the questions and, therefore, frames the issues. Reviewing the questions posed by the various CBS reporters in this *48 Hours* episode, a clear pattern emerges which is anything but neutral. In part two, for instance, Robert Krulwich interviews Pittston Coal Group president Mike Odom on the company's financial status:

KRULWICH: This is a tough business, and the Pittston Company has its problems. [to Odom] I'm looking at your sales of coal. That's your basic business. And I see that in 1986 you sold some; in 1987 you sold less; in 1988 you sold still less again.

ODOM: But we mined less coal last year than we did the previous year, and less then than the previous year. You're also seeing that the price of coal is going down.

KRULWICH: And what's more, Pittston's competitors are not just nearby coal companies. Pittston goes head to head with mines in Australia, South Africa, New Zealand. [to Odom] So I sense that this company is in a squeeze. There are more producers, and this pie is not getting any bigger. If I'm right on these observations, you have a problem, a business problem don't you?

ODOM: That's correct.

KRULWICH: How are you going to be able to beat the Australians or the Chinese?[18]

Of course, this final question was rhetorical. It was meant to make it clear that Pittston would be able to compete with the Australians or Chinese only if American mine workers could be content with a reduced standard of living. What is worse is that in the exchange, Krulwich spoke for the company more persuasively than did Odom, who seemed reluctant to jump to the economic conclusions Krulwich invited. Indeed, through the rest of the program the impression that Pittston's coal operation was floundering and that the miners were being unreasonable by refusing necessary concessions dominated the interviewers' questions. The union leadership was not given a chance to respond to this analysis. Neither the union president Trumka nor the union vice-president and chief negotiator Cecil Roberts was interviewed. Had they been, perhaps the information that in 1988 coal generated 32 percent of Pittston's sales revenues and 53 percent of its operating profits might have come to light.[19] In fact, the mine workers' productivity at Pittston's union operations had increased by 72 percent over the previous four years and the company officially asserted at its declaration of impasse that its demands were not made for economic reasons. Pittston, according to CEO Paul Douglas, was "in good financial condition, and pleading neither poverty nor an inability to pay any union demand. To set the record straight once and for all, the books would not disclose a financial justification for concessions."[20]

Instead of giving the union leadership a chance to respond to the question of Pittston's economic condition, in a segment near the end of the program, Eric Engberg asks Gail Gentry, the disabled miner who was the two thousandth person to be arrested for civil disobedience, to respond to the reasonableness of the union's position.

ENGBERG: [to Gail Gentry] You know you hear a lot of talk about how we don't need higher pay for union members and more benefits we need less. I mean you're swimming upstream aren't you?

GENTRY: Yes we are. We are swimming against the current. But this is not a strike about economics, it's about survival. It's about basic survival for my family and the workin' miner's family.

Krulwich's questions to Odom reflected a sympathy and understanding that is totally missing from the question put to Gentry. As is common in strike coverage, the company's official was asked about a management position while the union position was sought from an ordinary striker. Though Gail Gentry's response was thoughtful and well phrased, he fell into the trap set by the reporter by appearing to concede that the union's strike goals were impractical.

Similarly, Engberg quizzes strike coordinator Marty Hudson about the union's attempt to publicize Gentry's arrest. Again the question is essentially hostile.

> ENGBERG: But, Marty, this is the kind of stuff that when Reagan's people were doing it at the White House, people like you were complaining about how it's image-making.
>
> HUDSON: Well, it's image-making, but I tell you what . . . it works! Perception is reality, and it's not using Gail Gentry. It's Gail Gentry making a statement about what happened to him.

The question as Engberg phrases it assumes that the union is wrong in attempting to affect public opinion and is reminiscent of Nick Ravo's comment in the *New York Times* that the Geenwich demonstration was a "public relations ploy." Yet earlier, when Pittston's Mike Odom was conducting one of his daily press conferences, no such imputation was made that this was an unethical media manipulation. In fact, just the opposite was implied.

> KRULWICH: Mike Odom is willing to say that the union has done a very slick public relations job, and that he has some catching up to do. Almost every day Mike Odom holds a press conference.
>
> ODOM: Well, there's not a lot to report today from out in the field.
>
> KRULWICH: He distributes pictures of what he calls union sabotage.

The conclusion from all this is that the union has contrived an unfair media advantage and that the poor but honest company is suffering as a result. This interpretation, however, fails to recognize that the mine workers actually had very little success in influencing the national media coverage, which typically is interested in labor disputes only when they result in violence. Despite what Krulwich called the union's "slick" public relations, very little coverage was given to the strike, and the only national coverage of the two thousandth arrest was this same CBS episode of *48 Hours* accusing the union of slick public relations.

The clearest indication of the program's bias, however, is in its presentation of picket-line violence. The crew could find no "newsworthy" examples of violence to film while they were there, except for an incident in which a union picket was the victim of a hit-and-run accident by a replacement worker, so CBS resorted to video archives and fictionalized film accounts of historic events and interviews with veterans of those bygone days.

Part 7, entitled "Union Spirit," was an interview with two retired miners in Matewan, West Virginia, now a nonunion coal operation but once the scene of the bloodiest labor wars in this country's history. The title implies that the miners really want to perpetrate violence, and that civil disobedience is not the true union spirit. The two veteran mine workers call the strategy stupid and boldly call for the miners to get their guns and shoot it out as they did in the past. Complementing this portrayal is a short clip from the feature film *Matewan*. Though that film contained more scenes of company thugism than of union violence, the clip selected was of a final scene in which a miner's mother repeatedly shoots at the body of a dead company agent.

The United Mine Workers' strike leaders were doing everything they could to keep their strike peaceful and nonviolent, but the effect of this program was decidedly inflammatory. Mark Arnold of UMWA District 11 reported that miners in Indiana walked off their jobs after seeing the segment, and in Pittston, a supervisor's pickup truck was blown up in a rash of violent incidents that an article in the *Kingsport Times-News* believed was related to the call to arms televised on *48 Hours*.[21]

The Mine Workers' Joe Corcoran best expressed the primary defect of the *48 Hours* episode when he said, "It's fundamentally entertainment and it's not journalism."[22] As he explained, the program looked only at the effects, not the causes, of the strike, and did not tell why the workers went on strike and why they were willing to suffer so much deprivation and insult by staying on strike for so long. The suffering of the company and the scabs was well documented, but the miners were portrayed as comfortable, conniving, and on the verge of brutality.

Conclusions

The overall pattern of the Pittston coverage raises fundamental questions about what Edith Efron called "selectivity" and Norman Isaacs called the "gatekeeping" powers of the news media. In deciding what is news, the media immediately cast the story in the light of their own preconceptions and agendas.

In Chapter 6 attention was drawn to "pack journalism," the apparent connection between the coverage of a lead paper and the other dailies. In addition to revealing how inextricably the media are tied to their own preconceptions, the Pittston coverage reveals the crucial position held by the wire services in determining what the rest of the country may or may not know. This study also demonstrates the large difference that may develop between local, small-town presses and large urban presses. Comparing the generally favorable treatment in the smaller local papers covering the Pittston strike to the much higher levels of antipathy evident in the local Maui paper covering the Kupau case, it seems fair to say that the local press is most likely to express the prevailing community attitudes when emotions are running high. When the community is not deeply involved or in the case of distant urban newspapers, the attitudes of the editors are more likely to prevail.

Editors' attitudes are usually shaped long before the events their papers cover occur. The media expect violence to be a good story and do not question whether it is representative. If the strike does not fit the stereotype, instead of attracting press interest to the perceived deviation, it is ignored.

The use and abuse of headlines by their placement, their wording, and even their grammatical structure can slant even an article that is fairly cast. Fortunately, people who read the entire article are not as likely to be swayed by a problematic headline. Unfortunately, the vast majority of the public is likely to read only the headline.

As Joe Corcoran observed, often the best coverage may be found at the extremes, in conservative business publications on one end and liberal or left-wing journals and the labor press on the other. To the extent that this might be true it is probably because representatives of the extremes of the political spectrum are deeply committed and, therefore, care enough to dig more deeply into the issues than is the disinterested reporter who is on assignment and rushing to meet a news deadline.

Coverage of the Pittston strike is a prime example of one of the greatest defects in the news media's treatment of organized labor. Labor stories should be covered by trained labor reporters who are committed to the subject, not by staff writers who have only a general understanding of the basic legal principles of labor relations.

Finally, coverage of the Pittston strike suggests a most unwholesome class prejudice underpinning the prevailing anti-union attitudes. The disturbing theme in the mine workers' coverage that unions are no longer relevant in today's economy carries with it the sinister message that our blue-collar work force is no longer relevant either.

The 1989 Pittston Strike: A Timeline

Background

1986 Pittston Coal Group's parent corporation opens Pyxis Resources, a nonunion, parallel coal company in Pittston.

1987 *May 19:* The Pittston Coal Group withdraws from the Bituminous Coal Operators Association, the multiemployer bargaining coalition with which the United Mine Workers of America had been negotiating as a single entity for the past two decades.

November: Pittston Coal Group and the UMWA begin formal bargaining.

1988 *February 1:* The Mine Workers' contract with Pittston expires as negotiations continue.

November: The UMWA brings suit against Pittston for violating antidiscrimination provisions of ERISA (the federal pension protection law).

November 9: After a year of bargaining, Pittston, without prior notice, declares an impasse, announces it has made its "last best offer," and refuses to continue bargaining.

1989 *January:* Pittston advertises in the coalfield newspapers for "full-time replacement workers."

March 23: The regional NLRB office in Cincinnati charges Pittston with twenty-five violations of federal labor law.

April 3: Region 9 of the NLRB charges Pittston with additional unfair labor practices and announces its plans to investigate further allegations.

Strike Chronology (April 1989 to December 1989)
April

5 The UMWA goes on strike against the Pittston coal operators over contracts affecting 1,900 miners.

6 Pittston cancels health insurance for strikers and laid-off miners.

13 Virginia State Court Judge Donald McGlothlin, Jr., issues an injunction limiting the number of pickets.

18 "The Daughters of Mother Jones," a women's auxiliary of strikers' wives and supporters, stage a sit-in at Pittston's office in Lebanon, Virginia, where they occupy the lobby for thirty hours.

This timeline is based partially on "Anatomy of a Coal Strike" as compiled by the *Roanoke Times and World-News*, January 2, 1990.

21 Judge McGlothlin issues another injunction, which limits the number of pickets at seventeen more mines.

24 The UMWA stages its first demonstration of civil disobedience; strikers block mine entrances by sitting down in the paths of coal trucks. Over two hundred arrests; several strikers are hospitalized for arrest-related injuries.

25 High school students, mostly children of miners, walk out of classes at high schools throughout southwestern Virginia. Another two hundred miners arrested for civil disobedience.

30 Rev. Jesse Jackson arrives in Wise County, Virginia, to address a UMWA rally of ten thousand miners.

May

2 Seven miners, three of whom require hospitalization, are injured after a company security vehicle runs them down on the picket line.

10 The UMWA attends a Pittston annual shareholders' meeting in Greenwich, Connecticut, waging a nearly successful proxy fight to protest the company's treatment of the miners. Nuns are arrested in the civil-disobedience demonstrations.

16 Judge McGlothlin holds the UMWA in contempt for disobeying his injunction and orders $616,000 in fines, including $13,000 each against UMWA strike organizers Marty Hudson and Jackie Stump.

24 Gail Gentry, a permanently disabled Pittston miner whose health care was cut off, becomes the two thousandth person arrested for civil disobedience and is filmed by a CBS TV crew filming a documentary.

U.S. District Court for Western Virginia issues a temporary restraining order for the NLRB, prohibiting the UMWA from blocking Pittston operations.

30 Actor Ned Beatty joins the miners on the picket line.

June

2 Judge McGlothlin issues confiscatory fines against the union, starting at $500,000 and doubling each day.

5 U.S. District Court Judge Glen Williams jails strike leaders Marty Hudson, C. A. Phillips, and Jackie Stump for contempt of court.

7 Talks with the federal mediator break off.

9 Pittston unilaterally declares the contract talks at an impasse.

10 Pittston unilaterally implements the terms of its last contract pro-

posal, as Richard Trumka advises the company that the union has rejected Pittston's declaration of impasse.

11 Over ten thousand miners conclude a "March for Justice" that started on June 7 in Logan, West Virginia, and ended in Charleston.

12 Wildcat sympathy strikes break out across three states involving forty-five thousand miners (one third of the nation's mine workers) in support of the 1,600 Pittston strikers.

15 CBS airs the program, *48 Hours*: "On Strike!" hosted by Dan Rather and featuring miners, mineowners, scabs, and state police.

16 A dynamite charge destroys the pickup truck of a Pittston supervisor and damages his home in Russell County, Virginia.

18 UMWA opens up "Camp Solidarity" to house and feed the hungry and dispossessed strikers.

19 Strike leaders Marty Hudson, C. A. Phillips, and Jackie Stump, jailed on June 5, are released.

26 Federal Judge Dennis Knapp issues an injunction against the wildcat sympathy strikes.

July

4 United Farm Workers president Cesar Chavez addresses a rally of Pittston strikers at St. Paul, Virginia.

7 The NLRB issues another complaint against Pittston, charging the company with unfair labor practices, and certifies the ULP status of the Pittston strikers.

11 The U.S. House Subcommittee on Labor-Management Relations announces it will investigate the Pittston dispute.

17 The wildcat sympathy strikers return to work at the urging of UMWA president Trumka.

19 Contract talks resume.

25 UMWA vice-president Cecil Roberts is arrested on state and federal charges for taking part in a sit-down demonstration at Pittston's Moss No. 3 plant.

27 Judge McGlothlin fines the UMWA an additional $4.5 million for violating Russell County Circuit Court injunctions.

August

4 A U.S. House subcommittee report concludes that the legal system has failed to treat Pittston and the UMWA equally in their labor dispute.

17 A Pittston foreman is injured when his car is struck by rocks.

18 Pittston suspends contract talks, citing as rationale the previous day's violence.

21 UMWA vice-president Roberts is inexplicably acquitted of all charges by Judge McGlothlin.

23 AFL-CIO president Lane Kirkland, UMWA president Trumka, and other national labor leaders are arrested at a sit-down demonstration at the Russell County Courthouse.

24 The NLRB files a second unfair labor practice complaint against Pittston.

September

17 Ninety-eight striking miners and a United Methodist minister, all Pittston shareholders, take over Pittston's Moss No. 3 plant.

18 Judge McGlothlin imposes another $13.5 million in fines against the UMWA.

20 The UMWA peaceably ends its occupation of the Pittston plant in compliance with an order issued by U.S. District Court Judge Williams.

October

4 In Washington, D.C., the UMWA's executive board votes to apply for admission to the AFL-CIO as a member union.

5 Judge McGlothlin levies another $6.9 million in fines against the UMWA for violating his injunction.

14 Secretary of Labor Elizabeth Dole announces she will appoint a special "supermediator" to resolve the dispute between Pittston and the UMWA.

24 Secretary Dole selects former labor secretary William Usery as the supermediator.

November

7 Jackie Stump, a UMWA strike leader, wins a seat in the Virginia House of Delegates, soundly defeating in a write-in campaign the incumbent, Don McGlothlin, father of Judge McGlothlin.

December

7 Camp Solidarity II opens in Logan, West Virginia, and begins housing strikers and supporters.

8 Judge McGlothlin increases the fines against the union by another $33.4 million for violating his injunction.

27 New Beckley Corporation files a $60 million suit against the UMWA under the federal RICO statute.

31 After four days of around-the-clock bargaining, a tentative settlement is reached.

8. Labor's Response

Image Enhancement

A Free Press? Anybody in the ten-million-dollar category is free to try to buy or found a paper. . . . As to us, we are free to buy a paper or not as we wish.
—A. J. Liebling, *The Wayward Pressman*

In view of the formidable barrage of negative imagery the media have directed against unions over the years, it is surprising that labor's response has not been more aggressive. Only in the past ten years have a few of the larger internationals and the AFL-CIO begun to commit some of their limited resources to public relations with the fervor formerly applied only to direct organizing campaigns. Indeed, only in the past decade has organized labor considered public relations as an integral part of its overall organizing program.

A complete history of the public relations efforts of the AFL-CIO is related in the second chapter of Sara Douglas's 1983 dissertation at the University of Illinois, later published as *Labor's New Voice* (1986). Douglas shows how the response of organized labor to the treatment it has received has slowly evolved from avoidance and defensiveness into a greater willingness to use radio, and television particularly, in special, though somewhat isolated, target campaigns during select organizing drives, strikes, or contract negotiations.[1] No doubt her critique of this history lent support to the fledgling AFL-CIO video production studio, known as the Labor Institute for Public Affairs (LIPA), founded in 1982, and of the first coordinated national media campaign to enhance labor's image and promote unionization, the "Union, Yes!" program of 1988–89.

As Douglas's study reveals, labor's response has evolved in four steps. To begin with, public relations to most unions meant simply their internal newsletter, or house organ. In the early days of the movement, "labor leaders," as historian Jack Barbash noted, "did not care very much what the 'capitalist' press thought about them or their unions."[2] The focus of the labor press was on providing simple and direct communication between the union leadership and the rank and file, with the underlying assumption that union members will ignore the media bias once they are presented with the official union perspective.

A second response that labor developed early to improve its image was in reaction to the media stereotypes from the 1920s and 1930s that portrayed organized labor as the tool of foreign anarchists and, in a modified form, was popularized again in the 1940s and 1950s as red-baiting. To counter the image that they were unpatriotic or un-American, many unions undertook community service projects and other programs designed to impress the public with the civic-mindedness of union leadership and that unions are institutionally consistent with free enterprise and the "American Way."

Labor's third response to specific incidences of media bias was to counterattack. This defensive response has typically included resort to media councils or ombudsmen, use, in broadcast media, of equal time provisions under FCC regulations, and, more recently, media-monitoring activities by which union members or recruited analysts systematically record, analyze, and evaluate one medium's treatment of a given union or of labor in general. The Machinists project in the early 1980s was the most comprehensive example of such monitoring and provided the model.

Finally, as the quotation in the epigraph from A. J. Liebling suggests, labor's fourth response to the negative media portrayals it has suffered includes use not only of its own internal press but direct access to the local and national mass media.

As Douglas has carefully detailed, a large number of attempts were made by various labor unions to improve their public image and to combat the anti-union stereotypes that dominate media portrayals. The ILGWU and the United Auto Workers (UAW) developed particularly compelling and innovative media campaigns. But even these early efforts were handicapped by two basic problems that fatally limited their ability to reach the numbers of people necessary effectively to influence the weight of American public opinion. To begin with, because the financial resources of any single union or local thereof are limited, it is very difficult to sponsor a concerted, multimedia program. As a result, when such campaigns were attempted, they usually employed only one communications medium and were waged in a single geographical area. Following the traditional brand-name advertising approach familiar to the unions' media advisers, such campaigns featured the union's name, often without using the word *union* in the copy but focusing on its occupational or craft designation. A large number of unions do not even have the word *union* in their name but use words such as *association, federation, organization,* or *brotherhood.*

Unfortunately, unions are lumped together in the public consciousness. The conduct or reputation of any one union, good or bad, is imputed generally to the labor movement as a whole. That, for example, the National Education Association (NEA) representing teachers, is not an affiliate of the AFL-CIO is a distinction relevant only to NEA members and labor relations professionals. To the public, a union is a union and, therefore, intrinsically tied to all other unions. For years, labor's response to this misconception has been either to ignore it or for individual unions to spend their limited funds on campaigns in the hope of distinguishing their union from the rest.

This lack of unity and purpose in labor's response has been its greatest handicap. It has, until recently, resulted in the inability of the American labor movement to effectively coordinate a national multimedia response promoting a general image of labor unions that could appeal to a spirit of union solidarity rather than disparate professional or craft identities.

The one noteworthy exception to the reluctance and awkwardness of early union efforts to use the media was the International Ladies' Garment Workers' Union. Not only was the ILGWU the first union to write and run a special advertising supplement to its history published in the *New York Times* in 1959, but in 1937 the ILGWU produced and staged its own drama, *Pins and Needles,* a comedic revue that featured the problems of garment workers in the Depression. In 1950, the ILGWU produced a classic film, *With These Hands,* depicting the struggles of the immigrant garment workers who formed the backbone of the ILGWU. In 1975 the union popularized the inspiring song "Look for the Union Label," in a series of nationally run television and radio advertisements.[3]

The ILGWU projects were exceptional in their sophistication. Though the union's membership was based primarily in New York, it realized the importance of reaching a national audience. Likewise, its commitment to a multimedia approach that focused on the larger issue of "union label" instead of its own union name was unusual and uniquely effective. Clearly, most union leaders had viewed such media efforts as a huge sinkhole, swallowing their funds and producing little hard evidence of effectiveness. Unlike money spent on an organizing campaign or negotiations, the effectiveness of which can be measured, the net effect of public opinion campaigns was almost impossible to measure accurately. Labor's leadership, therefore, was ordinarily disinclined to risk the commitment. As a consequence, for most of its history, communications departments of most union locals were given short shrift. For this reason, V. O. Key noted in the 1960s:

> Union leadership has no impressive record in propagandizing its own members. Many members remain unaware of issues that the leadership regards as of prime importance to the union itself. Of those members who have opinions many take positions that depart from the official union line. . . . Yet if a mass-membership organization meets limited success in managing the attitudes of its own members, how much more ineffective must be campaigns of propaganda designed to settle like a mist over the population generally.[4]

Key's characterization of union public relations efforts as propaganda is reasonable because they were a response to the media-entrenched anti-union propaganda. But a comparison of the way unions have managed "persuader activities" to the efforts of business or political interests reveals labor's historic disadvantage. Jacques Ellul, for instance, writing a few years after Key, observed that "union propaganda has a character of its own: it is much more 'human,' costs less, uses the devotion of union members, their close human contact, and so on."[5] In other words, it was propaganda that attempted to work outside rather than through the media.

Today, however, there is evidence of a growing determination by many unions to respond actively to the distorted images created by the media. As Gary Hubbard, communications director for the United Steelworkers, has remarked, "Any union in today's society that doesn't have good communication with its members and the public will not survive."[6] There is no doubt that this sentiment is shared by the new generation of labor leaders throughout the country.

In the mid–1970s several Hawaii unions successfully instituted a labor education television series, *Rice & Roses*, that aired weekly on KHET, the state's public television channel, for sixteen years. Funded through the University of Hawaii's Center for Labor Education and Research, this program featured thirty-minute labor documentaries, histories, and panel discussions under the general supervision of a Labor Advisory Committee. The producers were given a free hand to control their programming, and *Rice & Roses* soon developed a reputation for fairness and innovation in its approach to a wide variety of labor issues. Not the tool of any one union, it provided the public viewing audience with insights into workers' perspectives not available on commercial television. Unfortunately, its limited production budget prevented the program from growing technologically with the rest of that medium through the 1980s, and it enjoyed only a statewide rather than national distribution.

In 1985, after a decade of declining union membership, the AFL-CIO reviewed its organization and structure and issued a report designed to improve its response to a newly evolved labor force and turn the tide of its national organizing efforts. It is significant that the entire third section of the report concerned the improvement of the labor movement's communications, including the following recommendations:

3.1   Efforts should be made to better publicize labor's accomplishments.

3.2   Union spokespersons need training in media techniques.

3.3   Efforts must be made at every level to better inform reporters about unions and trade unionism.

3.4   The AFL-CIO should develop a pilot project for a targeted area to test the usefulness of advertising to improve the public's understanding of labor.

3.5   Interferences with the right of workers to form a union should be forcefully brought to the attention of the general public to develop public support for labor law reform.[7]

Since that report was released, considerable progress has been made. Current examples of labor's response to its media portrayal may be broadly classified into two basic categories: media monitoring and advocacy advertising.

Media Monitoring

Labor's media-monitoring activities are by no means unique or original to the labor movement. Conservative interest groups have probably been more involved in monitoring than all the other groups put together. Accuracy in Media (AIM), for example, employs a twenty-member staff that continuously monitors national news stories to complain of errors and misinformation prejudicial to its conservative agenda. A plethora of advocacy groups, from the National and World Council of Churches to the Media Project of the National Organization for Women and the Arab-American Anti-Discrimination Committee, monitor the media either to make sure their members are not ignored or to record and formally protest misrepresentation and stereotypes. According to a study done by graduate students in journalism at American University in Washington, D.C., the AFL-CIO by comparison has been less direct in its reaction to media bias: "The AFL-CIO simply snubs journalists from offending news organizations. Interviews with federation president Lane Kirkland are never granted to the non-union Cable News Network, whose owner, Ted Turner, has made clear his dislike for unions."[8] The AFL-CIO treatment of Turner is not a proper example because it is likely that it was prompted less by his network's portrayal of labor than by his anti-union employment practices. And yet this strategy of avoidance, probably learned from the example of the White House, has been commonly used by labor. Often newspapers, in consideration of this strategy, either quietly drop the reporter's byline or reassign stories that are negative to their local unions to protect their regular labor reporters from losing future access. Such "snubbing" has usually, at least in the case of labor, been in response to very specific and localized stories, not the product of any organized or systematic monitoring program.

No extensive media-monitoring project for labor was conducted until the *IAM Television Report* in 1980 (five years before the AFL-CIO report), carried out by the International Association of Machinists. This project was remarkable in its scope, considering entertainment as well as news programming and national as well as local broadcasts across the country. Though the effectiveness of this or any response is difficult to gauge, the Machinists' staff who worked on this project noticed a difference in the attitude of network officials and news reporters following the survey. Editors and reporters, they found, were much more attentive and responsive to the union's concerns.[9]

Also in 1980, Sara Douglas and a team of researchers at the University of Illinois monitored three local newspapers in a month-long project categorizing labor stories thematically.[10] With the Machinists' survey clearly in mind, this study revealed many of the same basic patterns of bias in local newspapers that the Machinists had found in television programming. But the Illinois study was not a union response per se, though it was obviously union-inspired and designed to complement the Machinists' study.

For the most part, unions have not made systematic efforts to survey and evaluate the media attention they have received. Rather, unions have tended to respond to specific instances of a given medium's portrayal. Walter Kupau, for instance, the business manager of Hawaii's Carpenters Union, Local 745, responding to the abuse he was receiving in the press, cited the *Honolulu Advertiser* for its crusade against him and his union's organizers.[11] The following year, the local president of the Teamsters in Hawaii, Art Rutledge, complained about a similar series of stories in the *Advertiser* that improperly imputed guilt to the union leadership.[12] In each of these cases, however, the only satisfaction granted the complainant was the single item in the paper voicing the complaint, which was heavily outweighed by the number of articles that constituted the offending portrayal.

It is this hopelessly one-sided advantage that the press has in presenting its opinions to the public that Liebling had in mind when he remarked that freedom of the press belongs only to those who own one. As a result, most labor unions have not bothered to express their complaints directly to the news media, or, if they do, they do not tend to use the formal vehicles that their community or local press have instituted.

Rutledge's complaint was unusual in that it was directed to the paper's ombudsman. But no aggrieved union or its leader in Hawaii ever brought a complaint of media bias to the Honolulu Community Media Council that was established in 1970 to deal with such problems.[13] This aversion to making formal responses seems to be endemic to labor's relationship with newspapers, which has a long history of antagonism.

Labor has shown a much greater inclination to respond to television coverage. As Ralph Arthur Johnson described in his article "World without Workers: Prime Time's Presentation of Labor," the Steelworkers were able to turn their objections to a network series into an opportunity for positive public relations: "In a recent striking example, NBC's short-lived drama, 'Skag,' may have distorted the image of steelworkers, but the image created was tangible. The United Steelworkers resourcefully created a public debate about the lack of its authenticity and capitalized on the opportunity to inform the public about the function of labor unions."[14] Instances of media distortion are rarely seen as opportunities. More often labor has avoided raising its objections for fear of calling even more public attention to the distorted portrayals. Certainly this can be the result if the objections, after being publicized, are not followed by an educational program of the kind the Steelworkers developed after *Skag*. To be effective, labor's response must go beyond a mere objection and commit resources to reeducation. Beyond what is usually considered rebuttal, the response must be a form of what lawyers call "redirect."

After the Machinists' monitoring project, another extensive union-sponsored survey of television coverage was conducted by Local 37 of the American Federation of State, County and Municipal Employees (AFSCME). This New York City local was concerned about the TV news coverage it was receiving and so, in 1981, it organized 294 members into fifty-four teams to monitor TV newscasts on all seven New York channels for a four-week period. The subsequent report demonstrated that 55 percent of the time when a city employee or service was criticized it was not given the opportunity to answer. Mayor Edward Koch in particular, the survey revealed, was given wide latitude. Nine times out of ten, his statements went unchallenged, a deference shown to no other figures in the survey.[15] This survey, however, was directed at a specific problem peculiar to one union local and did not include questions on the general patterns of union portrayal, of which the local's complaint may have been only a symptom.

The basic weakness of monitoring that is so finely focused is that it misrepresents the true scale of the problem. This is not to say that labor's reaction to specific instances of media bias is unwarranted. The Communications Workers of America, for example, mounted a very successful campaign against MCI for a series of ads featuring comedienne Joan Rivers in what they perceived as an insulting portrayal of their members. Such defensive maneuvers are often necessary and valuable in the context of the workers' self-image, but they have left unaddressed the larger issue of the media's portrayal of unions and unionization.

Norman Isaacs, former president of the National News Council, in his book *Untended Gates*, endeavored to show the viability of self-regulatory bodies such as ombudsmen and media councils as avenues of redress for media bias.[16] A tireless monitor of newspaper improprieties, Isaacs formed his theory based on the premise that the overall treatment accorded most groups is fair and that media councils and independent ombudsmen are needed to pass judgment on the isolated examples of abuse that are bound to crop up occasionally. Labor's response to its media portrayal, particularly in its monitoring efforts, has been hampered by its tendency to accept unchallenged this same premise.

Recently, however, several union newsletter editors in Hawaii have developed an innovative approach to media monitoring on the state level. In 1988, editors representing five different unions formed the Hawaii Association of Labor Editors to pool their technical expertise and deal with statewide problems that affect the entire labor movement. One of the first issues they addressed was the problem of press relations with the state's major newspaper and television reporters.

Using research and data collected for this study, the labor editors began a series of informal discussions with the principal labor reporters. Eventually, the group was able to develop a set of guidelines that it submitted to the Honolulu Community Media Council in September 1989. The proposed guidelines consist of five primary recommendations:

1. Remain neutral.
2. Refer to labor leaders by their proper title.

3. Do not "play up" labor disunity.
4. Do not perpetuate popular misconceptions.
5. Give coverage to positive stories about labor.[17]

Though the Media Council did not immediately adopt the proposed guidelines, the dialogue with the council as well as with the local reporters has helped to sensitize both the media and the community to labor's problems.

Advocacy Advertising

Beyond monitoring the treatment labor is receiving in the media, more and more unions are taking steps to reform their portrayal. Though such campaigns are always costly and almost unpredictable in their outcome, the dramatic decline in union membership experienced in the late 1970s and early 1980s has spurred the labor movement to reconsider its traditional aversion to professional media advertising.

In 1985, the year of the landmark AFL-CIO reassessment, Plumbers and Steamfitters Local 33 in Des Moines, Iowa, began a campaign to promote the union's image as part of its ninety-fifth anniversary celebration, essentially designed as an organizing campaign. Six commercials were aired on local channels, particularly during broadcasts of local ball games. Emphasizing the quality and stability of union labor and the high standards of craftsmanship fostered by union apprenticeship programs, the ads were designed to appeal to contractors, potential members, and the public at large.

All six of the commercials, as their ninety-fifth anniversary video explained, were responses to the long years of biased portrayals in the popular media. One of the most effective ads showed a union hard hat with an American flag on it, placed in a large vise and gradually being crushed as the announcer read the following script:

> Remember when "Made in USA" meant craftsmanship? We do. But there are those in this country who would cheapen American labor, and their pressure is building every day. With every wage agreement that's broken, with every safety standard that's allowed to slip, with every reduction in accident and health benefits, the quality of American labor is cheapened. Isn't it time the pressure stopped? Let's keep quality, and build union. We're the Plumbers and Steamfitters of Local 33.[18]

Without naming a specific adversary, this ad skillfully portrayed union workers as victims of economic policies that ultimately depreciate not just our currency but our work ethic as well. And though these ads were focused on the Plumbers and Steamfitters, like the ILGWU union label campaign a decade earlier, they aimed at the larger issue of union-made products and therefore had a spillover benefit to all unions in the area.

A second ad showed a young construction worker returning home from work, his face lined with worry and apprehension, while the voice-over read:

> Nine years ago Jack Ferris went to work for a nonunion company. They promised him job security, decent wages and profit-sharing for his skills as a plumber. Today, Jack's dreams were shattered, so were the promises. He was laid off. Jack and his family have to start over . . . alone. Things might have been different. He could still have his rights if he'd belonged to the union. Maybe you should look into the union. For more information call this number. We're the Plumbers and Steamfitters of Local 33.[19]

Focusing on the issue of job security, traditionally the most persuasive union organizing feature, this ad appealed not just to would-be plumbers but to a wide variety of workers who were likely to be anxious about their future employment.

Certainly the balance of such campaigns throughout the nation have been directed toward specific local issues. In Hawaii, for instance, the Hotel Employees and Restaurant Employees Union, Local 5, ran a $50,000 to $60,000 media campaign supporting a particularly difficult round of bargaining in 1987.[20] And in 1988 the National Education Association ran a set of three commercials produced by Beber Silverstein and Partners of Miami, Florida, which aired in the fall on over-the-air and cable news, news analysis, and public affairs programming. These ads featured association members and presented common issues facing teachers in bargaining throughout the country, including teacher shortages, overcrowded classes, and noncompetitive salaries, but they targeted political action and support for legislative changes in the November elections.[21]

In 1989 the United Auto Workers launched a media campaign with a somewhat broader target. In two ten-day segments designed for national television in April and June, the UAW sought to turn national attention on anti-labor business practices. In one thirty-second spot called "Products," newsreel images of American success in production dissolve into images of a frenzied Wall Street trading floor as the narrator contrasts market manipulation and buyouts with the products of American labor made idle by plant closings and foreign investments.[22] These ads were broadcast in more than twenty-one market areas in Washington, New York, Chicago, Los Angeles, and Detroit on Cable News Network, Financial News Network, and ESPN.[23]

Another form of advocacy advertising that has become popular recently in the labor movement is image advertising. Unlike most of the previous media campaigns, image advertising is not directed toward the achievement of a specific union goal such as organizing or bargaining. Image advertising targets the general public rather than union members or recalcitrant employers. And, unlike political spots, image advertising is not focused on a specific public outcome so much as a general improvement in the public attitude toward unions.

Historically, labor has resisted this form of media use. Over thirty years ago, officials of the AFL-CIO spoke disdainfully of such advertising. As one spokesman remarked, "It's not like selling soap. You can't just sing a jingle that says 'Love that AFL-CIO.' "[24] By the end of the 1980s, the AFL-CIO launched a nationwide program that is succeeding in reforming public opinion through the use of jingles and media imagery virtually identical to the way Madison Avenue has marketed soap, cigarettes, and political candidates since the days of Albert Lasker.

In Hawaii, the Carpenters Union, Local 745, after suffering abuse in the local press from 1983 to 1986, produced and telecast a series of thirty-second commercials that began airing in December 1987. Designed to air on holidays, the various spots used a seasonal message. The first Christmas spot, for instance, was set to a bright musical score with the words:

> If what they say is true
> That holiday good cheer
> Is really what we built
> For others through the year,
> Let's celebrate together
> Families strong and fast.
> Good deeds without measure
> Friendships built to last.
> Building a better Hawaii
> Folks like you and me.
> Merry Christmas, Hawaii,
> From Santa's Carpenters.[25]

So understated was the message of this and the Carpenters' other commercials that they were virtually subliminal. The spot was run eighteen times in prime-time slots on the four network television channels in the two weeks before Christmas. Similar spots were run on Father's Day and Thanksgiving, giving the general impression of greeting cards and subtly identifying the union with the most cherished institutions in the state.

In October 1987, the AFL-CIO convention approved the inauguration of a $13 million media campaign unlike anything ever attempted before. Placed in the charge of the AFL-CIO's Labor Institute for Public Affairs, this new campaign would be the product of careful market research and, according to the convention resolution, be dedicated "to raise the level of public understanding of unions and of the AFL-CIO; and to increase both the predisposition of a new generation of American workers (20 to 40 years old) to union organization and those workers' understanding of how unionism responds to their own needs and concerns."[26]

By the spring of the following year, LIPA was ready to launch the two-year project under the theme "Union, Yes!" As the *Wall Street Journal* noted, the ads were created by the New York advertising firm of Lois Pitts Gershon Pon/GGK and featured TV stars Tyne Daly and Howard Hesseman as well as movie star Jack Lemmon.[27] The ads were aired on network television and on local stations in thirteen large cities beginning on May 11, 1988.

But the "Union, Yes!" program was successful primarily because it overcame the two greatest handicaps dogging union media campaigns in the past. First, "Union, Yes!" is a multimedia, long-term program. Designed to appear for two years on television, radio, billboards, and print media throughout the nation, "Union, Yes!" is not a onetime effort with a hit-and-run effect. Second, "Union, Yes!" is an AFL-CIO-sponsored campaign designed to improve the public's attitude about unions.

But the best aspect of this campaign has been its adaptability to local-issue campaigns that complement and enhance the national theme. More than 120 union sponsors have used the special "Union, Yes!" radio spots in conjunction with their own organizing campaigns, and an estimated two hundred billboards have been put up nationwide.[28] The American Federation of State, County and Municipal Employees used the campaign's radio and television ad to promote its successful organizing drive at Harvard University. And in Pennsylvania, the "Union, Yes!" message was used by the state AFL-CIO in its legislative campaign to increase that state's minimum wage.[29]

Not only did the AFL-CIO invest in market research in its design of the campaign, but it began public opinion surveys almost immediately after the program started to gauge the campaign's effectiveness. By the end of July, it could report that many who had seen the television ads earlier in the year had changed their attitudes significantly.[30]

Organized labor has, it seems, turned a corner in its willingness and commitment to the sophisticated use of mass media to respond to the onslaught of negative portrayals it has suffered at the hands of the national commercial news and entertainment media. Though it remains to be seen whether the hard lessons it has learned over the years will result in ongoing programs of media monitoring and advocacy advertising, such as corporate America has been engaged in since the 1950s, the success of its organizing efforts in the 1990s will probably determine the future course of the labor movement's response to its media portrayal as well as its survival as a viable economic and social force in the future of American society.

9. The Eight Lenses

...the guilèd shore
To a most dangerous sea...
The seeming truth which
        cunning times put on
To entrap the wisest.
       —William Shakespeare, *The Merchant of Venice*

Maureen Williams at the University of Massachusetts at Amherst has studied the patterns of news media attention to organized labor and described the change over the years as a progress "from incendiary to invisible."[1] Although I agree with Williams that labor is not getting the direct attention it once did, I would conclude that the image of labor has not been reduced to invisibility so much as it has been refocused and filtered into more subtle, indirect projections than before. Contemporary American media are most likely to refer to labor in the sideswipes and subliminal representations when labor or unionization is not the center of the story, but is attacked briefly in passing. As the previous chapters have shown, this pattern of abuse often conforms to Cirino's thirteen forms of bias and fits into Parenti's seven generalizations of media treatment of labor disputes summarized in the Introduction.

Each medium tends to focus on a particular facet of an overall labor union stereotype. The movies most often focus on the perceived connection between organized crime and organized labor. Only occasionally, in deference to the imagined liberalism of the film industry, does it honor the weak or unsuccessful attempts of minorities to unionize. Television portrayals tend to emphasize the pettiness or foolishness of union bargaining goals and take the cinematic portrayals a step further by portraying good unionists out of power and generally suppressed by their local or national leaders, whose power is considered excessive, out of touch, and corrupt. Television and print news share a preference for using employers as sources, which causes them to adopt the employer's perception of the issues as the basic premise of their reports. Just as commonly, when covering labor disputes, they attempt to adopt a position that supposedly advocates the interests of a general public, which they define to contain only victims of the strike action, not victims of the collective personnel policies established by national and local employers' councils. Furthermore, local newspapers, as illustrated in chapter 6, can become so caught up in a chamber-of-commerce mentality that they come to regard aggressive labor organizing as a criminal activity and are unable, as a result, to consider alternate interpretations of labor activism. And, in addition to all the other components of the stereotype mentioned above, the favorite target of the cartoon images of labor unions is the worthless, unproductive, overpaid blue-collar work force, which is considered the unhappy but inevitable result of unionization.

There are in addition a series of what might be called "lenses" coloring and distorting the different media portrayals of organized labor. In this study I have isolated at least eight of these lenses that have traditionally and consistently distorted the media images of labor unions and their leaders. Collectively they define the media stereotype of organized labor, which reporters, editors, and script writers see and then amplify:

1. Labor unions protect and encourage unproductive, usually fat, lazy, and insubordinate workers.
2. America is unable to compete internationally in open markets because big, powerful unions have forced the nation's employers to pay exorbitant union wages to unproductive laborers.
3. Although some very poor and abused workers (particularly women and immigrants) may need to form unions to protect themselves, big international unions usually fail to represent the interests of such workers.
4. Union leaders, because they do not come from the educated/ cultured (privileged) classes, are more likely to be corrupted by the power they achieve than are business or political leaders.
5. Unions should be volunteer societies organized and led by unpaid, unprofessional staffs of selfless workers; union dues should not be used to pay anyone's salary.
6. There was a time, long ago, when unions were necessary (when some of our older friends and relatives were in the movement), but now things are different. Employers are enlightened and would not generally try to abuse their workers. In the few cases where they might, new federal laws (Fair Labor Standards Act, the various civil rights acts, and the Occupational Safety and Health Act) can provide reasonable protection against employer abuse.
7. Unions institutionalize conflict. Unions came into being to solve

a specific labor relations problem. They solved the problem and, instead of going away, they remain to dredge up conflict where there would otherwise be perfect harmony.

8.   All unions are the same. All unions are, therefore, accountable for the corruption or excess of any one union or union leader and share the guilt or shame.

Unlike Cirino's thirteen forms of bias or Parenti's seven misrepresentations, these eight lenses operate as underlying values often absorbed so thoroughly into the conception of labor relations held by the press and entertainment media that the resulting portrayals of organized labor will necessarily be guided into further negative stereotypes.

The impact of this labor stereotyping on public opinion or on labor's ability to organize and bargain effectively is difficult to quantify because there are many variables at work. Not only have the media images been warped and permuted over the years, but the reach of the media has extended deeper into the American psyche. A. J. Liebling correctly observed that "the lazy mind, faced by recurrent but changing problems, takes refuge in a formula."[2] To the average American who is not personally involved in the country's labor movement, organized labor is a distant but recurrent phenomenon. Like foreign news and its geography, labor news and its arenas hum steadily in the background of consciousness, generally without requiring a personal decision or impinging on daily affairs. It is on such a benumbed or indifferent consciousness that the media are most influential. As V. O. Key, Jr., discovered, "In the short run the effects of the media probably are greatest on topics for which readers and viewers have only the vaguest internalized norms or standards for independent judgement."[3] The results of this study's survey of high school students (Appendix A) indicate how mistaken that image is likely to be in a generation whose knowledge of labor relations has been formed by the media considered here.

The media, whether news or entertainment, electronic, cinematic, or print, share a civic responsibility scrupulously to avoid stereotypical portrayals of races, ideologies, and institutions. Stereotypes are largely formed by ignorance, and the labor stereotype is no exception. Lack of informed coverage has been the bane of the labor movement since its inception. The media regularly resort to experts in medicine and law when treating these subjects, but it is assumed that anyone with a casual knowledge of current affairs can fairly and accurately describe labor relations. Newspapers encourage rotation rather than stability of their labor beat and qualified experts in TV news reporting are ordinarily employer representatives. These news media need to seek out and train reliable and objective experts, versed in the complexities of labor history as well as labor law and capable of researching and representing the issues of the disputes they report. Likewise, the producers of film and TV dramas, who regularly hire military, police, medical, and legal consultants to assure accuracy of plot and detail, need to accord the same respect to their treatment of labor scripts. Ignorance feeds a stereotype just as education destroys it. Like it or not, our media are our most influential and pervasive educators. Richard S. Salant, former president of CBS News, asserted, "Our job isn't . . . to give people what they're interested in. Our job is to provide people with the basic data that make democracy work."[4] Like all educators, the media have a responsibility to their students as well as to their subjects.

Conservative media critics have complained over the past twenty years that America's "media elite" have systematically pursued a liberal agenda of political and social issues. For the most part, such arguments rely on a definition of liberalism that is limited to policies affecting defense spending, federal funds for social programs, and advocacy of civil rights causes. The rights of labor to organize and bargain collectively have been removed from that liberal agenda so that not even its conservative critics can find traces of sympathy to the labor movement in the media they have so single-mindedly harangued otherwise.

It is difficult to say exactly why or even when this separation of traditional liberalism from the cause of labor occurred. To some extent, the labor movement may have itself contributed to this political disaffiliation. Labor's response to the red-baiting of the McCarthy era involved a considerable amount of reactionary reorganization. To counter the image that labor unions were unpatriotic or un-American, many unions undertook community service projects and other programs designed to impress the public with the civic-mindedness of union leadership and with the theme that unions are institutionally consistent with free enterprise and the American Way.

Labor's conservative response at that time may have led to its being dropped from the liberal agenda for much the same reason that, as Christopher Lasch commented, American liberals turned their backs on the likes of Archie Bunker. Both the labor movement and exponents of liberalism were ultimately interested in moving up the social ladder of acceptance. The labor movement saw the old Wobbly/socialism as its weak underbelly in its public relations struggles. At the same time, American liberals came to regard the unlettered and uncontrolled strength of their own blue-collar progenitors as a social embarrassment. It may be said they sold each other out for a better seat on the American omnibus.

Progressivism yielded up the labor movement as it devolved into liberalism in the 1950s. Richard Pells's careful analysis of the development of social philosophies espoused by American intellectuals in the 1940s and 1950s identified the significance of the postwar political climate as it was reflected in the works of such influential writers as William Whyte and David Riesman:

> Reading Whyte or Riesman, one sensed a profound shift in language, or in the connotations assigned to the same words. What the writers of the 1930s called "community," the postwar intelligentsia labeled "conformity." Cooperation now became "other-direction"; social consciousness had turned into "groupism"; solidarity with others implied an invasion of privacy; "collectivism" ushered in a "mass society"; ideology translated into imagery; economic exploitation yielded to bureaucratic manipulation; the radical activist was just another organization man.[5]

Likewise, the union organizer became another organization man; and union solidarity was viewed as misplaced loyalty.

By the 1980s, under the Reagan onslaught, liberalism metamorphosed again into "neo-liberalism." To the extent that this political philosophy has been championed by the media, it now admittedly excludes the promotion of organized labor from its agenda. Media sympathy for the working class in the United States is reserved almost exclusively for the utterly powerless and egregiously victimized. To the extent that organized labor is successful at developing bargaining power in any sector of the work force, it is vilified and attacked. In 1982 the *Washington Post* published a "neoliberal manifesto" written by Charles Peters, editor of the *Washington Monthly*, that minced no words regarding the changed neoliberal attitude toward labor: "If neo-conservatives are liberals who took a critical look at liberalism and decided to become conservatives, we are liberals who took the same look and decided to retain our goals but to abandon some of our prejudices. We still believe in liberty and justice and a fair chance for all, in mercy for the afflicted and help for the down and out. But we no longer automatically favor unions and big government or oppose the military and big business."[6]

By 1982, this declaration came as no surprise to labor. If anything, the startling revelation in Peters's "manifesto" must have been whatever led him to believe that liberals of the recent generation had any "prejudice" that favored unions. Even in the traditional "progressive" stronghold of Amherst, Massachusetts, which rallied behind Cesar Chavez's grape boycotts and supported the candidacy of Jesse Jackson over favorite son Michael Dukakis, a local organizing drive by the United Food and Commercial Workers in 1986 was hard-pressed to find any support in the local press. Instead, as Harold P. Schlechtweg described in his account of the dispute, "The public image, skillfully projected in the press, was of a liberal community speaking with one voice to defend a cherished community institution against the irrational attack of a large outside union."[7] It was of no concern that the wages and benefits paid by that cherished local institution were significantly lower than the standard wages in the area. It is an old saw that charity begins at home, but apparently liberalism ends there.

There never were a great number of media advocates for labor. Even Heywood Broun and A. J. Liebling were not products of a liberal press so much as they were knights errant to the pack of their peers. More recently there has been no lone media voice to uphold the rights of union labor.

Two hundred years ago, Alexis de Tocqueville observed that "the influence of the liberty of the press does not affect political opinions alone, but extends to all opinions of men, and modifies customs as well as laws." He realized that "the influence of a power is increased in proportion as its direction is centralized" and that "the only way to neutralize the effect of the public journals is to multiply their number."[8] Similarly, A. J. Liebling predicted "that labor unions, citizens' organizations, and possibly political parties yet unborn are going to back daily papers. These will represent definite, undisguised points of view, and will serve as controls on the large profit-making papers expressing definite, ill-disguised points of view."[9] Like Tocqueville, he realized that diversity of expression provides the best guarantee of freedom of speech. Unfortunately, neither Tocqueville nor Liebling could have imagined the frightening degree to which the American media would be centralized in our day.

Labor, therefore, cannot afford the luxury of backing a larger variety of daily papers. The labor movement can hope to deal with the power of the national media only on a national level. For this reason, as I indicated in the previous chapter, labor must be unified and accept the inescapable reality that unions are lumped together in the public consciousness. The "Union, Yes!" campaign is a good example of an effective response, but if this two-year campaign is not followed by similar national efforts, its momentum will be swallowed up by the sheer volume of negative media portrayals such as this study has documented. Surely the time is past when labor unions can ignore the impact of the mass media.

Appendix A

Results of High School Labor Survey

Correct responses appear in bold print.

	Maui	Kalani	Radford	Total	Percent
		Number of respondents from:			

	Maui	Kalani	Radford	Total	Percent
1. Which of these countries has the largest percentage of its workers represented by labor unions?					
a) England	3	10	8	21	5
b) Japan	13	32	52	97	21
c) USA	73	122	127	322	70
d) W. Germany	3	8	4	15	3
e) Australia	0	1	3	4	1
2. Which of the above countries has the lowest percentage of its workers represented by labor unions?					
a) England	7	12	23	42	9
b) Japan	32	61	58	151	33
c) USA	3	6	19	28	6
d) W. Germany	20	32	38	90	20
e) Australia	30	59	56	145	32

3. What percentage of American workers are now represented by a union?

a) 11	2	3	2	7	1
b) 17	11	19	36	66	15
c) 24	38	67	76	181	40
d) 33	33	82	83	198	44

4. The "Right-to-Work" Committee exists to

a) help create more jobs in the economy	16	26	48	90	20
b) defend workers unfairly dismissed	53	87	93	233	51
c) outlaw contracts which require union membership	10	24	27	61	13
d) none of the above	12	31	27	70	16

5. All unions have the right to strike.

a) True	69	132	146	347	75
b) False	23	41	51	115	25

6. If a union official doesn't like one of his members, he doesn't have to help him.

a) True	11	20	24	55	12
b) False	81	152	173	406	88

7. In the last national election, all the big unions endorsed the Democratic party's presidential candidate.

a) True	47	77	103	227	50
b) False	45	89	92	226	50

8. What percentage of contract talks result in strikes?

a) 2	20	32	27	79	17
b) 6	32	46	67	145	32
c) 12	32	68	77	177	39
d) 26	8	22	26	56	12

9. What percentage of
strikes are called
without an
authorization vote of
the membership?

a) 0 to 1	35	36	41	112	25
b) 2 to 6	31	52	67	150	33
c) 7 to 12	18	55	66	139	30
d) 13 to 18	8	24	23	55	12

10. The right of state
and county workers to
be represented by a
union is protected by
federal law.

a) True	78	125	152	355	78
b) False	14	40	45	99	22

11. After paying their
dues, union workers
make about the same
as nonunion workers in
comparable
employment.

a) True	39	66	87	192	42
b) False	53	102	110	265	58

12. What percentage of
labor unions are
corrupt?

a) less than 1	18	34	36	88	19
b) about 5	44	50	86	180	40
c) nearly 10	30	50	50	130	29
d) close to 25	0	32	25	57	12

13. List one main reason you wouldn't want to be represented by a labor union:

Unions are always going on strike.

Unions are too powerful.

Unions are corrupt.

Unions are greedy and selfish.

Unions are ruining the country.

Union leaders (bosses) are overpaid.

Union dues are too high.

Unions are not democratic but are un-American.

Unions protect bad workers.

Unions are no longer needed.

Appendix B

American Movies Dealing with Labor Unions

Capital vs Labor (26 March 1910)
Vitagraph
   Director: Van Dyke Brooke
   Stars: Maurice Costello, Harry T.
   Morey, and Earle Williams

A Martyr To His Cause (1911) Essanay
Film Mfg.
   Screenwriter: Arthur McMackin

Intolerance: The Modern Story
(1916) D. W. Griffith
   Director: David Wark Griffith
   Screenwriter: David Wark Griffith
   Stars: Robert Harron, Mae Marsh,
   Miriam Cooper, Sam De Grasse,
   Walter Long, and Monte Blue

Alice's Egg Plant (1925) Walt Disney
   Director: Walt Disney

Men of Steel (1926) Milton Sills
   Director: George Archainbaud
   Screenwriter: Milton Sills
   Star: Milton Sills

The Power and the Glory (1933) Fox
   Director: William K. Howard
   Screenwriter: Preston Sturges
   Stars: Spencer Tracy, Colleen Moore,
   Ralph Morgan, and Helen Vinson

I Believed in You (1934) Fox
   Director: Irving Cummings
   Screenwriter: William Conselman
   Stars: Rosemary Ames, Victor Jory,
   and John Boles

Riffraff (1935) MGM
   Director: J. Walter Ruben
   Screenwriters: Frances Marion, Anita
   Loos, and H. W. Hanemam
   Stars: Spencer Tracy, Jean Harlow,
   and Mickey Rooney

Black Fury (1935) Warner Brothers
   Director: Michael Curtiz
   Screenwriters: Abem Finkel and Carl
   Erickson
   Star: Paul Muni

Modern Times (1936) Chaplin Studios/
United Artists
   Director: Charlie Chaplin
   Screenwriter: Charlie Chaplin
   Stars: Charlie Chaplin and Paulette
   Goddard

Dead End (1937) United Artists
   Director: William Wyler
   Screenwriter: Lillian Hellman

Stars: Humphrey Bogart, Joel McCrea, and Sylvia Sidney

Racket Busters (1938) Warner Brothers
Director: Lloyd Bacon
Screenwriters: Robert Rossen and Leonardo Bercovici
Stars: Humphrey Bogart and George Brent

Our Leading Citizen (1939) Paramount
Director: Al Santell
Storywriter: Irvin S. Cobb
Screenwriter: John C. Moffitt
Stars: Bob Burns and Susan Hayward

The Devil and Miss Jones (1940) RKO
Director: Sam Wood
Screenwriter: Norman Krasna
Stars: Jean Arthur and Robert Cummings

How Green Was My Valley (1941)
Twentieth Century-Fox
Director: John Ford
Screenwriter: Philip Dunne
Stars: Walter Pidgeon and Maureen O'Hara

An American Romance (1944) MGM
Director: King Vidor
Storywriters: Herbert Dalmas and William Ludwig
Stars: Brian Donlevy, Ann Richards, Walter Abel, and Horace McNally

Fountainhead (1949) Warner Brothers
Director: King Vidor
Screenwriter: Ayn Rand
Stars: Gary Cooper and Patricia Neal

The Whistle at Eaton Falls (1951)
Columbia
Producer: Louis de Rochemont
Director: Robert Siodmak
Screenwriters: Lemist Esler and Virginia Shaler
Stars: Lloyd Bridges and Dorothy Gish

Salt of the Earth (1954) Independent
Productions Corp.
Director: Herbert J. Biberman
Screenwriter: Michael Wilson
Stars: Rosaura Revueltas and Juan Chacon

On the Waterfront (1954) Columbia
Director: Elia Kazan
Screenwriter: Budd Schulberg

Stars: Marlon Brando and Eva Marie Saint

Inside Detroit (1956) Columbia
Director: Fred F. Sears
Screenwriters: Robert E. Kent and James B. Gordon
Stars: Dennis O'Keefe and Pat O'Brien

Edge of the City (1957) MGM
Director: Martin Ritt
Screenwriter: Robert Alan Arthur
Stars: Sidney Poitier and John Cassavetes

The Garment Jungle (1957) Columbia
Director: Vincent Sherman
Screenwriter: Harry Kleiner
Stars: Lee J. Cobb, Kerwin Matthews, Gia Scala, and Richard Boone

The Pajama Game (1957) Warner
Brothers
Directors: George Abbott and Stanley Donen
Screenwriters: George Abbott and Richard Bissell
Stars: Doris Day and John Raitt

Slaughter on Tenth Avenue (1957)
Universal
Director: Arnold Laven
Screenwriter: Lawrence Roman
Stars: Walter Matthau and Richard Egan

Never Steal Anything Small (1959)
Universal
Director: Charles Lederer
Screenwriter: Charles Lederer
Stars: James Cagney and Shirley Jones

The Trouble with Girls (1969) MGM
Director: Peter Tewksbury
Screenwriters: Arnold and Lois Peyser
Stars: Elvis Presley and Marlyn Mason

The Molly Maguires (1970) Paramount
Director: Martin Ritt
Screenwriter: Walter Bernstein
Stars: Sean Connery and Richard Harris

Joe Hill (1971) Sagittarius Production/
Paramount
    Director: Bo Widerberg
    Screenwriter: Bo Widerberg
    Stars: Thommy Berggren and Anja
Schmidt

Sometimes a Great Notion (1972)
Universal
    Director: Paul Newman
    Screenwriter: John Gay
    Stars: Paul Newman, Henry Fonda,
and Lee Remick

Bound for Glory (1976) United Artist
    Director: Hal Ashby
    Screenwriter: Robert Getchell
    Star: David Carradine

Which Way Is Up? (1977) Universal
    Director: Michael Schultz
    Screenwriters: Carl Gottlieb and Cecil
Brown
    Stars: Richard Pryor and Lonette
McKee

Blue Collar (1978) Universal
    Director: Paul Schrader
    Screenwriters: Paul and Leonard
Schrader
    Stars: Richard Pryor, Yaphet Kotto,
and Harvey Keitel

F.I.S.T. (1978) United Artists
    Director: Norman Jewison
    Screenwriters: Joe Eszterhas and
Sylvester Stallone
    Star: Sylvester Stallone

Norma Rae (1978) Twentieth Century-
Fox
    Director: Martin Ritt
    Screenwriters: Irving Ravetch and
Harriet Frank, Jr.
    Stars: Sally Field and Ron Leibman

Power (1979) Columbia
[Television]
    Director: David Gerber
    Screenwriter: Ernest Tidyman
    Stars: Joe Don Baker and Karen
Black

Steel (1979) Davis/Panzer Production
    Director: Steve Carver
    Screenwriter: Leigh Chapman
    Stars: Lee Majors, George Kennedy,
and Jennifer O'Neill

The Mysterious Stranger (1982)
Great Amwell-Nebraska ETV
    Director: Peter H. Hunt
    Screenwriter: Julian Mitchell
    Stars: Chris Makepeace and Lance
Kerwin

Silkwood (1983) Twentieth Century-Fox
[ABC Pictures]
    Director: Mike Nichols
    Screenwriter: Nora Ephron and Alice
Arlen
    Stars: Meryl Streep and Cher (Bono)

Kentucky Woman (1983) Twentieth
Century-Fox
    Director: Walter Doniger
    Screenwriter: Walter Doniger
    Stars: Cheryl Ladd, Ned Beatty, and
Philip Levien

Blood Feud (1983) Twentieth Century-
Fox
[Selznick/Glickman Productions]
    Director: Michael Newell
    Screenwriter: Robert Boris
    Stars: Robert Blake and Cotter Smith

Teachers (1984) United Artists/MGM
    Director: Arthur Hiller
    Screenwriter: W. R. McKinney
    Stars: Nick Nolte, Lee Grant, and
Judd Hirsch

The River (1984) Universal
    Director: Mark Rydell
    Screenwriters: Robert Dillon and
Julian Barry
    Stars: Sissy Spacek and Mel Gibson

Two Fathers Justice (1985) A. Shane
Company
    Director: Rod Holcomb
    Screenwriter: David J. Kinghorn
    Stars: Robert Conrad and George
Hamilton

Act of Vengence (1985) Telepictures
Production (HBO)
    Director: John Mackenzie
    Screenwriter: Trevor Armbrister
    Stars: Charles Bronson and Ellen
Burstyn

Gung Ho (1986) Paramount
    Director: Ron Howard
    Screenwriters: Edwin Blum, L.
Gantry, and Babaloo Mandell
    Stars: Michael Keaton and Gedde
Watanabe

Armed and Dangerous (1986)
Columbia-Delphi V Productions
   Director: Mark L. Lester
   Screenwriters: Harold Ramis and
   Peter Torokvei
   Stars: John Candy and Eugene Levy

Wall Street (1987) Twentieth Century-
Fox
   Director: Oliver Stone
   Screenwriters: Stanley Weiser and
   Oliver Stone
   Stars: Charlie Sheen, Michael
   Douglas, Martin Sheen, and Hal
   Holbrook

Robocop (1987) Orion Pictures
   Director: Paul Verhoeven
   Screenwriters: Edward Neumeier and
   Michael Miner
   Stars: Peter Weller and Nancy Allen

Matewan (1987) Cinecom International/
Red Dog Films
   Director: John Sayles

   Screenwriter: John Sayles
   Stars: Chris Cooper and James Earl
   Jones

Frank Nitti: The Enforcer (1988)
Leonard Hill Films
   Director: Michael Switzer
   Screenwriter: Lee David Zlotoff
   Stars: Anthony LaPaglia and Vincent
   Guastaferro

Robocop 2 (1990) Orion Pictures
   Director: Irvin Kershner
   Screenwriters: Edward Neumeier and
   Michael Miner
   Stars: Peter Weller and Nancy Allen

Darrow (1991) American Playhouse
   Director: John David Coles
   Screenwriters: William Schmidt and
   Stephen Stept
   Stars: Kevin Spacey and Chris
   Cooper

Selected Documentaries

The People of the Cumberlands (1937)
Frontier Films
   Directors: Sidney Meyers and Jay
   Leyda
   18 minutes

Man and Dust (1940) Dial Films
   Producers: Lee and Sheldon Dick
   17 minutes

Native Land (1942) Frontier Films
   84 minutes

With These Hands (1950) ILGWU
   Writer: Harold Rome
   Stars: Arlene Francis and Sam
   Levene
   50 minutes

Harvest of Shame (1960) CBS-TV
   54 minutes

The Inheritance (1964) Amagalmated
Clothing Workers
   Director: Harold Mayer
   Writer: Millard Lanpell
   60 minutes

Bullet Bargaining at Ludlow (1965)
KOA Radio-TV
   Producer: KOA Radio-TV Denver
   23 minutes

Huelga (1967) King Screen
   53 minutes

The Rise of Labor (1968)
Metropolitan Broadcasting
   30 minutes

With Babies and Banners (1975) New
Day Films
   Directors: Anne Bohlen, Lyn
   Goldfarb, and Lorraine Gray
   45 minutes

Union Maids (1975) New Day Films
   Directors: Julia Reichert, Miles
   Mogulescu, and James Klein
   48 minutes

Harlan County, U.S.A. (1976) Cabin
Creek Films
   Director: Barbara Kopple
   Producer: Barbara Kopple
   103 minutes

*Eugene Debs and the American
Movement* (1978) Cam. Doc.
   Producer: Cambridge Documentary
   Films
   42 minutes

The Wobblies (1979) First Run Features
   Directors: Stewart Bird and Deborah
   Shaffer

Screenwriters: Stewart Bird and
Deborah Shaffer
89 minutes

The Willmar 8 (1980) California
Newsreel
   Director: Lee Grant
   Producer: Mary Beth Yarrow
   55 minutes

The Life and Times of Rosie the Riveter
(1980) Clarity Educational Productions
60 minutes

Selected Foreign Labor Films

Strike (1924) Russia: Goskino
   Director: Sergei Eisenstein
   Screenwriters: Sergei Eisenstein and
   Valeri Pletnyov
   Stars: A. Antonov, Mikhail
   Gomarov, and Maxim Shtraukh

The Stars Look Down (1941) Britain:
I. Goldsmith Productions
   Director: Dr. A. J. Cronin
   Screenwriter: J. B. Williams
   Stars: Michael Redgrave and
   Margaret Lockwood

The Organizer (1964) Italy: Lux Film-
Vides-Mediterranée Cinema
   Director: Mario Monicelli
   Screenwriters: Age and Scarpelli,
   Mario Monicelli
   Stars: Marcello Mastroianni and
   Renato Salvatori

Crime, Inc.: The Mob at Work (1984)
Thames Television
   Directors: Ken Craig and Ian Stuttard
   Writer: Martin Short
   51 minutes

American Dream (1991) Barbara
Kopple and Arthur Cohn
   Director: Barbara Kopple
   100 minutes

*Out of Darkness: The Mine Workers'
Story* (1991) Labor History and Cultural
Foundation
   Directors: Barbara Kopple and Bill
   Davis
   100 minutes

Coup pour coup (Blow for Blow) (1971)
France: Red Ball Films
   Director: Marin Karmitz
   Producers: Marin Karmitz/Cinema
   Services/W.D.R.
   Stars: garment workers in Rouen
   American release, March 1975

I'm All Right Jack (1960) Britain:
British Lion
   Director: John Boulting
   Stars: Peter Sellers

The Angry Silence (1960) Britain:
British Lion/Beaver
   Director: Guy Green
   Screenwriter: Bryan Forbes
   Stars: Richard Attenborough,
   Michael Craig

Business as Usual (1988) Britain
   Stars: Glenda Jackson and John Thaw

Appendix C

Network News Specials and Documentaries about Labor Unions on American Television

Compiled from Daniel Einstein, *Special Edition: A Guide to Network Television Documentary Series and Special News Reports, 1955–1979* (Metuchen, N.J.: Scarecrow Press, 1987), and *Video Source Book,* 7th ed., National Video Clearinghouse (New York: 1985).

December 30, 1951: CBS
See It Now
CIO leader John L. Lewis was interviewed in West Frankfort, Illinois, on the subject of mine safety. Films of Harold Stassen's press conference. Jet pilot in Korea discusses Russian MIG aircraft. Winston Churchill celebrates his seventy-seventh birthday. (E. 3466)

October 16, 1954: CBS
Person to Person
American Federation of Musicians president James Caesar Petrillo in Chicago. (E. 2893)

January 8, 1954: CBS
AFL President George Meany in Bethesda, Maryland. Singer Ethel Waters in Brooklyn. (E. 2905)

January 15, 1956: NBC
"Labor's New Look"
Report on the impact on the United States and its economy of the recent merger of two major labor organizations into the AFL-CIO. Guests include the organization's president, George Meany; vice-president, Walter Reuther; secretary-treasurer, William Schnitzler; and Charles Sligh of the National Association of Manufacturers. (E. 5383)

May 8, 1957: ABC
"Senate Labor Investigating Committee Highlights"
Highlights of Dave Beck's testimony were aired by ABC on May 9, 10, 14, 15, and 16.
(E. 5419)

August 20, 1957: ABC
"Senate Labor Investigating Committee Highlights"
Highlights of Teamster official James R. Hoffa's testimony before the Senate. Other
excerpts from Hoffa's testimony were aired by ABC on August 21, 22, and 23. (E.
5427)

October 13, 1957: NBC
"Outlook"
Filmed report on life in Bulgaria. Report on the launching into orbit of the Soviet
Sputnik satellite. Report on Teamsters' Union "boss" James Hoffa. (E. 2850)

January 5, 1958: NBC
"Look Here"
United Mine Workers president and pioneer labor leader John L. Lewis. (E. 2427)

September 25, 1958: NBC
"Man against the Senate"
Report on the Senate investigation into the activities of Teamsters Union "boss" James
R. Hoffa. (E. 5495)

June 24, 1959: CBS
"Hoffa and the Teamsters"
Report on Teamsters Union "boss" James R. Hoffa, currently under investigation by
the Senate. (E. 5550)

November 25, 1960: CBS
CBS Reports: "Harvest of Shame"
Broadcast on Thanksgiving evening, this program dramatically brought to national
attention for the first time the plight of American migrant farm workers and the shocking
conditions in which they live, travel, and labor in American fields and orchards. Included
are interviews with Labor Secretary James P. Mitchell, Senator Harrison A. Williams,
and farm officials. Edward R. Murrow (E. 895)

December 9, 1960: ABC
"Featherbedding?"
Representatives of labor management in the home building and railroad industries
comment on the practice of limiting a worker's chores so as to create jobs for others.
(E. 737)

January 7, 1961: NBC
"Should Public Employees Have the Right to Strike?"
With Michael J. Quill, president of the Transport Workers Union, and former con-
gressman Fred A. Hartley, coauthor of the Taft-Hartley Act. Moderator: Gabe Pressman. (E. 2674)

July 27, 1961: CBS
"At the Source: Walter Reuther"
Interview with United Auto Workers president Walter Reuther. Topics discussed include Reuther's role as co-chairman of the Tractors for Freedom Committee, which
unsuccessfully attempted to make a deal for the release of some Cuban political prisoners. Also discussed are the current UAW contract talks. (E. 5664)

March 7, 1962: NBC
David Brinkley's Journal
Investigation of Labor Secretary Arthur Goldberg's concept of the five-hour work day,

focusing on the Electrical Workers Union, which operates on that schedule. Workers are seen at "think" schools and recreational facilities provided by their union. (E. 1557)

April 13, 1962: CBS
Eyewitness to History: "The Big Steel Scrap"
Report on the reaction of government and labor to the recent steel price increase includes statements by JFK, RFK, Labor Secretary Arthur Goldberg, U.S. Steel president Roger M. Blough, and Steelworkers Union leader David G. MacDonald. Also, a look at a recently automated steel plant in Indiana. (E. 1833)

September 2, 1962: ABC
Editor's Choice: "Labor Day, 1962: Milestone"
Examination of the changing status and shape of organized labor in the United States Interviews with David McDonald, president of the Steelworkers Union, and James Carey, president of the Electrical Workers Union. Also, a talk with James F. Lincoln, director of an electric company whose employees have a profit-sharing plan. (E. 1699)

1963: CBS
Biography: "John L. Lewis" (E. 829)

April 1, 1963: NBC
David Brinkley's Journal: "Inside Jimmy Hoffa"
Profile and interview of Teamster "boss" Jimmy Hoffa, focusing on the activities of his union in the East and Midwest. Hoffa responds to Brinkley's questions on the Senate Labor hearings, Attorney General Robert Kennedy, and the image of the Teamsters Union. (E. 1598)

April 9, 1963: ABC
Bell & Howell Close-Up! "The Miners' Lament"
Report on the issues and arguments behind recent violence in the eastern Kentucky coal regions. Kentucky governor Bert T. Combs discusses union versus nonunion friction. Cameras reveal bombed homes, impoverished towns, and thousands of unemployed miners. (E. 776)

March 5, 1965: ABC
F.D.R.: "Strife!"
Chronicle of the labor/management conflicts of the early 1930s: the San Francisco and Minneapolis general strikes; West Virginia coal strikes; the split of labor into AFL and CIO camps; and the efforts of unions to gain collective bargaining powers. Interviews with Eleanor Roosevelt, New York City mayor Robert F. Wagner, and labor leader James Casey. (E. 1907)

August 2, 1966: CBS
"The Airline Strike: What Price Settlement?"
Examination of issues involved in the current strike and a look at how they might be resolved. (E. 6126)

November 15, 1966: CBS
CBS Reports: "The State of the Unions"
Study of the history and present activities of American labor unions and of how the American public perceives these organizations amid charges of racism, parochialism, and excessive power. Also, a look at how unions act to improve conditions among the dispossessed, focusing on Cesar Chavez and the United Farm Workers of California. Senator Wayne Morse, Labor Secretary Willard Wirtz, and AFL-CIO president George Meany are interviewed. (E. 1028)

September 23, 1969: CBS
"Challenge in the Coal Mines: Men against Their Unions"
Report on dissident elements within the United Mine Workers and the split between the union's long-entrenched leadership under its president W. A. "Tony" Boyle and a new breed of concerned miners led by Joseph Yablonski. (E. 6396)

January 18, 1970: NBC
Frank McGee Reports: "Report on the Steel Union Crisis"
Examination of crime in Washington, D.C., in the aftermath of President Richard Nixon's anti-crime program inaugurated in February 1969. A look at the effects of sonic booms in Boron, California. (E. 2187)

March 22, 1970: NBC
Frank McGee Reports: "The Strike of the Mailmen"
Entire show is devoted to reports on the current strike by U.S. postal employees. (E. 2195)

March 22, 1970: CBS
"Strike!: Crises in the Post Office"
Special report on the postal strike. (E. 6428)

August 31, 1970: ABC
Now: "Unions and the Blacks"
Report on the opinions of union leaders, workingmen, and rank and file union members regarding the current status of blacks in the construction industry and efforts on the part of black workers to join labor unions. Civil rights leader Jesse Jackson is among those interviewed. (E. 2736)

1972
"Asian Garden Strike," 15 min. Chinese for Affirmative Action
In 1972 workers of the Asia Garden Restaurant went on strike. In this program the workers and employers discuss working conditions. [VSB, p. 85]

March 19, 1972: CBS
60 Minutes
Jack Anderson and the ITT scandal. Report on George Meany and President Richard Nixon. Examination of marriage laws and the Equal Rights Amendment. "Point/Counterpoint": The topic is equal rights for women. (E. 3731)

September 12, 1972: NBC
NBC Reports: "Pensions—the Broken Promise"
Examination of the inequities and insecurities of pension systems that all too frequently do not pay back veteran workers who are helpless to do anything about it. Pension victims from New York to California relate their stories. The program won American Bar Association and Peabody awards and stirred Congress into dealing with the problem in its pensions reform law of 1974. However, the Federal Communications Commission (FCC) cited the show as a "one-sided documentary that created the impression that injustice and inequity were widespread in the administration of private pension plans." NBC went to court over the matter and after three years and a number of decisions and opinions, the Court of Appeals turned the case back to the FCC, which then decided it would no longer seek compliance from the network. (E. 2541)

1974
"Chinatown Report: Lee Mah Strike"
(40841) 60 min. KQED San Francisco. Chinese for Affirmative Action
In this program a bilingual (Cantonese, English) panel and audience discuss the dispute between eighteen workers who were laid off by the Lee Mah Electronics Corporation in California. [VSB, p. 247]

November 30, 1974: ABC
ABC News Close-Up: "Hoffa"
Profile of former Teamsters' president Jimmy Hoffa, who had been sent to prison in 1967 for jury tampering and was released under presidential commutation by Richard Nixon in 1972 on the condition that he stay out of union affairs until 1980. Investigation into Hoffa's rise to power discloses some previously unknown facts surrounding his conviction and sentence commutation. Interview with current Teamster "boss" Frank E. Fitzsimmons and with Hoffa himself. (E. 14)

1975
"Labor Unions: A Question of Violence," 15 min. CBS/Carousel Film & Video (American Film Festival: Blue Ribbon Award)
Confrontation between a successful, independent, nonunion building contractor in Philadelphia and the construction union. [VSB, p. 785]

April 11, 1976: CBS
60 Minutes
"Norman Lear": Profile of one of TV's most successful producers. "Do the Teamsters Own Alaska?": Report on union power and influence. "Hoffa": Discussion with Mrs. Jimmy Hoffa and with former Hoffa associates regarding the former Teamster official's disappearance. (E. 3857)

October 3, 1976: CBS
60 Minutes
"Unions, Money, and Politics": Examination of the influence and power of U.S. labor unions. "Something Rotten in Arizona": Report on the murder of Phoenix newspaper reporter Don Bolles. "Oriana": Interview with Italian journalist Oriana Fallaci. (E. 3876)

March 13, 1977: CBS
60 Minutes
"Target: J. P. Stevens": As Mike Wallace says, "This is the story of big labor versus J. P. Stevens." Also "Ivory Tower Cop": Profile and interview of criminologist and policeman Dr. George Kirkham. "Natasha": Profile of ballerina Natalia Makarova. (E. 3698)

December 20, 1977: NBC
NBC White Paper: "Trouble in Coal Country"
Examination of the difficult task America faces in trying to make coal its major energy source and the problems this effort is creating for miners, the coal industry, and environmentalists. Also, a look at mine safety, strip mining, and United Mine Workers efforts to aid striking miners. (E. 2576)

July 14, 1978: ABC
ABC News Close-Up: "Asbestos—the Way to Dusty Death"
Investigation into the biggest industrial killer in history reveals the health dangers of working with asbestos, risks that have been known for years by federal agencies. Focus on Philadelphia and Groton, Connecticut, shipyards includes interviews with victims and physicians. (E. 48)

November 18, 1978: CBS
60 Minutes
"Student Strike Enders": Report on students in Tacoma, Washington, who sued to end a teachers' strike. "The Dieter's Disease": Profile of a teenage girl suffering from anorexia. (E. 4279)

December 3, 1978: CBS
60 Minutes
"Taking on the Teamsters": Examination of efforts to "reform the giant union" by

rank-and-file members. "Remember Pearl Harbor?": A look at Japan's self-defense forces. "From Burgers to Bankruptcy": Investigation into how many people invested and lost money in Wild Bill's fast food restaurants. (E. 3987)

March 6, 1979: CBS
CBS Reports: "Inside the Union"
A look at the labor movement as experienced by members of Local 1010 of the United Steelworkers at the East Chicago, Indiana, Inland Steel plant. Included are films of internal battles between rank-and-file members and union officials. (E. 1135)

1983
"John L. Lewis"
24 minutes, WGBH Boston/King Features Entertainment
John L. Lewis, president of the United Mine Workers, who employed aggressive tactics to improve the lot of miners, is the subject of this program. [VSB, p. 756]

June 5, 1983: CBS
60 Minutes
"The Palestinians": Yasir Arafat is interviewed about Arab terrorism and the future of the PLO. "Uncle Sam Doesn't Want You": A look at the army's concerns about homosexuals in the armed forces. "Trouble Brewing": An unsympathetic look at the AFL-CIO boycott of Coors Brewery. (Originally broadcast 26 September 1982).

March 5, 1983: NBC
NBC Reports: "Labor in the Promised Land."
A report on the problems faced by the AFL-CIO in its attepts to organize workers in Houston, Texas. Reporter: Mike Jensen. Writers: Mike Jensen, Tom Spain, Marilyn Nissensen.

July 26, 1988: ABC
Nightline
"The TV Writers' Strike." A completely one-sided critique of the 1988 Writers' Guild strike that treats the writers as unwitting traitors in the network's losing battle with cable and video tape programming. As Greenfield says, it was "the worst case of bad timing since General Custer showed up at the Little Big Horn." Reporter: Ted Koppel. Correspondent: Jeff Greenfield.

January 31, 1989: PBS/CPB
Frontline
"The Battle for Eastern Airlines." Produced for release a month before the Eastern Airlines strike of 1989, this was a detailed account of the ups and downs of the Machinists' relationship with Eastern's previous owners and revealed a pattern of union responsiveness to concessions where corresponding concessions were made to joint decision making. With Judy Woodruff. Producer: Alex Gibney. Correspondent: Robert Kuttner

June 15, 1989: CBS
48 Hours "On Strike"
Dan Rather hosts a report on the opening of the Pittston coal mine strike of 1989. Interviews with miners and company management, this report sees the plight of the miners as a model for the lost cause of American labor as it struggles to maintain old strategies in new times.

April 1, 1990: CBS
60 Minutes
"Trouble: *Daily News*" Mike Wallace describes the untenable situation the pressman's union has put itself in as it draws nearer to an inevitable confrontation with the *New York Daily News*.

April 17, 1990: PBS/CPB
Frontline "New Harvest, Old Shame"
Thirty years after Edward R. Murrow's powerful "Harvest of Shame," this hour-long documentary looks at the lack of progress in the national and local responses to the plight of the country's eight hundred thousand migrant farm workers.

Appendix D

Plot Synopses of American TV Dramas
Dealing with Labor

Compiled from scripts and other documents at the Annenberg Television Script Archive, Annenberg School of Communications, University of Pennsylvania. Date given is airdate; an * indicates script date; +/0/− indicates whether portrayal of unions was positive, neutral, or negative. All quotations are referenced to pages of the scripts at the Annenberg Archive.

1. *All in the Family* (September 17, 1974) CBS: Saturday 8:00 P.M.
   − Episode: "The Bunkers and Inflation"
   Authors: Don Nicholl, Michael Ross, and Bernie West
   Studio: Tandem Productions
   Stars: Carroll O'Connor, Jean Stapleton, and Rob Reiner

Synopsis: Archie's union down at the plant decides to go out on strike.

2. *All in the Family* (September 21, 1974) CBS: Saturday 8:00 P.M.
   − Episode: "Archie Underfoot"
   Authors: Don Nicholl, Michael Ross, and Bernie West
   Studio: Tandem Productions
   Stars: Carroll O'Connor, Jean Stapleton, and Rob Reiner

Synopsis: Archie's still on strike, and when he's not out picketing, he's in Edith's way at home.

3. *All in the Family* (September 28, 1974) CBS: Saturday 8:00 P.M.
   − Episode: "Edith the Job Hunter"
   Authors: Don Nicholl, Michael Ross, and Bernie West

Studio: Tandem Productions
Stars: Carroll O'Connor, Jean Stapleton, and Rob Reiner

Synopsis: With no money coming in, Edith is forced to take a job . . . in the Jeffersons' cleaning store.

4. *All in the Family* (October 5, 1974) CBS: Saturday 8:00 P.M.
  – Episode: "Archie's Raise"
     Authors: Don Nicholl, Michael Ross, Bernie West
     Studio: Tandem Productions
     Stars: Carroll O'Connor, Jean Stapleton, and Rob Reiner

Synopsis: The strike has been settled and Archie goes back to work with a 15 percent raise. He is pleased until his son-in-law, Mike, points out that he is behind the rise in the cost of living.

5. *Serpico* (June 30, 1976*) NBC: Friday 10:00 P.M.
  – Episode: "Every Man Must Pay His Dues"
     Author: Brad Radnitz
     Studio: Paramount
     Stars: David Birney and Tom Atkins

Synopsis: Set in Brooklyn, John Maloney, a rough but big-hearted Irishman, is running for president of his local truckers' union (BTC). Show opens with his campaign worker and close friend, Ed Demarest, killed in car bomb explosion. Maloney's campaign speech, "Is that the kind of man you want at the head of your union? Do you want to go on putting up with violence and the sweetheart deals that Powell's been negotiating with management for six years?" (p. 5). "Look at your paychecks. In three years we've had a total raise of seven percent! I've got the facts and figures to have shown three hundred percent increases in profit! . . . Your *wives* aren't getting any of that profit! Your *kids* aren't getting any of that profit! *You* aren't getting any of that profit!" (p. 6). "But management is. Jack Powell is! And when somebody like me steps up to challenge that fact! Somebody dies! Somebody gets murdered!" (p. 7). Serpico foils Powell's attempt to have Maloney assassinated. Powell ends up going to jail, but Maloney loses the election. Quote from script: "In the back seat is Jack Powell, forties, a Jimmy Hoffa type, tough, rough, king of his mountain and not about to be dethroned" (p. 11).

6. *Gibbsville* (August 31, 1976*; November 26, 1976) NBC: Thursday 10:00 P.M.
  + Episode: "Andrea"
     Author: Edward Adler (John O'Hara)
     Studio: Columbia/ David Gerber Productions
     Stars: Gig Young and John Savage

Synopsis: Senator Barton Styler is in Gibbsville, Pennsylvania, for a fact-finding session on mine safety, intended to be only a whitewash. Andrea Cooper, fiancée to Judge Walter Mulligan, is new in town also. She was once a lover of Ray Whitehead, a newspaperman on the *Gibbsville Courier*, who is intent on presenting the miners' side of the safety problems. In the meantime Tad Kelly, the union's information officer, is organizing a play on John L. Lewis's life. The three miners scheduled to testify are bribed, and when Whitehead tries to investigate he is attacked by thugs hired by the jealous judge; he narrowly escapes with his life and a few broken ribs. Andrea is spurned by the judge, and after apologizing to Ray in his hospital room, she leaps out the window to her death.

7. *Phyllis* (September 9, 1976*; October 18, 1976) CBS: Monday 8:30 P.M.
  o Episode: "Boss or Buddy or Both or Neither"

Author: Earl Pomerantz
Studio: MTM Enterprises
Stars: Cloris Leachman and Henry Jones

Synopsis: San Francisco garbage workers' strike. Phyllis is the assistant to Dan Valenti, who is the supervisor in charge of the situation. Two weeks into the strike, Dan is appointed mediator. Paralleling the conflict between the city and the union is Phyllis's bad feelings toward Dan after she learns he's been taking advantage of her good nature and treating her like his secretary. At the mediation the management and labor teams have to mediate between Phyllis and Dan. As the negotiations wind down at 6:00 in the morning, the issues of the strike became humorously intertwined with Phyllis's complaints against Dan, but finally a settlement is reached when Dan agrees to pay for the dress Phyllis bought earlier when she thought he had invited her to a dinner she arranged for him. The union refuses to sign its agreement until Dan accepts these conditions.

8. *Executive Suite* (September 27, 1976) CBS: Monday 10:00 P.M.
   – Episode: "The Trap," Part 2 of Augmented Pilot
   Authors: Barbara Avedon, Barbara Corday, and Henry Slesar
   Studio: Metro-Goldwyn-Mayer
   Stars: Mitchell Ryan, Stephen Elliott, and Sharon Acker

Synopsis: A subplot in the episode shows Harry Ragin, the shop steward at a chemical plant (Cardway Chemical) in southern California, angered by the news that Brian Walling, the owner's son, is working at the plant where there has been a rash of layoffs. A Chicano women at the plant passes out and is taken to the hospital. Harry goes to see Don Walling, Brian's father, about the layoffs. Don likes Harry but defers to the union leadership. Harry says: "You know, there's union management . . . and there's union rank and file. You talk to the wrong guys . . . you come up with the wrong answers" (p. 19).

9. *All's Fair* (October 4, 1976) CBS: Monday 9:30 P.M.
   – Episode: "The Perfect Evening"
   Author: Gy Waldron
   Studio: T.A.T. Communications Co. Productions
   Stars: Richard Crenna and Bernadette Peters

Synopsis: In the second half of the program, conservative Richard Barrington and his liberal girl friend Charley are coming home from a movie and find a picket line in front of Richard's condominium. Charley: "These poor men have every right to better their working conditions by negotiating with their money-grubbing, labor-exploiting employers! The rotten tightwads." Richard: "Charley, it's a condominium. I own my own apartment. I'm one of the rotten tightwads" (p. 21). Charley grabs a picket sign and joins the line with the strikers. When asked what he's got against unions, Richard says, "I resent the way labor unions pose as the workingman's friend when actually they're nothing but elite clubs for the organized few. Most people out of work can't even get into a union. And not only that—if you clowns get what you want, the maintenance costs on my apartment will go right through the roof. The whole idea of *my* having to pay more money just because *you* join a union makes my blood boil" (p. 24). Senator Joplin passes by and tells them the strike will probably be settled soon so Richard finally agrees to leave until it is settled.

10. *The Quest* (November 17, 1976) NBC: Wednesday 10:00 P.M.
    – Episode: "Welcome to America, Jade Snow"
    Author: Anthony Lawrence
    Studio: Columbia Pictures TV
    Stars: Kurt Russell and Tim Matheson

Synopsis: Historical scene (perhaps 1870s) in California, and the plot involves mine workers and the Knights of Labor. The mining company, AMPAC (American Pacific), is bringing in Chinese workers as scabs to break the miners' strike. The representative of the mine owners admits frankly that he not only intends to break the strike but to eliminate all the white miners. H. P. Pierson says: "John Chinaman is a marvelous discovery" (p. 26). After the strikers are fired, they get violent with the Chinese scabs, who are the focus of the program's sympathy. The hero of the series, Quentin, comes to the aid of the Chinese as he comes to despise the selfishness and racism of the strikers. Though in the end, Pierson is fired and the guilty striking miners are banished from the territory, the final impression is that the strike was an extension of racial rather than industrial conflict, and the victims were the scabs, not the striking miners.

11. *Gibbsville* (December 9, 1976) NBC: Thursday 10:00 P.M.
- Episode: "Manhood"
  Author: John T. Dugan (John O'Hara)
  Studio: Columbia/David Gerber Productions
  Stars: Gig Young and John Savage

Synopsis: Reporter Ray Whitehead is investigating a story about a murdered Pennsylvania miner, Martin Dubcek. He soon learns that Dubcek was a supporter of Matt Ryan, candidate for treasurer in the upcoming union election, who claims that he will set up a credit union so the miners will not need to use the local loan shark, Ed Haney. At the union meeting Sean Banigan proposes that they take care of Haney themselves, but Ryan talks them out of it. Later, Sean Banigan goes to Jim Malloy, Ray's fellow reporter, with the suspicion the Ryan has been paid off by Haney. As Jim tells the unionists at their gathering, "Don't you get it? Haney wanted Ryan to be your treasurer. So they can loot the union" (p. 56).

12. *Executive Suite* (December 13, 1976) CBS: Monday 10:00 P.M.
- Episode: "What Are Patterns For?"
  Author: Don Brinkley
  Studio: Metro-Goldwyn-Mayer
  Stars: Mitchell Ryan, Stephen Elliott, and Sharon Acker

Synopsis: It is a continuation of the previous subplot with the complication that Harry Ragin is beginning a relationship with Walling's daughter Stacey. Rutledge, a corporation board member, and Walling discuss Ragin's proposal to establish a preventive medical program with regular exams to check the daily effects of CD–7, the pesticide they produce, but Rutledge believes the existing union medical plan is adequate. "Ragin's group" is referred to as different from the union. Rutledge believes Ragin should be fired, but Walling decides against it.

A woman shop steward, Donnalee, and Ragin meet with the workers after receiving the employer's letter rejecting their requests. Ragin instigates a protest "slowdown." Walling offers Ragin a foreman's job, to promote him out of the union, but Ragin is undecided.

13. *Laverne and Shirley* (December 21, 1976*) ABC: Tuesday 8:30 P.M.
- Episode: "Lonely at the Middle"
  Author: Jack Winter
  Studio: Paramount: Miller-Milkis
  Stars: Penny Marshall and Cindy Williams

Synopsis: The Cappers and Labelers Unit of the union is gathered for a strike meeting. Henry Wanda (played by Pat McCormick), described in the script as "a very fat man . . . all fired up," is addressing them. They are all told that picket duty will be for sixteen hours with eight hours off and that they are to dress up as though they are ragged and pregnant. Shirley Feeney (Cindy Williams) is against the strike and argues with Laverne

De Fazio (Penny Marshall): "Every year we go out on strike and what do we wind up with? A nickel raise that doesn't make up for all the money we lose by striking" (p. 5). Shirley talks the unit out of striking and negotiates a promotion for herself, the institution of a suggestion box, and a "worker of the week" program. When she starts using Taylor time/efficiency methods to increase productivity but actual productivity of the group drops 20 percent, Shirley is demoted back to the line. The episode ends with Lenny and Squiggy singing their new labor song: "If we strike when the union is hot."

14. *Eight Is Enough* (January 10, 1977*; March 24, 1977) ABC: Wednesday 8:00 P.M.
–   Episode: "Pieces of Eight"
    Author: Greg Strangis based on book by Thomas Braden
    Studio: Lorimar Productions
    Stars: Dick Van Patten and Betty Buckley

Synopsis: Mr. Bradford, acting editor of a Sacramento newspaper while his boss is vacationing in Europe, suddenly finds himself having to deal with a series of crises, including a "wildcat strike" of the paper's printers' union (p. 13). A stab at blue-collar workers is revealed on page 13A of the script in which the following direction appears: "Nancy, in hardhat, cut-offs, T-shirt inscribed with some inane blue-collar slogan, and a pack of smokes rolled in one sleeve, sits side-saddle on a motorcycle." The following exchange also indicates the anti-labor position of the writers:

MARY: C'mon Dad. You don't really do *work*. You're management.

BRADFORD: I've seen the enemy and she is mine.

JOANNIE: Don't blame Mary. She's just basically pro-labor.

BRADFORD: And habitually anti-father. [Bradford shakes his head, moves to the portable bar to mix a drink.] (continuing; gloomy) I don't think any of you see the real issue here. Strikes like this are notorious for dragging on. It could break the back of the paper. (p. 15)

Bradford becomes so worried about the loss of income the strike might mean to his family that he gives in and lets his wife go to work against his better judgment. But the strike is settled early.

15. *The Fitzpatricks* (February 7, 1977*; August 22, 1977) CBS: Tuesday 8:00 P.M.
–   Episode: Pilot aka "It's a Great Life"
    Author: John Sacret Young
    Studio: Warner Brothers TV
    Stars: Bert Kramer, Mariclare Costello, and Michelle Tobin

Synopsis: Detroit steelworkers are on strike. Mike (played by Bert Kramer) expresses his disgust: "Sooner or later they're going to settle on something they could've settled on weeks ago. . . . I hate 'em, the management, and maybe the union too. The last couple a years have been lousy for steel, layoffs, inflation, but we're striking. I'm for it, I guess. Always have been. [and] I'm just sick of the whole rotten load" (p. 16).

16. *Barney Miller* (March 24, 1977) ABC: Thursday 9–9:30 P.M.
–   Episode: "Strike, Part 1"
    Author: Reinhold Weege
    Studio: Four D/Columbia Pictures TV
    Star: Hal Linden

Synopsis: The squad goes on an unauthorized strike leaving Barney to run the station alone.

17. *Barney Miller* (March 31, 1977) ABC: Thursday 9:00 P.M.
— Episode: "Strike, Part 2"
   Author: Reinhold Weege
   Studio: Four D/Columbia Pictures TV
   Star: Hal Linden

Synopsis: While the squad is still on strike, Barney deals with a man-hungry spinster.

18. *Alice* (July 6, 1977*; August 12, 1977) CBS: Wednesday 9:30 P.M.
+ Episode: "The Bus"
   Author: Chris Hayward
   Studio: Warner Brothers TV
   Stars: Linda Lavin and Philip McKeon

Synopsis: A subplot set in a diner somewhere between San Diego and the Grand Canyon starts with two union organizers trying to persuade Alice to join. Mel, her boss, describes himself as a New Dealer (pp. 6–7) but draws the line at industrial workers. Later Vera and Alice use the threat of unionization to pressure Mel into paying them overtime while Mel is catering to a bus company that might contract to stop regularly at his diner.

19. *What's Happening!!* (July 19, 1977*; September 22, 1977*) ABC: Thursday 8:30 P.M.
— Episode: "One Strike and You're Out"
   Director: Michael Warren
   Studio: T.O.Y. Productions
   Author: Rick Mittleman
   Stars: Ernest Thomas and Haywood Nelson

Synopsis: Raj, who is working at Pronson's Supermarket, is upset because the boss has not provided an employee lounge as promised in the union contract. Raj talks Harold, his union steward, into confronting the boss. The next thing they know they are taking a strike vote. In the meantime, Raj learns that his mother is sick and the family can't afford to lose his paycheck. But it's too late because the rest of the workers vote to strike. For two weeks he's able to hide it from his mother until (version 1), at the end of the program, the boss agrees to negotiate the problem of the lounge. But the twist is that to get the lounge they had to agree to layoff one worker, who turns out to be Raj. In version 2 Raj decides to cross the picket line and is clubbed with a picket sign carried by a big striker from the meat department. Recuperating at home, he learns that the strike was settled when Pronson agreed to put in the lounge if he could lay off one worker, Irene, his own mother.

20. *Carter Country* (August 17, 1977*) ABC: Thursday 9:30 P.M.
— Episode: "Union vs. the Confederacy"
   Author: Sheldon Bull
   Studio: T.O.Y. Productions
   Stars: Victor French and Kene Holliday

Synopsis: Police Chief Roy Mobey explains to Baker how he "negotiates" improvements for the force with Mayor Burnside. Baker is surprised that no lawyers, judges, or unions were involved. The chief says, "Union? This is Clinton Corners, Baker. We're all like members of a big family here. . . . We don't need any union" (p. 8). As it turns out, the mayor is getting legal advice to be tough, so the chief's negotiating doesn't work this year. The chief then goes home sick and Baker organizes a bout of "blue-flu" just as the mayor is expecting a motorcade for the governor's visit. The mayor gives in and agrees to negotiate with the chief, who proudly exclaims at the end of the program: "Did I tell you guys? Did I tell you? And we didn't need any unions, or any of their big city-negotiators. All we needed was Chief Roy Mobey!" (p. 36)

21. *Quincy* (October 21, 1977) NBC: Friday 10:00 P.M.
－ Episode: "Murder by Self"
   Author: William Froug
   Studio: Universal TV
   Star: Jack Klugman

Synopsis: In East Los Angeles Quincy is investigating the apparent suicide of David Brady, a young Anglo (Irish) lawyer who was engaged to marry a young Chicano woman and was working as a fund-raiser for Roberto "Beto" Cruz, the charismatic leader of the "Farm Workers' Alliance," one of "two labor unions, long at each other's throats, fighting to represent nearly a hundred thousand farm workers" (p. 15). Tony Gordon, president of the Philadelphia-based Labor Brotherhood, is soon implicated. The script describes the latter's union hall: "A modern, impressive structure, as befits a labor organization as rich and powerful as the FWA is weak and struggling" (p. 36). Gordon tells Quincy: "Well, lemme tell you a couple of things, Doctor. We did bust a few heads. That's how you run a labor union when you're getting started and you got a bunch of company goons to hassle with" (p. 31). In the end it turns out that David was killed by Beto's aide Luis, whom David discovered was getting a kickback for smuggling illegal aliens across the border.

22. *Maude* (November 7, 1977) CBS: Monday 9:30 P.M.
－ Episode: "The Doctor's Strike"
   Author: William Davenport
   Producer: Bud Yorkin-Norman Lear-Tandem Productions
   Stars: Beatrice Arthur and Bill Macy

Synopsis: Arthur Harmon, Maude's doctor, is upset about the possibility of a local doctors' strike planned to force the hospital to pay the physicians' escalating malpractice insurance. Maude points out the inconsistency of Arthur's beliefs: "Well, here you are, all set to lead a doctor's strike. And yet you're the man who's been against unions striking ever since I've known you. In fact, you're the man who said, 'If the immigrant farm workers don't like it here, let 'em swim back where they came from' " (p. 9). Then, in the middle of writing a prescription for his old friend Walter, Arthur learns that the strike has started and he has to tear up the prescription and let Walter fend for himself. Arthur struggles with the conflict between his professional ethics and the union strike until the end of the program. Finally Arthur caves in and scabs, doing the right thing by his patients, which even his fellow doctors and the strike leader accepts wisely.

23. *The Jeffersons* (December 10, 1977*) CBS: Saturday 9:00 P.M.
＋ Episode: "Florence's Union"
   Authors: Andy Guerdat, Steve Kreinberg, Patt Shae, and Jack Shae
   Studio: T.A.T. Communications/NRW Productions
   Stars: Isabel Sanford and Sherman Hemsley

Synopsis: The Jeffersons' maid, Florence (Marla Gibbs), is working with Cassy Kincaid (Dorothy Meyer), president of the "United Sisterhood of Household Technicians, Local Number Two," to organize the maids in her building. George Jefferson decides to support the union drive when he thinks an influential neighbor is also supportive. When he finds the opposite is the case, he quickly switches sides. But when this Mr. Big comes by to see if his maid is joining the union, he insults Louise, George's wife, as well as the maids. George gets angry and sends him packing, pledging to support the maids.

24. *Quincy* (January 27, 1978) NBC: Friday 9:00 P.M.
－ Episode: "Passing"
   Author:
   Studio: Universal TV
   Star: Jack Klugman

Synopsis: The plot involves the Amalgamated Factory Workers Union in Los Angeles. Quincy finds a motorcycle gang member with a real human skull ornamenting his bike. They impound the skull and learn that it belonged to David Lockwood, a labor leader who embezzled two and a half million dollars in union funds; both Lockwood and the funds had been missing for over two years. Quincy suspects the current president of the union, Sal Jarrett. As Quincy says: "It's common knowledge that your Mr. Jarrett was working hand in glove with the mob ever (sic) before he gained control of this union" [p. 17]. In a surprise twist at the end, it turns out that Bricker, one of Lockwood's old friends, was the real embezzler and murderer.

25. *Hawaii Five–0* (February 2, 1978) CBS: Thursday 9:00 P.M.
 – Episode: "A Short Walk on the Long Shore"
  Author: Richard DeLong Adams
  Studio: CBS-TV
  Stars: Jack Lord and James MacArthur

Synopsis: In Honolulu rebel dockworker Anton Krebs is running against Jackson Croft for the presidency of the Longshore local. After charging Croft with criminal corruption, extortion, and violence before a crowd of reporters, Krebs is shot to death by a professional hit man. Croft then threatens the governor with a dock strike unless and until McGarrett finds the killer and exonerates him before the union election. Working on a lead that the case is related to drug traffic, McGarrett pretends to leave town but takes on a secret identity and teams with FBI investigators to crack the case. Acting like a recently laid-off seaman, McGarrett discovers that it was Krebs who was supposed to be the mobsters' handpicked candidate. The mob killed him because he was getting too independent and arrogant when it looked like he might win the election.

26. *The Ted Knight Show* (February 21, 1978*) CBS: Saturday 8:30 P.M.
 – Episode: "Strike"
  Author: Barry Rubinowitz
  Studio: Paramount Pictures
  Star: Ted Knight

Synopsis: The women of Roger Dennis's (Ted Knight) escort service in New York City go on strike (without forming a union) in protest of the terrible treatment they usually are accorded by the "Wolves Conventioneers" who have contracted with Roger for their service. The escorts want "double time for conventions and time-and-a-half for all dates where food is thrown" (p. 20). Finally, when his brother Burt comes over to applaud his business acumen, Roger realizes he has been unfair to his "girls" and concedes to their demands, more because he can't stand Burt than because he is pro-employee.

27. *The Incredible Hulk* (May 26, 1978) CBS: Friday 8:00 P.M.
 – Episode: "The Waterfront Story"
  Authors: Paul Belous and Robert Walterstorff
  Studio: Universal TV
  Star: Bill Bixby

Synopsis: Banner (the Hulk) is staying at a waterfront cafe in Galveston, Texas, run by the widow of the former union president as the new union election heats up between Cliff McConnel (good guy) and Tony Palomino (bad guy). Both want Josie, the widow, to endorse their candidacy. When she favors Cliff, thugs come to ransack Cliff's office and Josie's cafe, but David overhears Cliff plotting with his men and learns that it was Cliff who had the previous president killed and is responsible for the thugs wrecking his office and the cafe. Of course, the Hulk jumps in and saves Josie from Cliff and his corrupt cronies.

28. *Hizzoner* (September 1, 1978*) NBC: Thursday 8:00 P.M.
- Episode: [#3] ""Mr. Perfect"
  Author: Deborah R. Baron
  Star: David Huddleston

Synopsis: In a subplot Hizzoner, the mayor, is trying to keep track of the negotiations surrounding a local musicians' strike, which he wants to see settled before a big benefit for the city orphanage. He calls the union and management representatives together like a federal mediator and threatens to keep them together until they reach a settlement. In one short scene (one page long, p. 36) they bargain the whole contract easily.

29. *Sword of Justice* (September 13, 1978*) NBC: Saturday/Sunday 10:00 P.M.
o Episode: "Blackjack"
   Authors: Glen A. Larson and Michael Sloan
   Studio: Universal TV
   Star: Dack Rambo and Bert Rosario

Synopsis: In Cincinnati Jack Cole is working on a federal task force on organized crime. He goes after "union boss" Vincent Conti, who illegally put $10 million of union funds into a Las Vegas casino, then retrieved the money in winnings at the blackjack table. Conti is audited and found out. The head of the federal task force is killed in an explosion, and another union officer planning to testify against Conti is running for his life as Jack rescues him and traps Conti and the mobsters in their Las Vegas scam.

30. *The Rockford Files* (September 22, 1978) NBC: Friday 9:00 P.M.
- Episode: "Tears on the Skillet"
  Author: Stephen J. Cannell
  Producer: Universal/Cherokee Productions
  Stars: James Garner and Noah Beery

Synopsis: The action occurs between Los Angeles and Cripple Creek, Arkansas, and involves a fictional union of truckers—I.T.T.W., Local 214. Rockford's father, Joseph, driving an eighteen-wheeler across the country, jackknives his truck and ends up in the hospital. The police find that he was carrying illegal cargo, and the union pulls his card (throws him out) for driving a nonunion run even though he had been a member for forty years. Joseph: "These guys from the union . . . they're saying I was ignorant of working rule eight. In '56 I was on the strike committee, 'member, sonny?" He continues: "Me'n fifteen other guys helped write working rule eight. (from memory) 'Any member attempting to, or participating in either long or short hauls, county, state or city, without union authorization or consent, will be judged to be a scab operator . . . and if adjudged guilty . . . will lose all health, welfare and pension benefits and will be permanently suspended from the I.T.T.W. Local and International' " (p. 17). In Arkansas they find Clement Chen, who tells them the sausages Joe was carrying were made in Mexico because, "If we were producing in the U.S., with all the union restrictions, it would cost us eighty-five cents a unit. In Mexico, with everything exactly the same, we're getting them in L.A., F.O.B. my food distributing company for thirteen cents a unit" (p. 52).

31. *Grandpa Goes to Washington* (November 16, 1978*) NBC: Tuesday 8:00 P.M.
- Episode: "The Union Boys"
  Author: Paul West
  Studio: Paramount Television Productions
  Stars: Jack Albertson and Sue Ann Langdon

Synopsis: A union official of the Kitchen Workers, Local 37, tells Mama he is putting a picket line up around her Mama Matrella's Restaurant because she does not hire union workers, but Mama realizes that pressure is being put on her because her son is trying to "clean up the union." Mama says, "It's a good union, but this is a rotten local. The president of the local, Ed Crandall [Allan Miller], should be in prison" (p. 8). When the senator offers to get involved, his aide says, "Don't fight the unions, Senator. It's bad politics." But the senator doesn't listen. Lou Matrella tells Sen. Joseph Kelley about the corruption and "sweetheart deals" Crandall makes. Kelley calls for a hearing into the union and charges Crandall with using a goon squad to keep control over the members and rigging the elections. But another senator tells him, "Labor *is* a sacred cow. You go taking out after unions and your next election you'll be able to count your votes on your fingers" (p. 17). Later Lou confronts Crandall and after an argument leaves saying, "You know what the union is? Just another rip-off in a rip-off world" (p. 24). When Lou prepares to testify at the hearings, his leg is broken by Crandall's goons. Fortunately, at the end of the program, just as it looks as though the senator's investigation is going to be canceled, the national union president, Meyer Brockman (Victor Jory), shows up at the local's meeting to help the senator and Lou turn Crandall out of office. In a stirring speech about the history of the labor movement, Brockman reaffirms the high purpose of unions and pleads with the rank and file to testify against Crandall.

32. *CHIPS* (April 18, 1979*) NBC: Thursday 8:30 P.M.
   – Episode: "Candi"
      Authors: William D. Gordon and James Doherty
      Studio: Metro-Goldwyn-Mayer
      Stars: Larry Wilcox and Erik Estrada

Synopsis: In a subplot about police officers in California, in the middle of tracking down some crooks, the CHIPS team finds out that the Palma Vista Police Department has just gone on strike. According to Getraer, "The cops there called the strike at this time because there's a big stock-car race coming up" (p. 16). They have to go to Palma Vista to substitute (scab) for the striking officers. Shamelessly, they cross the PVPD picket line, insulting the local officers as they go.

33. *Lou Grant* (June 11, 1979*) CBS: Monday 10:00 P.M.
   o Episode: "Slammer"
      Author: Johnny Dawkins
      Studio: MTM Enterprises
      Star: Edward Asner

Synopsis: In a subplot, negotiations between the Pressmen's Union lawyers and the lawyers at the *Los Angeles Tribune* degenerate until the new union president and Charlie Hume (Mason Adams) sit down alone together and hammer out an agreement unfettered by legal advice. At the end of the show, Hume is trying to stockpile paper because of a rumor he picked up about a possible lumbermen's strike.

34. *One in a Million* (January 15, 1980) ABC: Tuesday 8:30 P.M.
   + Episode: "Executive Dad"
      Authors: Bill Box and Dick Westerschulte
      Studio: T.O.Y./Columbia TV Production
      Stars: Shirley Hemphill, Richard Paul, and Carl Ballantine

Synopsis: Shirley's father, Raymond Simmons, a city bus driver, has been on strike for three weeks and is driving his wife crazy. Shirley is persuaded to put him to work as a secretary at her corporation. Not only does he begin to drive Shirley and the other executives crazy, but after a few weeks he organizes 127 of the firm's secretaries to go out on strike as well. Happily, Shirley supports her father and the secretaries' demands, which are portrayed as reasonable. In the end, Shirley and her father sit down and informally negotiate a settlement. On the same day, the city settles with the bus drivers and the show ends happily.

35. *Taxi* (January 29, 1980) ABC: Thursday 9:00 P.M.
– Episode: "Shut It Down, Part 1"
   Authors: M. Jocobson, M. Tolkin, H. Gewirtz, and I. Praiser
   Studio: Paramount
   Stars: Judd Hirsch, Marilu Henner, and Danny DeVito

Synopsis: Enraged by a series of accidents and near accidents, the cab drivers of the Sunshine Cab Company want to walk out in protest. Elaine Nardo (Henner) talks them into working through their union procedure first. Banta (Tony Danza), the most recent victim of the unsafe equipment, is quickly elected steward to confront Louis (DeVito), but Banta is soon flattered and cajoled into giving up the "grievance." Then Elaine is elected to try, but she is bluntly rebuffed by the owner, Louis's boss. So they call a strike. In the meantime, Louis brags to Alex (Hirsch) that he is doctoring the company books so the upcoming hearing on their safety complaints will make the company look good and force the union officials to call off the cabbies' strike. Alex gets Louis worried about possible damnation for lying under oath, so Louis agrees to negotiate with Elaine. Louis, a disgusting lecher, then agrees to grant all the union demands if Elaine will go out on a date with him.

36. *Taxi* (February 5, 1980) ABC: Thursday 9:00 P.M.
– Episode: "Shut It Down, Part 2"
   Authors: M. Jocobson, M. Tolkin, H. Gewirtz, and I. Praiser
   Studio: Paramount
   Stars: Judd Hirsch, Marilu Henner, and Danny DeVito

Though Elaine tries to keep her "deal" with Louis a secret, Alex figures it out. He tries to talk Elaine out of it, but she reluctantly goes out on her date with Louis, who, at the end of the date, wrestles her to the ground in a lecherous embrace.

37. *Trapper John, M.D.* (February 24, 1980) CBS: Sunday 10:00 P.M.
o   Episode: "Strike" Annenberg # Trap018
    Author: Kenneth Berg
    Studio: Frank Glickman and Don Brinkley/Twentieth Century-Fox
    Star: Pernell Roberts

Synopsis: The nurses at San Francisco Memorial Hospital go on strike. Ben Calvert, a professional union negotiator, has been hired by the nurses. Shortly after he gets there, though, he has a heart attack and needs to be hospitalized himself. His old girl friend, Starch, a striking nurse, helps keep the strike going for him while he must decide whether to have dangerous surgery or forsake the stress of labor relations as a profession. The nurses are torn between their professional commitment to nursing and the demands of the strike. In the end, Ben has his operation after working out a settlement with the administrator, the pompous Arnold Slocum.

38. *Eight Is Enough* (November 1, 1980*) ABC: Wednesday 8:00 P.M.
– Episode: "Strike" Annenberg # Eight066
   Author: Bruce Shelly
   Studio: Lorimar Productions
   Stars: Dick Van Patten and Betty Buckley

Synopsis: The pressmen at the *Sacramento Register* are on strike and his friends on the line want Tom Bradford, a columnist, to honor their picket line. He crosses the line and goes inside to be pressured by management to write attacks on the union and then to be trained to run the presses while the strike is on. Angered by these orders, Bradford goes out and joins the picket line and prepares a pro-labor editorial. At home, Abby praises him as a "closet Samuel Gompers" (p. 30). But when he goes to work the next day with his new editorial, the editor tells him that "corporate has decided to shut us down" (p. 34)—that is, a lockout—for the duration of the strike because the cost of maintaining the skilled crew is too high. Mounting financial pressures make life hard at the Bradfords', so at the urging of his accountant, Tom Bradford reluctantly applies for unemployment insurance. Back at the picket line, Bradford tells Joe he's changed his mind about the strike because "this strike is unfair to innocent bystanders" (p. 53). In the end, Bradford sets up a meeting between Joe, the strike leader, and his editor, Mr. Randolf, and his son Nicholas shares his insight about a barter system he tried to set up: "If the other guy can't give what you want, then you've got to want something he can give or else nobody gets anything" (p. 67). This gets the two sides talking, and before they leave that day, the strike is settled.

39. *Archie Bunker's Place* (November 22, 1980) CBS: Sunday 8:00 P.M.
+   Episode: "Wildcat Strike" [#0205] Annenberg # Archie035 +036
    Authors: Stephen Miller and Mark Fink
    Studio: Tandem Productions
    Star: Carroll O'Connor

Synopsis: Jose, one of Archie's cooks, cuts his finger and has to go to the hospital to get it stitched up. Because he is uninsured, Jose and his fellow workers expect Archie to pay for it, but Archie refuses. When confronted with his contradictory feelings about unions, Archie answers, "That was different. When I worked on the loading dock, we needed a union. We were up against a bunch of tyrants. Does this look like the face of a tyrant?" (p. 13). Murray, Archie's partner, asks Archie to reconsider, but Archie says, "Would you listen to the liberal here? Murray, don't you know nothin'? Once you start in with the unions, they take over. They're like a bad rash" (p. 14). Then Archie rants: "Don't youse people know who's behind them unions? It's all Mafia guys. Whatever you get they'll make you pay for it. . . . What about Jimmy Hoffa?" (p. 16). When Murray hears the cost, he retreats. Archie chides him: "Oh, listen to Mr. Big Union Man here. When it comes to spending your own money, you liberals are all the same: you gotta reach into your own pocket to find your heart" (p. 17). Archie fires Samantha, the union proponent, and the rest of his workers decide to strike in protest. In the cold weather, they are picketing and freezing. Veronica complains that "the man upstairs is taking their side," and Mr. Van Ranseleer rejoin: "You have to remember, he is management" (p. 36). But Van Ranseleer brings them together and Archie finally agrees to talk to the strikers, at which point the strike seems to be over and the episode ends with the workers singing their own version of "Look for the Union Label (Ladle)."

40. *The Incredible Hulk* (December 6, 1980) CBS: Friday 8:00 P.M.
o   Episode: "Deep Shock" Annenberg # Inhulk039
    Author: Ruel Fischmann
    Studio: Universal TV
    Star: Bill Bixby

Synopsis: Working on a construction site with a union crew, David Banner (the Hulk) hears the shop steward talking to the men about their imminent layoff. Later, after an industrial accident in which David is almost electrocuted, the men are considering a wildcat strike to protest the loss of jobs and the automation of the plant they are working on. The steward, Edgar Tucker, an older worker with a medical problem, is then called in by the company and forced to retire. Worse still, he learns that all the benefits he had promised his men are not going to be honored by the company when they are all laid off in a few days. The men turn on Edgar and accuse him of selling out to management for his retirement package. So Edgar breaks into the electrical generating plant's control room and takes it over (à la *Black Fury*). Threatening to destroy the plant unless they stop the layoffs, Edgar nearly kills himself and would have destroyed the plant but for the Hulk's intervention. In the epilogue or "tag" scene, Edgar finds out that the company has relented about the benefit packages and will be keeping the workers longer than expected to clean up the mess.

41. *House Calls* (December 10, 1980*) CBS: Monday 9:30 P.M.
- Episode: "No Balls, One Strike" Annenberg # House008
  Authors: Tom Chehak, Kathy Greer, and Bill Greer
  Studio: Universal City Studios
  Stars: Wayne Rogers, Lynn Redgrave, and Sharon Gless

Synopsis: Administrative assistant Ann Anderson is trying to negotiate a raise for the (nonunion) nurses and orderlies, but the administrator, Conrad Peckler, refuses to grant any raises to an unorganized, unofficial representative. She gets up a petition and gives it to Johnny, one of the orderlies, who formally presents their demands to Peckler. Peckler threatens to fire him and everyone whose name is on the petition so the orderlies and nurses go on strike (without a union). After a few days of trying to make things work without the staff, the doctors are getting upset. Dr. Charley Michaels, the key figure in the series, says, "I'll tell you why they're on strike ... because they went too far ... going in and making all those demands. They backed themselves into a corner! You know how cheap Peckler is" (p. 16). Later, when they find out Charley was the one who told the workers they should organize, Norman says, "Charley ... When you say organize to underpaid workers, they *always* strike" (p. 22). At the end of the program, Charley and Ann convince Peckler that the strike is costing more than it would to settle, so the strike ends and everyone is happy again.

42. *Lou Grant* (December 23, 1980*) CBS: Monday 10:00 P.M.
- Episode: "Strike" [#0510] Annenberg # Lougr071
  Author: April Smith
  Studio: MTM Enterprises
  Star: Edward Asner

Synopsis: The story opens on the difficult negotiations at the *Los Angeles Tribune* over the question of automation and two hundred existing jobs with Hume versus Bronsky of the Print Media Workers Guild, Local 5503. This scene cuts to the newsroom, where Rossi is describing to Lou a case of assault in the police holding cell. Hume interrupts with his account of the bargaining: "The *London Times* had the same situation: wanted to automate, unions wouldn't allow it. Boy it was bitter. ... The unions shut the paper down eleven months. The *London Times* almost folded" (pp. 6–7). Rossi bemoans the union leadership: "Our future is being decided by a bunch of loudmouths, who love to make speeches just to hear themselves talk" (p. 8). At the meeting that Rossi goes to a strike vote is taken and all but Rossi enthusiastically vote for it. Back at the newsroom Rossi finds that all the reporters who did not go to the meeting are against the strike. Animal compares the strike to Vietnam: "I'm telling you we're just foot soldiers. The Pynchons and Bronskys don't care about us" (p. 27). When the strike does start, though, Rossi, Animal, Donovan, and Billie all go out, leaving Lou and Hume alone with a few scabs to write the paper. After two weeks, the strike is still on. Lou and Hume are commiserating. Hume says, "I guess I've got this old fashioned loyalty to the printed word. It's powerful. And vital to the expression of human thought. The printed word is in danger in this country, and I believe it's got to be saved. Too many newspapers have been killed by strikes" (p. 51). Ironically, Billie is disturbed by the press coverage the strike is getting: "I can't believe how the other papers are covering the strike. Look how they distorted this. Wages are not the issue. They make the printers look greedy" (p. 56). A little later Billie is hit in the head by a flying rock as she chases after a "scab truck." The scene switches to the editorial conference room where Lou, Hume, and the other editors are reading, and one of them remarks: "Look how they've distorted the issues to make management seem greedy" (p. 58). Lou can't take it any more and tells Hume he has got to leave. He goes out to join the strikers, but a little later Pynchon comes in to tell them the strike is settled; the union has accepted automation for a guarantee of $20,000 to each worker displaced.

Norma Rae (January 23, 1981*) NBC Pilot: November 21, 1981?
(Because this program was not aired, it is not numbered and was not included in the Chapter 2 analysis.)
o   Episode: 60 minute pilot
    Author: Carol Evan McKeand
    Studio: Saracen Productions and Rose and Asseyev Productions in association with Twentieth Century-Fox Television

Synopsis: The place is Okalona, Georgia, and the plot concerns textile workers. At the Teeter Towel Company, Norma Rae Webster, aged thirty, is helping Reuben Marshasky, the organizer for the Fabric Workers' Union of America, to form a union at her plant. Her ex-husband, Frank Osborn, now a company spy, is remarried, but his new wife cannot have children so he's trying to take his and Norma Rae's son away from her. Osborn takes her to court. Reuben tries to help her, but she refuses legal counsel. After being accused in court of having a loose reputation, Norma Rae is still able to make a convincing plea about her love and maternal interest in her boy, and the episode ends with the judge dismissing Osborn's suit.

43. *Lou Grant* (March 14, 1981) CBS: Monday 10:00 P.M.
o   Episode: "Compesinos" [#0513] Annenberg # Lougr074
    Author: Michael Vittes
    Studio: MTM Enterprises
    Star: Edward Asner

Synopsis: The plot concerns farmworkers in the San Joaquin Valley, California. An old high school acquaintance of Rossi's, now a union organizer, calls him about their strike in Ortega. Rossi is assigned to write about how a promising high school football player ended up as a union organizer. The farm owners have brought in scabs from Mexico to work in the fields, and Rossi's friend Hernandez has brought an old 1960s farm labor activist, the Reverend Holstrom, to speak to the strikers. Rossi learns of the bad working conditions and wages that caused the strike. Meanwhile, back at the newsroom, Lou is moving articles to accommodate a full-page ad by the growers attacking the strike. In Ortega, after interviewing one of the growers, Rossi goes to a demonstration at the jailhouse which gets out of hand and Rossi is arrested as part of the crowd. In jail, Rossi is able to interview the Reverend Holstrom, who asks Rossi where he stands. Rossi says: "That's my job—to report both sides. I've got to stay objective." Holstrom responds: "How convenient. You can hide behind your objectivity and never have to decide for yourself what's right or wrong" (p. 35). Hume and Lou tell Mrs. Pynchon they are planning to run the story on the strike. Interestingly, the automation of farmwork is opposed by Hume and Lou (note opposite attitude in an earlier episode about a newspaper strike). After talking to the growers, Rossi and Donovan try to set up a meeting between one of them and Hernandez. It fails because their personal relationship has soured. Hernandez, therefore, is seen as prolonging the strike because of a personal grudge. On the picket line, violence erupts and Hernandez is shot and killed. Geyer, the one farm owner who knew Hernandez, signs the contract in remorse, and the strike starts to cool down, so Hume dispassionately pulls the reporters off the story and wraps it up.

44. *WKRP in Cincinnati* (October 21, 1981) CBS: Wednesday 8:30 P.M.
–   Episode: "The Union" [#1002] Annenberg # Wkrp041
    Author: Blake Hunter
    Studio: MTM Enterprises
    Stars: Gary Sandy, Gordon Jump, and Loni Anderson

Synopsis: Venus, Johnny, Bailey, and others get letters from the Brotherhood of Midwestern Radio Workers encouraging them to organize a union. Those three are for it but Les Nessman is not. He says: "I'll make a deal with you. I'll join the union if you can tell me where Jimmy Hoffa is" (p. 15). Herb tells Carlson, who becomes irate. Mrs.

Carlson tells her son to start a rumor that she will sell the station if it goes union. Andy tries to stay between the Carlsons and the staff, but he is management, after all. He tells Mr. Carlson: "I'd make a deal with the devil to put some money into this station" (p. 38). This he does and when it comes to a vote, the union loses five to four. But Mrs. Carlson starts putting more money into the station as promised. It is a happy ending.

45. *Hill Street Blues* (November 3, 1981*) NBC: Thursday 10:00 P.M.
  –   Episode: "Cranky Streets" [#1405] Annenberg # Hillst022
      Authors: Steven Bochco, Michael Kozoll, and Robert Crais
      Studio: MTM Enterprises
      Stars: Daniel J. Travanti and Charles Haid

Synopsis: In a subplot, at roll call, Sergeant Esterhaus briefs the station on the impasse in the police officers' negotiations and the city's early rejection of all their proposals. Later in the episode, Esterhaus gets more bad news about the bargaining and news of a possible wildcat strike. Lieutenant Hunter complains about the "road to Socialism" that unionism represents and almost gets into a fight with Lieutenant Calletano over his racist remarks. Throughout the various scenes, officers comment to each other about the increased stress of the possible union walkout. Furillo notes: "I don't believe this! ... The negotiating committee hits a snag and we're all tearing at each others' throats" (p. 40).

46. *Hill Street Blues* (November 4, 1981*) NBC: Thursday 10:00 P.M.
  –   Episode: "Chipped Beef" [#1406] Annenberg # Hillst023
      Authors: Steven Bochco, Michael Kozoll, and Robert Crais
      Studio: MTM Enterprises
      Stars: Daniel J. Travanti and Charles Haid

Synopsis: In a subplot, Esterhaus's roll call proclaims: "Item ten, the union situation. Word is the city got down to serious bargaining yesterday. But let's not raise any expectations or put down any thousand dollar deposits on Caribbean love nests yet" (p. 2). And later Renko (Charles Haid) snaps: "Wish that union we pay all them dues to would get us some money, you know?" (p. 11). Then Bobby Hill reminds him of all the money he has wasted on motorcycles, girls, cowboy boots, motor boats, and the like.

47. *Fame* (November 13, 1981*) NBC: Thursday 8:00 P.M.
  –   Episode: "The Strike" [#2702] Annenberg # Fame006
      Authors: Danny Jacobson and Barry Vigon
      Studio: Metro-Goldwyn-Mayer/UA TV
      Stars: Debbie Allen and Lee Carreri

Synopsis: The plot involves a New York teachers union. After showing how involved the students at the School for the Arts are in their projects, Miss Sherwood tries to talk Mr. Shorofsky into attending the union strike meeting. He does not believe public employees should have the right to strike. At the meeting the teachers passionately discuss the repercussions on their students and their projects if they strike with the rest of the public school teachers. Shorofsky has come and speaks against the strike because of its harm to the students and the divisiveness it will create, but the vote favors striking. While the teachers picket, the students try to work out their projects on their own. Outside in the rain, Shorofsky reluctantly reports to picket duty under the threat of a fine from strike headquarters. Lydia Grant, the dance teacher/drama coach, though on strike, wants to work with her students at night on their performance project, but Miss Sherwood talks her out of it. But then Leroy catches Miss Sherwood, the English teacher, at home to ask her if she can help him with his pronunciation and elocution for the play. With tears in her eyes, she finally agrees to accept a token fee for tutoring him after hours. At the end of the episode the striking teachers are happily, proudly sneaking a peak at the dress rehearsal of their students for the play that they have managed to keep afloat on their own.

48. *Lou Grant* (November 23, 1981) CBS: Monday 10:00 P.M.
+ Episode: "Hometown" [#1504] Annenberg # Lougr084
   Author: Micelle Gallery
   Studio: MTM Enterprises
   Star: Edward Asner

Synopsis: The action occurs in a Goshen, Michigan, glass bottle factory. Lou goes back to his hometown for his aunt's funeral. At the Goshen Glass Factory, tracking down an old acquaintance, Lou finds out how a string of corporate buyouts and deals has left this factory in the lurch, scheduled for shutdown, even though it is still producing as well as before. Lou decides to do a story on the plant because the corporate headquartes are in Los Angeles. Back in Los Angeles, Billie finds out from corporate headquarters that the decision to close the factory was made because that subsidiary was not growing fast enough, and only 250 workers out of the corporation's 85,000 were affected. The city fathers and the union (Local 462) back in Goshen do not have much to say about it. Lou writes the stories, which annoy the corporation. In the meantime, the workers in Goshen are trying to engineer an employee stock ownership plan. The episode leaves them hopeful and determined but uncertain of success.

49. *Quincy* (February 4, 1982*) NBC: Wednesday 10:00 P.M.
− Episode: "Flight of the Nightingale" Annenberg # Quincy131
   Authors: Gene Church and Paul Edwards
   Studio: Universal TV
   Star: Jack Klugman

Synopsis: In a subplot, in a hospital already plagued by short staffing and overloading, a patient gets the wrong medication partly because the doctor failed to note a change on the patient's chart. The nurse is blamed and suspended. Fellow nurses decide to strike over her suspension and the work-load problems. The nurses are torn between their professional ethics about patient care and their desire to protest the bad conditions. Over and over again, doctors and nurses exclaim that the real losers in the strike are the patients. Meanwhile, Lynne, the suspended nurse, who has now decided to quit the profession, is persuaded by one of the doctors to cross the picket line and help calm one of her patients before a big operation. The striking nurses abuse and jeer her as she crosses the line. At the same time, Quincy has discovered that the patient she was supposed to have killed did not, in fact, die from the change in medication but from an unrelated condition. The whole strike and its final resolution are described without reference to a nurses' union.

50. *Trapper John, M.D.* (March 29, 1982*) CBS: Sunday 10:00 P.M.
− Episode: "John's Other Life" Annenberg # Trap069
   Author: Jerry Ross
   Studio: Frank Glickman Productions
   Star: Pernell Roberts

Synopsis: In a subplot, a San Francisco hospital is suffering from a garbage collectors' strike. Dr. Stanley Riverside is furious at the "rabble-rousing" strikers. The central plot is about the medical treatment of a former syndicate figure. As rumors circulate about the syndicate, it gets all mixed up with the garbage strike until Riverside thinks the mob is behind the strike.

51. *Voyagers!* (November 1, 1982*, possible air date: December 19, 1982) NBC: Sunday 7:00 P.M.
+ Episode: "Merry Christmas, Bogg" Annenberg #57215
   Author: Bruce Shelly
   Studio: Universal City Studios
   Stars: Jon-Erik Hexum and Meeno Peluce

Synopsis: A subplot concerns Pennsylvania factory workers. The voyagers, Phineas Bogg and Jeffrey Jones, bounce back and forth in time between Washington in 1776 and Pennsylvania in 1892, where Sam Gompers is leading a factory workers strike. Gompers is described by the boy voyager as "the greatest labor leader America ever had" (p. 19), and as they watch him, a squad of strikebreaking goons attacks the strikers with clubs, one of them making off with a cash box containing the union strike fund. It is Christmas Eve and the union needed the money to keep the strikers' morale up. Gompers is suspected of stealing the money for himself and the whole AFL and the strike in Pittsburgh seems lost. The voyagers retrieve the gold, and history is saved together with the strike and the AFL.

52. *Benson* (November 25, 1983) ABC: Friday 8:00 P.M.
 – Episode: "Labor Pains" [#100] Annenberg # Benson107
    Author: Brill Boulware
    Studio: A Witt/Thomas/Harris Production
    Stars: Robert Guillaume and James Noble

Synopsis: Benson is negotiating on behalf of the governor with the road workers. Their leader, Stump Walker (John C. Beecher), comments, "As far as the workin' man is concerned, there ain't no such thing as a fair contract" (p. 2). Later, in the midst of a terrible snowstorm, Benson is called back to the office because the road workers are on strike and are refusing to clear the streets. The bargaining reveals that Stump rejected the package without going to the membership with it because the snow gave him the upper hand in the negotiations. Stump does not trust Benson until the baby staying at the mansion gets sick and Stump finds out Benson is caring for it. That turns the tide, and Stump agrees to put his men back to work while he and Benson renegotiate their contract.

53. *Empire* (February 1, 1984) CBS: Wednesday 8:30 P.M.
 – Episode: "Episode Six" [#3329] Annenberg # Empire006
    Authors: Jim Geoghan, Lawrence Cohen, and Fred Freeman
    Studio: Humble Productions with Metro-Goldwyn-Mayer Film Co.
    Stars: Patrick MacNee, Dennis Dugan, and Cameron Mitchell

Synopsis: The action occurs at a Springfield missile plant. Ben's hothead father, Lou Christian (Cameron Mitchell), shows up to lead a union protest on the eve of a presidential visit. Lou, "an old union dog," was off living with a stripper until the union called him up. Ben complains to him, "The only place you ever took me was to picket... We'd march around a factory somewhere, they'd beat us up and then we'd go home" (p. 9). Ben is worried about the pickets around the plant, but goes ahead with his plans. In the meantime, his father threatens to blow up the plant if the company refuses to negotiate the job transfers from their U.S. plant to a new African factory. Of course, the dynamite is a bluff, as Calvin Cromwell (Patrick MacNee), his old adversary, well knows. In the end, Lou admits to Ben that he got involved in the strike as an excuse to see him again. They let him negotiate, but the issue is moot when Ben learns that the plant in Africa was just appropriated by the king of that nation.

54. *St. Elsewhere* (October 3 and 10, 1984) NBC: Wednesday 10:00 P.M.
 – Episode: "Two Balls and a Strike"
    Authors: John Macius, Tom Fontana, and John Tinker
    Episode: "Strike Out"
    Author: Steve Bellow
    Studio: MTM Enterprises
    Stars: Christina Pickles and Ed Flanders

Synopsis: Nurse Helen Rosenthal (Christina Pickles) fanatically leads a nurses' strike against the hospital's kindly, long-suffering administrators, Drs. Donald Westphall (Ed

Flanders) and Auschlander, while the scabbing nurses are portrayed as caring, selfless professionals. Later, Helen, after leading a protest against mandatory drug testing, becomes a drug abuser and kills a patient in her care.

55. *Silver Spoons* (December 9, 1984) NBC: Sunday 7:00 P.M.
–   Episode: "Beauties and the Beasts" [#0310]
    Authors: Robert Illes and James Stein
    Studio: Embassy TV
    Stars: Ricky Schroder, Joel Higgins, and Franklyn Seales

Synopsis: In a subplot at a toy factory, Ed Stratton (Joel Higgins) is negotiating with Big Jake Geoghan (not pictured), the Cuddly Toy union representative for his company's workers. Ed describes the union leader as an "animal" who "keeps his toupee on with staples" (p. 4). But after bitterness prevents Ed from being able to come to a settlement with Big Jake, Kate (Erin Gray) proposes an employee vegetable garden in lieu of pay raises and Jake accepts because he always wanted a garden but could not have one in his apartment.

56. *Simon and Simon* (February 14, 1985) CBS: Thursday 9:00 P.M.
–   Episode: "The Mickey Mouse Mob" [#58538]
    Author: Ross Thomas
    Studio: Universal TV
    Stars: Jameson Parker and Gerald McRaney

Synopsis: In a subplot, Dan Thacker is an international vice-president of the LDUW (described as one of the country's biggest unions) who is trying to get elected president of his union. He lends his car to his young attorney, who is blown up when he turns the ignition on. Thacker goes to Simon and Simon for help. It turns out that he is being blackmailed because he used to have a different name and went to Canada to evade the draft during the Vietnam war. He has decided to come clean about all that and wants their help to find the wife and kids he had deserted. They find her, and she turns out to be running the Delaporte mob (the Mickey Mouse Mob) and seems just as interested in keeping Thacker's former life a secret as he was. We soon learn that Thacker's blackmail, the car bomb, and everything else is part of a plot by his ex-wife's lawyer to take over that mob. But a heavy comes in from the East Coast and stops that plot and everything goes back to normal, except that the outcome of the union election is never revealed.

57. *Diff'rent Strokes* (March 9, 1985) NBC: Saturday 8:00 P.M.
o   Episode: "Blue Collar Drummond" [#0702]
    Authors: Robert Jayson and A. Dudley Johnson, Jr.
    Studio: Embassy TV
    Stars: Conrad Bain, Gary Coleman, and Todd Bridges

Synopsis: Phil Drummond (Conrad Bain) is negotiating with Bill Perkins (Barney Martin), a "die-hard labor Rep" (p. 1) at Drummond's home over dinner. The session ends with a lot of name-calling and no progress. Later, Phil's wife, Maggie (Dixie Carter), suggests that Perkins was right about Phil being out of touch with the workers. He decides to go to work in the factory to prove he can do the work as well as any of his employees. At the factory, Phil finds out how boring the work is, how unresponsive his managers have been to employees' suggestions, and how the workers have come to hate him for the way he distanced himself from their work, unlike his father, who knew them all by name. No return to the union negotiator is shown.

58. *Bronx Zoo* (January 20, 1988) NBC: Wednesday 10:00 P.M.
–   Episode: "The Long Gray Line"
    Authors: Patricia Jones, Donald Reicher, and Kathy McCormick
    Studio: MTM Enterprises
    Star: Edward Asner

Synopsis: Not unlike the film *Teachers*, in which Nick Nolte stood up heroically as an individual not with the teachers' union or with the school's administrators, the strike-breaking (scab) teacher in the *Bronx Zoo* is admired for his individuality and personal courage while the strikers are portrayed as mindless, uncaring, and selfish.

Moonlighting (March 22, 1988) ABC: Tuesday 9:00 P.M.
(This episode is not numbered since its reference to unions was not related to the plot.)
   Studio: Picturemedia Productions—ABC Circle Films
   Stars: Bruce Willis and Cybill Shepherd

Synopsis: Filmed during the Hollywood writers' strike, this episode may have inadvertently, and with the best intentions, trivialized the plight of the striking writers by ending one of their shows with a humorous dance routine that marched through the offices of the striking writers. The program, written before the strike, fell about seven minutes short, according to the show's producer, Jay Daniel. "Normally we just turn to the writing staff and say we need another scene here" (quoted in Judy Farah, Associated Press, "Writers' strike forces cast to improvise," Honolulu *Star-Bulletin* March 25, 1988: B-2). Without the opportunity to do that, Bruce Willis and Cybill Shepherd began singing "Wooly Bully" and danced through the offices of the show's five writers, who joined the silly skit carrying their picket signs.

59. *Designing Women* (January 2, 1989) CBS: Monday 9:30 P.M.
+   Episode: "Curtains"
    Authors: Pam Norris
    Studio: Bloodworth/Thomason Mozark Productions
    Stars: Dixie Carter, Royce D. Applegate, and Pat Li

Synopsis: The stars operate a small interior decorating company that gets a long-awaited big job. But the drapery manufacturer's workers go on strike. The interior decorators are themselves picketed and, at first, cross the picket lines and try to work at the drapery factory to rush their job through. There they realize how sorry the working conditions and wages are for the striking workers, and they join the strikers to pressure the draper to settle. This a a rare sympathetic view of a union and a strike.

60. *Wiseguy* (January 11, 1989) CBS: Wednesday 10:00 P.M.
−   Episode: "All or Nothing"
    Story Editor: John Schulian
    Studio: Stephen J. Cannell Productions
    Stars: Anthony Denison and Joan Chen

Synopsis: In the first of a two-part program, Denison portrays John Raglin, an FBI undercover agent investigating corruption in New York's garment district. Though the target of the probe is primarily a mob-run business, the fictitious "Fashion Union Workers of America" is portrayed as complicit with the owners and unconcerned with the plight of the Chinese immigrant garment workers. The program shows a heroic strike led by the young female immigrant, Maxine Tzu (Joan Chen). The father of the Jewish factory owner, who was himself once a union member, does not want to cross their picket line; his son, played by Jerry Lewis, dismisses the strikers as "commies."

61. *In the Heat of the Night* (March 28, 1989) NBC: Tuesday 9:00 P.M.
−   Episode: "Walkout"
    Author: Stephen Aspis
    Studio: Metro-Goldwyn-Mayer/UA TV—Fred Silverman
    Stars: Carroll O'Connor, Howard Rollins, and O. J. Simpson

Synopsis: In Sparta, Mississippi, Wade Britton, the new manager at the town's Thail River Industries plant, forces the union to strike by demanding major concessions. When the chief of police (Carroll O'Connor) hears about it, he tells his big city deputy, Virgil Tibbs, to prepare for a murder. The local black leader and councilman Lawson Stiles (O. J. Simpson), who has been trying to get jobs for the poor blacks there, is asked to provide scabs but refuses. A rival black leader (Darnell Williams) wants to scab because the union has not been accepting blacks as members. First the councilman, then the union leader, is murdered. The scabs come in with the new black leader and the strike gets more and more violent. Though, in the end, the murders turn out to be unrelated to the strike, the union is portrayed as a violent, red-neck, discriminatory institution, and the strike is seen as destructive and totally indefensible.

62. *Head of the Class* (May 3, 1989) ABC: Wednesday 7:30 P.M.
+ Episode: "Labor Daze"
 Author: Jerry Rannow
 Studio: Eustis Elias Productions/Warner Brothers Television
 Star: Howard Hesseman

Synopsis: As the semester is drawing to a close, the teachers are about to strike because of a planned "rollback" in wages. Charlie Moore (Hesseman) leads the teachers at his school on a prestrike slowdown in order to draw attention to their protest while the negotiations are stalled. At first the students in his class are angry because of their anxiety about an advanced placement history exam they have to take the following week. Two days later the slowdown becomes a work stoppage, and Moore refuses to teach (though he is still in the classroom with the students). Moore finally relents but teaches the class about labor history. He does such a good job that, when a replacement teacher is brought in, the class refuses to be taught by the "scab."

Notes

Notes to Introduction

1. Albert J. Zack, "The Press Bias on Labor," *AFL-CIO American Federationist* 84, no. 10 (1977): 1–7 (originally delivered in September 1977 to a symposium on business and the media at Georgia State University); John M. O'Keefe, "The Public vs. the Striker," *International Molders' Journal*, January 1922, pp. 27–28, as quoted in David J. Saposs, *Readings in Trade Unionism* (New York: Macmillan, 1927), 84.

2. Derek C. Bok and John T. Dunlop, *Labor and the American Community* (New York: Simon and Schuster, 1970), 36; John Tebbel, *The Media in America* (New York: Thomas Crowell, 1974), 373.

3. Jane Klain, ed., *International Television & Video Almanac*, 35th ed. (New York: Quigley, 1990), 26A.

4. V. O. Key, Jr., *Public Opinion and American Democracy* (New York: Knopf, 1961), 401.

5. Jacques Ellul, *Propaganda: The Formation of Men's Attitudes*, trans. Konrad Kellen and Jean Lerner (New York: Knopf, 1965), 9–10.

6. Robert S. Lynd and Helen Merrell Lynd, *Middletown: A Study in Modern American Culture* (New York: Harcourt, Brace & World, 1929), 78–79.

7. "Approval of Labor Unions Remains at Low," *Gallup Report*, August 1981, Report 191, pp. 6–7; "Long Slide in Approval of Labor Unions Comes to Halt," *Gallup Report*, June 1985, Report 237, pp. 30–31; Seymour Martin Lipset, "Unions in Decline," *Public Opinion* 9 (September–October 1986): 52–54.

8. The sample consisted of 462 seniors and juniors in three different high schools; see Appendix A.

9. Robert Cirino, *Don't Blame the People: How the News Media Use Bias,*

Distortion and Censorship to Manipulate Public Opinion (Los Angeles: Diversity Press, 1971), 43; the text of Vice-President Agnew's speech was reprinted in the *New York Times*, November 14, 1969, p. 24.

10. Efron quoted by Michael J. Robinson and Maura E. Clancey, "Network News, 15 Years after Agnew," *Channels* 4 (January–February 1985): 34; Herbert J. Gans, "Are U.S. Journalists Dangerously Liberal?" *Columbia Journalism Review* 24 (November–December 1985): 29–31.

11. William A. Rusher, *The Coming Battle for the Media: Curbing the Power of the Media Elite* (New York: Morrow, 1988), 88.

12. C. Wright Mills, "The Trade Union Leader: A Collective Portrait," *Public Opinion Quarterly* 9 (Summer 1945): 158.

13. Aaron Wildavsky, "The Media's 'American Egalitarians'," *Public Interest* 88 (Summer 1988): 94–104.

14. Harold Laski, *The American Democracy* (New York: Viking Press, 1948), 670.

15. Cirino, *Don't Blame the People*, 134–79.

16. Michael Parenti, *Inventing Reality: The Politics of the Mass Media* (New York: St. Martin's Press, 1986), 84–85.

Notes to Chapter 1

1. Philip S. Foner, "A Martyr to His Cause: The Scenario of the First Labor Film in the United States," *Labor History* 24 (1983): 103.

2. William M. Drew, *D. W. Griffith's* Intolerance*: Its Genesis and Its Vision* (Jefferson, N.C.: McFarland, 1986), 20–22.

3. Joseph A. Gomez, "History, Documentary, and Audience Manipulation: A View of 'The Wobblies,' " *Labor History* 22 (1981): 143.

4. A good review of these early short films from 1910 to 1929 can be found in Ken Margolies, "Silver Screen Tarnishes Unions," *Screen Actor* 23 (Summer 1981): 43–52.

5. Andre Sennwald, rev. of *Black Fury* in *New York Times*, April 11, 1935, p. 27.

6. Albert Maltz, "What Is Propaganda?" *New York Times*, April 28, 1935.

7. Francis R. Walsh, "The Films We Never Saw: American Movies View Organized Labor, 1934–1954," *Labor History* 27 (1986): 565–67; citing Hal Wallis, "inter-office memo," September 13, 1934, University of Southern California, Special Collections (USCSC).

8. Parenti, *Inventing Reality*, 84–85.

9. Bosley Crowther, rev. of *Reaching for the Sun* in *New York Times*, May 8, 1941, p. 21.

10. Walsh, "Films We Never Saw," 570–73.

11. Ibid., 572.

12. Bosley Crowther, rev. of *Salt of the Earth* in *New York Times*, March 15, 1954, p. 20.

13. Herbert Biberman, *Salt of the Earth: The Story of a Film* (Boston: Beacon Press, 1965), 86.

14. Bosley Crowther, rev. of *The Pajama Game* in *New York Times*, August 30, 1957, p. 12.

15. Margolies, "Silver Screen Tarnishes Unions," 43.

16. United States Department of Labor, *Semiannual Report of Inspector General, April 1, 1982–September 30, 1982* (Washington, D.C.: Government Printing Office, 1982): 53–64.

17. Masayoshi Kanabayashi, "Japanese Unions Slipping at Workplace, Emerge as an Intriguing Political Force," *Wall Street Journal*, July 8, 1989, p. A4.

18. Dorothy Rabinowitz, "Snap, Crackle and Pop," *Wall Street Journal*, June 3, 1991, p. A8.

19. Jeremiah C. McGuire, *Cinema and Value Philosophy* (New York: Philosophical Library, 1968), 73.

Notes to Chapter 2

1. Leila A. Sussman, "Labor in the Radio News: An Analysis of Content," *Journalism Quarterly* 22 (September 1945): 214.

2. Glasgow University Media Group, *Bad News* (London: Routledge & Kegan Paul, 1976), 267–68.

3. Martin Harrison, *TV News: Whose Bias? A Casebook Analysis of Strikes, Television and Media Studies* (Hermitage, Berks.: Policy Journals, 1985), 47.

4. Cirino, *Don't Blame the People*, 141–46, 174–78.

5. Klaus Bruhn Jensen, "News as Ideology: Economic Statistics and Political Ritual in Television Network News," *Journal of Communications* 37, no. 1 (1987): 8–27, quote on p. 15.

6. Herbert J. Gans, *Deciding What's News* (New York: Pantheon, 1979), 14, 46.

7. Jerry Rollings, "Mass Communications and the American Worker," in *Labor, the Working Class, and the Media*, ed. Vincent Mosco and Janet Wasko (Norwood, N.J.: Ablex, 1983), 138.

8. Cirino, *Don't Blame the People*, 166–68.

9. *CBS News Index*, vol. 12 (Ann Arbor: UMI, 1986), 847–49.

10. Interview with Clyde Hayashi, former president of the Federal Employees' Metal Trades Council, at Pearl Harbor, April 14, 1989.

11. Cirino, *Don't Blame the People*, 152–53.

12. William J. Puette, *Labor Dispute Picketing: Organizing a Legal Picket in Hawaii* (Honolulu: University of Hawaii, Center for Labor Education and Research, 1984), 9.

13. Cirino, *Don't Blame the People*, 136.

14. Robinson and Clancey, "Network News, 15 Years After Agnew," 39.

15. Daniel Einstein, *Special Edition: A Guide to Network Television Documentary Series and Special News Reports, 1959–1979* (Metuchen, N.J.: Scarecrow Press, 1987), 512–47; Roberta Lynch, "The Media Distort the Value of Labor Unions," *In These Times*, July 15–28, 1981, p. 17.

16. Mark Crispin Miller, "Deride and Conquer," in *Watching Television*, ed. Todd Gitlin (New York: Pantheon, 1986), 196.

17. *Frontline*, with Judy Woodruff, PBS, January 31, 1989.

18. "Trouble Brewing," *60 Minutes*, vol. 15, no. 38, reporter, Mike Wallace; producer, Allan Marayanes; CBS, September 26, 1982 (rebroadcast June 5, 1983).

19. Rockne Porter, "What 60 Minutes Didn't Tell You," *The Gavel* (Drake Law School), December 8, 1982.

20. "Trouble Brewing," 12.

21. A. David Sickler, Coors boycott national coordinator, AFL-CIO, "Memorandum To: Coors Boycotters" (October 8, 1982) Re: CBS/60 Minutes Coors Boycott Story, September 26, 1982.

22. Ibid., 13, 5.

23. Robert Miraldi, *Muckraking and Objectivity: Journalism's Colliding Traditions* (New York: Greenwood Press, 1990), 112.

24. Einstein, *Special Edition*.

25. Harvey Molotch, "Media and Movements," in *The Dynamics of Social Movements: Resource Mobilization, Social Control, and Tactics*, ed. Meyer N. Zald and John D. McCarthy (Cambridge, Mass.: Winthrop, 1979), 76.

26. Walter Cronkite as quoted in Stephan Lesher, *Media Unbound: The Impact of Television Journalism on the Public* (Boston: Houghton Mifflin, 1982), 55.

27. William Hoynes and David Croteau, "Are You on the Nightline Guest List?" *Extra* 2 (January–February 1989): 5.

28. Irving Howe and Michael Kinsley, "'Special Interests' and American Politics," *Dissent* 31 (Summer 1984): 270–74.

Notes to Chapter 3

1. Ralph Arthur Johnson, "World without Workers: Prime Time's Presentation of Labor," *Labor Studies Journal* 5 (Winter 1981): 200.

2. Joel Eisner and David Krinsky, *Television Comedy Series: An Episode Guide to 153 TV Sitcoms in Syndication* (Jefferson, N.C.: McFarland, 1984), 459–60.

3. Seymour Martin Lipset, ed., *Unions in Transition: Entering the Second Century* (San Francisco: Institute for Contemporary Studies Press, 1986), 81.

4. "Every Man Must Pay His Dues" by Brad Radnitz, *Serpico* (Annenberg Script Serpico02), 11.

5. Ibid., 5.

6. "Murder by Self" by William Froug, *Quincy* (Annenberg script Quincy027), 31, 36.

7. Johnson, "World without Workers," 202–3.

8. Christopher Lasch, "Archie Bunker and the Liberal Mind," *Channels* 1 (October–November 1981): 35, 63.

9. "Wildcat Strike" by Stephen Miller and Mark Fink, *Archie Bunker's Place* (Annenberg Script Archie036), 14, 17.

10. "The Perfect Evening" by Gy Waldron, *All's Fair* (Annenberg script Alfair006), 21, 24.

11. Daniel C. Hallin, "We Keep America on Top of the World," in *Watching Television*, ed. Gitlin, 33.

12. Parenti, *Inventing Reality*, 84–85.

13. "Strike" by Bruce Shelly, *Eight Is Enough* (Annenberg script Eight066), 67.

14. "Beauties and the Beasts" by Robert Illes and James Stein, *Silver Spoons* (Annenberg script Silver054), 4.

15. Parenti, *Inventing Reality*, 85.

16. United Artists/MGM (1984), director: Arthur Hiller; screenwriter: W. R. McKinney; starring Nick Nolte, Lee Grant, and Judd Hirsch.

17. Hallin, "We Keep America on Top of the World," 23.

18. Cirino, *Don't Blame the People*, 141–46.

19. *Norma Rae* "pilot" by Carol Evan McKeand (Annenberg script dated January 23, 1981).

20. Judy Farah, "Writers' Strike Forces Cast to Improvise," *Honolulu Star-Bulletin*, March 25, 1988, p. B2.

Notes to Chapter 4

1. Zack, "The Press Bias on Labor," 1.

2. Cirino, *Don't Blame the People*, 134–79; Parenti, *Inventing Reality*, 84–85.

3. Haynes Johnson and Nick Kotz, *The Washington Post National Report: The Unions* (New York: Pocket Books, 1972), 5.

4. Daniel Lazare, "State of the Union: The Newspaper Guild under the Gun," *Columbia Journalism Review* 27 (January–February 1989): 44.

5. Edmund M. Midura, "A. J. Liebling: The Wayward Pressman as Critic," *Journalism Monographs* no. 33 (April 1974): 3.

6. Quoted in Sidney Lens, *The Labor Wars: From the Molly Maguires to the Sitdowns* (New York: Anchor Books, 1974), 248.

7. Walter Lippmann, *Public Opinion* (New York: Harcourt Brace, 1922), 350.

8. Parenti, *Inventing Reality*, 85.

9. Maureen Williams, "The House of Labor and the Fourth Estate: Where the Middle Ground Is," *Labor Center Review* 8 (Spring 1986): 6.

10. Quoted in Charles P. Larrowe, *Harry Bridges: The Rise and Fall of Radical Labor in the United States* (New York: Lawrence Hill, 1972), 80.

11. William J. Puette, *The Hilo Massacre: Hawaii's Bloody Monday, August 1st, 1938* (Honolulu: University of Hawaii, Center for Labor Education and Research, 1988), 52–54.

12. Neil MacNeil, *Without Fear or Favor* (New York: Harcourt, Brace, 1940), 368.

13. Michael Hoyt, "Downtime for Labor: Are Working People Less Equal Than Others—Or Is Labor Just a Dead Beat?" *Columbia Journalism Review* 22 (March–April 1984): 37.

14. Curtis Seltzer, "The Pits: Press Coverage of the Coal Strike," *Columbia Journalism Review* 20 (July–August 1981): 70.

15. John A. Grimes "Are the Media Shortchanging Organized Labor?" *Monthly Labor Review* 110 (August 1987): 53–54.

16. *Honolulu Advertiser*, March 2, 1984, p. B4.

17. Leonard W. Doob, *Public Opinion and Propaganda* (New York: Henry Holt, 1948), 440–41.

18. Larry David Price, "The Role of Hawaii's Media in Shaping Perceptions of Selected Constituencies Regarding Collective Bargaining Process in Public Education" (Ed.D. diss., University of Southern California, 1985).

19. Cirino, *Don't Blame the People*, 154–59.

20. *Honolulu Advertiser*, October 13, 1982, p. A6, November 2, 1982, p. A-8.

21. Ibid., 29 February 29, 1983, p. A5; *Sunday Star-Bulletin and Advertiser*, December 2, 1987, p. A7.

22. T. E. Moore "Subliminal Advertising: What You See Is What You Get," *Journal of Marketing* 46 (Spring 1982): 38–47; and Ronnie Cuperfain and T. K. Clarke, "A New Perspective of Subliminal Perception," *Journal of Advertising* 14 (1985): 36–41.

23. David Ignatius, "The Press in Love," *Columbia Journalism Review* 16 (May–June 1977): 26.

24. Parenti, *Inventing Reality*, 85.

25. The former story was in the *Sunday Star-Bulletin and Advertiser*, June 24, 1987, the latter in the *Honolulu Advertiser*, March 11, 1988.

26. *Sunday Star-Bulletin and Advertiser*, June 28, 1987, p. A34.

27. Ibid., July 3, 1988, p. A28, June 26, 1988, p. A30.

28. "NewsMaker," Honolulu *Star-Bulletin*, November 12, 1987, featured Joan Husted, program director of the Hawaii State Teachers Association.

29. *Honolulu Star-Bulletin*, January 31, 1986, p. A6; *Honolulu Advertiser*, February 1, 1986, pp. A1 and A4.

30. "Report on 1984 Work Stoppages," *Labor Relations Reporter* (118 LRR 186), March 11, 1985; "Labor Experts Discuss Strike Tactic," *Labor Relations Reporter* (130 LRR 431), April 10, 1989.

31. Lippmann, *Public Opinion*, 350.

32. Zack, "The Press Bias on Labor," 4.

33. *Honolulu Star-Bulletin*, May 15, 1989, p. A1.

34. Hoyt, "Downtime for Labor," 39.

35. *Honolulu Star-Bulletin*, February 28, 1985, p. A1, March 2, 1985, p. A3.

36. Everett D. Martin, "Our Invisible Masters," *Forum* 81 (1929): 145.

37. A. A. Smyser, "News Won't Ever Please All People, All the Time," *Honolulu Star-Bulletin*, April 26, 1988, p. A16.

38. In 1975 the American Society of Newspaper Editors revised this "Code of Ethics" or "Canons of Journalism" and renamed it "A Statement of Principles." The last sentence of this quotation was excised.

Notes to Chapter 5

1. John Tebbel, *The Media in America* (New York: Crowell, 1974), 373.

2. Morton Keller, *The Art and Politics of Thomas Nast* (New York: Oxford University Press, 1968), 73–74.

3. Harry R. Rubenstein, "Symbols and Images of American Labor: Dinner Pails and Hard Hats," *Labor's Heritage* 1, no. 3 (1989): 37–38.

4. Keller, *Thomas Nast*, 263, fig. 174.

5. Ibid., 109.

6. *Puck*, March 31, 1886, reproduced in M. B. Schnapper, *American Labor: A Pictorial Social History* (Washington, D.C.: Public Affairs Press, 1972), 337.

7. *Puck*, March 16, 1887, reproduced in Schnapper, 140.

8. Corky Trinidad, in the *Honolulu Star-Bulletin*, March 2, 1989, p. A24.

9. *Honolulu Star-Bulletin*, July 16, 1988, p. A6, August 17, 1988, p. A15, August 22, 1988, p. A11.

10. Quoted in David Manning White and Robert H. Abel, eds., *The Funnies: An American Idiom* (New York: Free Press, 1963), 3.

11. Louis Rukeyser, "'Funnies' Having Last Laugh in Advertising," *Honolulu Star-Bulletin*, December 5, 1988, p. C1.

12. Mike Feinsilber, "Newspaper Comic Page a Serious Matter," *Honolulu Star-Bulletin*, April 13, 1989, p. E5.

13. Kathleen A. Hughes, "Zowie! Newspapers Poll Readers on Comic Strips," *Wall Street Journal*, June 15, 1988, p. 25.

14. Feinsilber, "Newspaper Comic Page."

15. Ibid.

16. Tom Gliatto, "It's a Blooming Shame," *Honolulu Star-Bulletin*, May 5, 1989, pp. B1 and 5.

17. Berke Breathed, "Bloom County," cartoon, *Honolulu Star-Bulletin*, October 21, 1987, p. G8.

18. Garry Trudeau, "Doonesbury," cartoons, *Honolulu Star-Bulletin*, July 4, 1988, p. B4, October 5, 1988, p. B4; *Sunday Star-Bulletin and Advertiser*, April 23, 1989.

19. Ibid., *Honolulu Star-Bulletin*, March 11, 1989, p. B4.

20. Brant Parker and Johnny Hart, "B.C.," cartoon, *Honolulu Star-Bulletin*, October 18, 1985, p. C6.

21. Ibid., *Sunday Star-Bulletin and Advertiser*, August 28, 1988, n.p.

22. Ibid., January 15, 1989, n.p.

23. Brant Parker and Johnny Hart, "Wizard," cartoon, *Honolulu Star-Bulletin*, August 25, 1987, p. B4.

24. Ibid., January 2, 1987, p. B4.

25. Ibid., January 11, 1990, p. G6.

26. Greg Howard, "Sally Forth," cartoon, *Honolulu Star-Bulletin*, May 11, 1991, p. B16.

27. W. B. Park, "Off the Leash," cartoon, *Honolulu Advertiser*, May 31, 1990, p. C6.

28. Francis Barcus, "The World of Sunday Comics," in *The Funnies*, ed. White and Abel, 201.

29. Hughes, "Zowie!" *Wall Street Journal*, June 15, 1988, p. 25.

Notes to Chapter 6

1. Gerald Gross, ed., *The Responsibility of the Press* (New York: Fleet, 1966), 406.

2. Everette E. Dennis, "Memo to the Press: Let's Have Fair Play," delivered at the Virginia Associated Press Newspapers Annual Meeting, Richmond, March 5, 1988, in *Vital Speeches of the Day* 54 (June 1, 1988): 500.

3. David L. Paletz and Robert M. Entman, *Media, Power, Politics* (New York: Free Press, 1981), 19–20.

4. According to their respective circulation departments, as of November 1988, the *Advertiser*'s daily circulation was 93,088, the *Star-Bulletin*'s was 97,950, and the *Maui News*'s was 17,400.

5. In 1983 about eight hundred employees of the two Honolulu dailies were represented by six different unions, according to an article in the *Honolulu Star-Bulletin*, April 11, 1983, p. A10.

6. Russ Lynch, "It's a Rough Road for Young Leader of Labor Group," ibid., December 13, 1969, p. B1.

7. Victor Lipman, "Interview with Walter Kupau," *Honolulu Magazine*, February 1985, p. 33.

8. See *Honolulu Advertiser* and *Honolulu Star-Bulletin*, May 18, 1977.

9. See Lynch, "It's a Rough Road for Young Leader of Labor Group"; Tom Coffman, "Kupau Wants Labor Unified," *Honolulu Star-Bulletin*, September 22, 1969; and "Firebrand Takes Key Labor Post," ibid., October 2, 1969.

10. "Carpenter's Pact Ups Wages 58%," *Honolulu Star-Bulletin*, October 2, 1980, p. A10.

11. "Carpenter Picket Line Breached," *Honolulu Advertiser*, September, 16 1980, p. A3; "Three Unions Crossing Carpenter's Picket Lines," *Star-Bulletin*, September 16, 1980, p. A4.

12. Within a year after the strike he was reelected by an overwhelming two-to-one margin; see "Carpenters Re-elect Kupau to Union Post," *Honolulu Star-Bulletin*, June 25, 1981.

13. Charles Turner, "Nonunion Work in Construction on the Upswing," *Honolulu Advertiser*, November 3, 1983, p. A10.

14. Ed Gorman and Marvin Gittler, eds., *Organizer's Handbook*, rev. ed. (Washington D.C.: Building and Construction Trades Department, AFL-CIO, 1990), pp. 41–48.

15. The full coverage of this story spanned four years. The tally of 1983 headlines is a sample meant to suggest the weight and character of each paper's overall treatment.

16. Interview with Phil Mayer, December 8, 1988.

17. See "Kupau Sees Plot Against Union," *Honolulu Advertiser* and "Kupau Claims Advertiser, U.S. Agencies Conspired," *Honolulu Star-Bulletin*, June 3, 1983, p. A10; and Walter Kupau's sister Jessica Kirk's letter, *Honolulu Advertiser*, December 2, 1983, p. A17.

18. Doob, *Public Opinion and Propaganda*, 440–41.

19. *Honolulu Advertiser*, June 23, 1981, p. A12.

20. Ibid., May 12, 1983, p. A1.

21. Walter Wright, "Contractor: Taped Union 'Threats'," ibid., May 17, 1983, p. A3.

22. Walter Wright, "Pending Cases Exempt from FOIA: FBI Probe Off Limits to Carpenters," ibid., May 25, 1983, p. A4.

23. "The Trials for Viet Vet, Wife Just Beginning," ibid., July 25, 1983, p. A1.

24. Paletz and Entman, *Media, Power, Politics*, 19, 201–2.

25. *Honolulu Star-Bulletin*, November 5, 1983, p. A1.

26. Ibid., October 26, 1983, pp. A1, A10; February 8, 1984, p. A16; April 30, 1984, p. A14.

27. *Honolulu Star-Bulletin*, October 30, 1987, p. A5.

28. "Kupau Says Reaganites Want to Bust the Unions," ibid., September 2, 1983, p. A7.

29. "Union Not Served by Racism Charges," *Maui News*, May 25, 1983, p. A9.

30. Jack Anderson, "Fighting Union Power" and "Labor Law With Loopholes," *Honolulu Star-Bulletin*, September 23, 24, 1983, p. A6.

31. *Reader's Digest*, July 1984; *Wall Street Journal*, December 29, 1983, article by Senator Charles E. Grassley; the *Washington Times*, October 26, 1983, article by Tom Diaz; the *New York Times*, September 12, 1983; the *Washington Post*, September 23, 25, 1983, two articles by Jack Anderson; *London Daily Mail*, "Why the Union Wants My Husband Dead!" September 6, 1983.

32. Walter Wright was considered by the *Advertiser* to be an investigative reporter (interview with Charles Turner, November 28, 1988).

33. "Deposition of Walter Mungovan," *C&W Construction v. Brotherhood of Carpenters and Joiners of America, Local 745*, CIVIL No. 83–0710 (U.S. District Court, District of Hawaii, February 1986), pp. 125–27.

34. Joanna Russ, *The Female Man* (Boston: Beacon Press, 1975), 196.

Notes to Chapter 7

1. Alexander Cockburn, "Their Miners and Ours—II," *Nation* 249 (October 16, 1989): 410–11.

2. Phill Kwik, "Pittston Power," *Nation* 249 (October 16, 1989): 409; "Media Watch: What Are They Afraid to Tell?" *People's Daily World* 4 (September 21, 1989): 2.

3. Jonathan Tasini, "Lost in the Margins: Labor and the Media" (A Special FAIR Report prepared for Fairness and Accuracy in Reporting, Sep. 1, 1990) in *Extra!* 3 (Summer 1990): 1–12.

4. *Richmond Times-Dispatch*, July 17, 1989.

5. Denise Giardina, "Solidarity in Appalachia," *Nation* 249 (July 3, 1989): 13.

6. Jude Wanniski, ed., *The 1989 Media Guide: A Critical Review of the Print Media's Recent Coverage of the World Political Economy* (Morristown, N.J.: Polyconomics, 1989), 41–49.

7. Interview with Patricia Edwards, United Mine Workers of America, in Washington, D.C., January 23, 1991.

8. Interview with Kenneth Gagala at the George Meany Center in Washington, D.C., January 25, 1991.

9. Nick Ravo, "Moving a Strike from Coal Pits to Suburbia," *New York Times*, July 5, 1989, p. 31.

10. Alexander Cockburn, "Their Miners and Ours," *Nation* 249 (August 21–28, 1989): 195.

11. Tasini, "Lost in the Margins," 9.

12. Interview with F. Kirsten Smith, United Mine Workers of America, in Washington, D.C., January 23, 1991.

13. Alecia Swasy "Coalfield Crisis," *Wall Street Journal*, July 17, 1989, p. A1.

14. Alecia Swasy, "United Mine Workers Union Applies to Rejoin AFL-CIO after Long Absence," *Wall Street Journal*, October 5, 1989, p. B10.

15. Greg Tarpinian, "Pittston: Rebirth of the Unions?" *Wall Street Journal*, November 20, 1989, p. A14.

16. Spiro T. Agnew, "Democracy Doesn't Need Picketers," *Wall Street Journal*, November 1, 1989, p. A12.

17. Tasini, "Lost in the Margins," 7.

18. *48 Hours*, "On Strike!" CBS Television, June 15, 1989 (unofficial transcript prepared by the author from a videotape of the original telecast).

19. United Mine Workers of America, *Betraying the Trust: The Pittston Company's Drive to Break Appalachia's Coalfield Communities* (information brochure, 1989).

20. Letter of Paul Douglas to UMWA, November 9, 1988.

21. Martha J. Hall, "CBS Show Catalyst?" *Kingsport Times-News*, June 17, 1989, pp. 1A, 12A.

22. Ibid., 12A.

Notes to Chapter 8

1. Sara U. Douglas, "Organized Labor and the Mass Media" (Ph.D. diss., University of Illinois, 1983), 26–72.

2. Jack Barbash, *The Practice of Unionism* (New York: Harper and Brothers, 1956), 287.

3. Douglas, "Organized Labor and the Mass Media," 78–79, 85.

4. Key, *Public Opinion and American Democracy*, 515–16.

5. Jacques Ellul, *Propaganda: The Formation of Men's Attitudes* (New York: Knopf), 227.

6. Joe Cosco, "Unions Polishing a Tarnished Image," *Public Relations Journal* 45 (February 1989): 18.

7. AFL-CIO, *The Changing Situation of Workers and Their Unions*, Report by the AFL-CIO Committee on the Evolution of Work (Washington, D.C.: AFL-CIO, 1985), 27–28.

8. Lois Breedlove et al., "Media Monitors: Most Are Simply Vigilant, But Some Are Vigilantes," *Quill* 72, no. 6 (1984): 18, 19.

9. Interview with Richard L. Schneider, IAM Grand Lodge representative, March 1, 1989.

10. Sara U. Douglas, Norma Pecora, and Thomas Guback, "Work, Workers and the Workplace: Is Local Newspaper Coverage Adequate?" *Journalism Quarterly* 62 (1985): 855–60.

11. Susan Manuel, "Kupau Claims Advertiser, U.S. Agencies Conspired," *Honolulu Star-Bulletin*, June 3, 1983, p. A10; Charles Turner, "Kupau Sees Plot Against Union," *Honolulu Advertiser*, June 3, 1983, p. A3; and Charles Turner, "Kupau Blasts GOP, Media, Management at Unity Breakfast," ibid., September 3, 1983, p. A3.

12. Charles Ware (ombudsman), "Fairness of Advertiser's Rutledge Suit Coverage," *Honolulu Advertiser*, May 6, 1984, p. B3.

13. Stuart Gerry Brown, "The Media Council after 15 Years," *Honolulu Advertiser*, January 13, 1986, p. A6.

14. Johnson, "World without Workers," 200; "'Skag': TV's Steel Soap a Factual Wipe-Out," *Steel Labor* 45 (February 1980): 7.

15. Edward Handman, "DC 37 News Watch Proves TV Puts Koch on a Pedestal," *Public Employee Press* (AFSCME, District Council 37 Newsletter), May 29, 1981, p. 5.

16. Norman E. Isaacs, *Untended Gates: The Mismanaged Press* (New York: Columbia University Press, 1986).

17. Mel Chang, "Media Handling of Labor Issues: Possible Guidelines," September 19, 1989.

18. Plumbers and Steamfitters Local 33, "95th Anniversary Video and 6 TV Commercials," videotape, Des Moines, Iowa, 1987.

19. Ibid.

20. Sandra S. Oshiro, "From Bargaining Table to TV Screen," *Honolulu Advertiser*, February 19, 1987, p. C9.

21. "HSTA, NEA Set to Broadcast Election-Year TV Commercials," *HSTA Teacher Advocate* 17 (September 1988): 5.

22. "UAW Ad Campaign," *Labor Relations Reporter* (130 LRR 509), April 24, 1989, p. 509.

23. Gregory A. Patterson and Louis Aguilar, "UAW Blasts Wall Street with Ad Blitz," *Wall Street Journal*, April 19, 1989, p. C1.

24. Roscoe Born, "Madison Avenue Techniques Considered by the AFL-CIO," *Wall Street Journal*, February 6, 1958, p. 5.

25. Carpenters Union, Local 745, television commercial, produced by Chun & Yonamine Advertising, December 14, 1987.

26. "Resolution No. 217," *Proceedings of the Seventeenth Constitutional Convention of the AFL-CIO* (Washington, D.C.: AFL-CIO, October 1987), 371.

27. "AFL-CIO Plans TV Ads to Boost Labor's Image," *Wall Street Journal*, May 11, 1988, p. 17.

28. "Accentuating the Positive about Your Union Membership," *Carpenter* (Magazine of the United Brotherhood of Carpenters) 109 (February 1989): 15.

29. "Union Yes Spots Aired Widely on Radio," *AFL-CIO News* 33 (June 11, 1988): 2.

30. "Union Yes: It's Working," ibid. (July 30, 1988): 4.

Notes to Chapter 9

1. Maureen Williams, "From Incendiary to Invisible: A Print-News Content Analysis of the Labor Movement," *Labor Center Review* 10 (Spring 1988): 23.

2. A. J. Liebling, "Foreign News," in *The Most of A. J. Liebling*, selected by William Cole (New York: Simon and Schuster, 1963), 159.

3. Key, *Public Opinion and American Democracy*, 400.

4. Salant speaking at taping of "Inside CBS News," Harrisburg, Pa., October 8, 1977; quoted in Paletz and Entman, *Media, Power, Politics*, 234.

5. Richard H. Pells, *The Liberal Mind in a Conservative Age: American Intellectuals in the 1940s and 1950s* (New York: Harper & Row, 1985), 247.

6. Charles Peters, "A Neo-Liberal's Manifesto," *Washington Post*, September 5, 1982, p. C1.

7. Harold P. Schlechtweg, "When Worlds Collide: Amherst's Progressives and the Picketing of Louis' Foods," *Labor Center Review* 11 (Spring 1989): 25.

8. Alexis de Tocqueville, *Democracy in America*, trans. Richard D. Heffner (New York: Mentor/New American Library, 1956), 91–93.

9. A. J. Liebling, *The Wayward Pressman* (1947; rpt. Westport, Conn.: Greenwood Press, 1972), 271.

Bibliography

Books and Theses

Adler, Richard P., ed. *All in the Family: A Critical Appraisal.* New York: Praeger, 1979.

American Society of Newspaper Editors. *Problems of Journalism: Proceedings of the 1975 Convention.* Washington D.C.: American Society of Newspaper Editors, 1975.

Barbash, Jack. *The Practice of Unionism.* New York: Harper and Brothers, 1956.

Barker, Martin. *Comics: Ideology, Power and the Critics.* Manchester, England: Manchester University Press, 1989.

Beharrell, Peter, and Greg Philo, eds. *Trade Unions and the Media.* London: Macmillan, 1977.

Bender, Martin. "An Introduction to Organized Labor in Television." Master's thesis, Michigan State University, 1969.

Biberman, Herbert. *Salt of the Earth: The Story of a Film.* Boston: Beacon Press, 1965.

Bok, Derek C., and John T. Dunlop. *Labor and the American Community.* New York: Simon and Schuster, 1970.

Bower, Robert T. *The Changing Television Audience in America.* New York: Columbia University Press, 1985.

Brooks, Tim, and Earle Marsh. *The Complete Directory to Prime Time Network TV Shows, 1946–Present.* 3d ed. New York: Ballantine Books, 1985.

Brown, Gene, ed. *The New York Times Encyclopedia of Film.* 13 vols. New York: Times Books, 1984.

Cantor, Muriel G. *Prime-Time Television: Content and Control.* Sage CommText Series, vol. 3. Beverly Hills: Sage, 1980.

CBS News Index. Vol. 12. Ann Arbor: UMI, 1986.

Cirino, Robert. *Don't Blame the People: How the News Media Use Bias, Distortion and Censorship to Manipulate Public Opinion.* Los Angeles: Diversity Press, 1971.

Couperie, Pierre, et al. *A History of the Comic Strip.* Translated by Eileen B. Hennesy. New York: Crown, 1968.

Crawford, Nelson Antrim. *The Ethics of Journalism.* New York: Knopf, 1924.

Dickinson, Burrus Swinford. "The Newspaper and Labor: An Inquiry into the Nature and Influence of Labor News and Comment in the Daily Press." Ph.D. diss., University of Illinois, 1930.

Doob, Leonard W. *Public Opinion and Propaganda.* New York: Henry Holt, 1948.

Douglas, Sara U. *Labor's New Voice: Unions and the Mass Media.* Norwood, N.J.: Ablex, 1986.

————. "Organized Labor and the Mass Media." Ph.D. diss., University of Illinois, 1983.

Downing, John. *The Media Machine.* London: Pluto Press Ltd., 1980.

Drew, William M. *D. W. Griffith's* Intolerance*: Its Genesis and Its Vision.* Jefferson, N.C.: McFarland, 1986.

Efron, Edith. *The News Twisters.* Los Angeles: Nash, 1971.

Ehrenreich, Barbara. *Fear of Falling: The Inner Life of the Middle Class.* New York: Pantheon, 1989.

Einstein, Daniel. *Special Edition: A Guide to Network Television Documentary Series and Special News Reports, 1959–1979.* Metuchen, N.J.: Scarecrow Press, 1987.

Eisner, Joel, and David Krinsky. *Television Comedy Series: An Episode Guide to 153 TV Sitcoms in Syndication.* Jefferson, N.C.: McFarland, 1984.

Ellul, Jacques. *Propaganda: The Formation of Men's Attitudes.* Translated by Konrad Kellen and Jean Lerner. New York: Knopf, 1965.

Fauss, Richard. *A Bibliography of Labor History in News Film.* 4 vols. Morgantown, W. Va.: Institute for Labor Studies, West Virginia University, 1980.

Fink, Conrad C. *Media Ethics: In the Newsroom and Beyond.* New York: McGraw-Hill, 1988.

Gans, Herbert J. *Deciding What's News.* New York: Pantheon, 1979.

Gertner, Richard, ed. *International Television Almanac.* 27th ed. New York: Quigley Publishing Co., 1982.

————. *International Television Almanac.* 33d ed. New York: Quigley, 1988.

Gitlin, Todd., ed. *Watching Television.* New York: Pantheon, 1986.

Glasgow University Media Group. *Bad News.* London: Routledge & Kegan Paul, 1976.

————. *More Bad News.* London: Routledge & Kegan Paul, 1980.

————. *Really Bad News.* London: Writers and Readers, 1982.

Gorman, Ed, and Marvin Gittler, eds. *Organizer's Handbook.* Washington, D.C.: Building and Construction Trades Department, AFL-CIO, 1990.

Graber, Doris A. *Processing the News: How People Tame the Information Tide.* 2d ed. New York: Longman, 1988.

Gross, Gerald, ed. *The Responsibility of the Press*. New York: Fleet, 1966.

Halberstam, David. *The Powers That Be*. New York: Dell, 1979.

Halliwell, Leslie. *Halliwell's Film Guide*. New York: Scribner's, 1977.

Harrison, Martin. *TV News: Whose Bias? A Casebook Analysis of Strikes, Television and Media Studies*. Hermitage, Berks.: Policy Journals, 1985.

Herman, Edward S., and Noam Chomsky. *Manufacturing Consent: The Political Economy of the Mass Media*. New York: Pantheon, 1988.

Hess, Stephen, and Milton Kaplan. *The Ungentlemanly Art: A History of American Political Cartoons*. New York: Macmillan, 1968.

Isaacs, Norman E. *Untended Gates: The Mismanaged Press*. New York: Columbia University Press, 1986.

Jarvie, I. C. *Movies and Society*. New York: Basic Books, 1970.

Johnson, Haynes, and Nick Kotz. *The Washington Post National Report: The Unions*. New York: Pocket Books, 1972.

Kauffmann, Stanley. *Before My Eyes*. New York: Harper & Row, 1980.

Keeley, Joseph. *The Left-Leaning Antenna: Political Bias in Television*. New Rochelle, N.Y.: Arlington House, 1971.

Keller, Morton. *The Art and Politics of Thomas Nast*. New York: Oxford University Press, 1968.

Kent, Noel J. "Islands under the Influence: Hawaii and Two Centuries of Dependent Development." Ph.D. diss., University of Hawaii, 1979.

Kessler, Lauren. *The Dissident Press: Alternative Journalism in American History*. Sage CommText Series, vol. 13. Beverley Hills: Sage, 1984.

Key, V. O., Jr. *Public Opinion and American Democracy*. New York: Knopf, 1961.

Key, W. B. *Subliminal Seduction*. New York: Signet, 1973.

Krippendorff, Klaus. *Content Analysis: An Introduction to Its Methodology*. Sage CommText Series, vol. 5. Beverly Hills: Sage, 1980.

Larrowe, Charles P. *Harry Bridges: The Rise and Fall of Radical Labor in the United States*. New York: Lawrence Hill, 1972.

Laski, Harold. *The American Democracy*. New York: Viking, 1948.

Lens, Sidney. *The Labor Wars: From the Molly Maguires to the Sitdowns*. New York: Anchor Books, 1974.

Lesher, Stephan. *Media Unbound: The Impact of Television Journalism on the Public*. Boston: Houghton Mifflin, 1982.

Lichter, S. Robert, Stanley Rothman, and Linda S. Lichter. *The Media Elite*. Bethesda, Md.: Adler & Adler, 1986.

Liebling, A. J. *The Most of A. J. Liebling*, Selected by William Cole. New York: Simon and Schuster, 1963.

———. *The Wayward Pressman*. 1947. Reprint. Westport, Conn.: Greenwood Press, 1972.

Lippmann, Walter. *Public Opinion*. New York: Harcourt, Brace, 1922.

Lipset, Seymour Martin, and William Schneider. *The Confidence Gap: Business, Labor, and Government in the Public Mind*. Rev. ed. Baltimore: Johns Hopkins University Press, 1987.

Lipset, Seymour Martin, ed. *Unions in Transition: Entering the Second Century*. San Francisco: Institute for Contemporary Studies, 1986.

Lynd, Robert S., and Helen Merrell Lynd. *Middletown: A Study in Modern American Culture*. New York: Harcourt, Brace & World, 1929.

McGuire, Jeremiah C. *Cinema and Value Philosophy*. New York: Philosophical Library, 1968.

Marc, David. *Deomographic Vistas: Television in American Culture*. Philadelphia: University of Pennsylvania Press, 1984.

Mills, C. Wright. *The New Men of Power: America's Labor Leaders*. New York: Harcourt, Brace, 1948.

———. *The Power Elite*. New York: Oxford University Press, 1956.

———. *Power, Politics and People*. Edited by Irving Louis Horowitz. New York: Oxford University Press, 1963.

———. *The Sociological Imagination*. New York: Oxford University Press, 1959.

Miraldi, Robert. *Muckraking and Objectivity: Journalism's Colliding Traditions*. New York: Greenwood Press, 1990.

Mosco, Vincent, and Janet Wasko, eds. *Labor, the Working Class, and the Media. The Critical Communications Review*, vol. 1. Norwood, N.J.: Ablex, 1983.

National Labor Service. *Television—Labor's New Challange*. New York: National Labor Service, 1954.

The New York Times Film Reviews. 5 vols. New York: Times Books and Garland Publishing, 1970.

Nyden, Philip W. *Steelworkers Rank-and-File: The Political Economy of a Union Reform Movement*. New York: Praeger, 1984.

Packard, Vance. *The Hidden Persuaders*. New York: David McKay Company, 1957.

Paletz, David L., and Robert M. Entman. *Media, Power, Politics*. New York: Free Press, 1981.

Parenti, Michael. *Inventing Reality: The Politics of the Mass Media*. New York: St. Martin's Press, 1986.

Pells, Richard H. *The Liberal Mind in a Conservative Age: American Intellectuals in the 1940s and 1950s*. New York: Harper & Row, 1985.

Petty, Richard E., and John T. Cacioppo. *Communication and Persuasion: Central and Peripheral Routes to Attitude Change*. New York: Springer-Verlag, 1986.

Peyton, Patricia, ed. *Reel Change: A Guide to Social Issue Films*. Emeryville, Calif.: Albany Press, 1979.

Price, Larry David. "The Role of Hawaii's Media in Shaping Perceptions of Selected Constituencies Regarding the Collective Bargaining Process in Public Education." Ph.D. diss., University of Southern California, 1986.

Puette, William J. *The Hilo Massacre: Hawaii's Bloody Monday, August 1st, 1938*. Honolulu: University of Hawaii, Center for Labor Education and Research, 1988.

————. *Labor Dispute Picketing: Organizing a Legal Picket in Hawaii*. Honolulu: University of Hawaii, Center for Labor Education and Research, 1984.

Rivers, William L., and Cleve Matthews. *Ethics for the Media*. Englewood Cliffs, N.J.: Prentice Hall, 1988.

Robinson, John P., and Mark R. Levy. *The Main Source: Learning from Television News*. Beverley Hills: Sage, 1986.

Roffman, Peter, and Jim Purdy. *The Hollywood Social Problem Film*. Bloomington: Indiana University Press, 1981.

Rollins, Peter C., ed. *Hollywood as Historian: American Film in a Cultural Context*. Lexington: University Press of Kentucky, 1983.

Roper Organization, Inc. *Public Perceptions of Television and Other Media: A Twenty-year Review, 1959–1978*. New York: Television Information Office, 1979.

Rowan, Ford. *Broadcast Fairness: Doctrine, Practice, Prospects*. Longman Series in Public Communication. New York: Longman, 1984.

Rowland, Willard D., Jr., and Bruce Watkins, eds. *Interpreting Television: Current Research Perspectives*. Sage Annual Reviews of Communications Research, vol. 12. Beverly Hills: Sage, 1984.

Rusher, William A. *The Coming Battle for the Media: Curbing the Power of the Media Elite*. New York: Morrow, 1988.

Russ, Joanna. *The Female Man*. Boston: Beacon, 1975.

Sagen, Maile-Gene, ed. *Ethics and the Media*. Monticello, Iowa: Iowa Humanities Board, 1987.

Saposs, David J. *Readings in Trade Unionism*. New York: Macmillan, 1927.

Schnapper, M. B. *American Labor: A Pictorial Social History*. Washington, D.C.: Public Affairs Press, 1972.

Schulberg, Budd. *On the Waterfront: A Screenplay*. Carbondale: Southern Illinois University Press, 1980.

Siebert, Fred S., Theodore Peterson, and Wilbur Schramm. *Four Theories of the Press*. Urbana: University of Illinois Press, 1956.

Simmons, Steven J. *The Fairness Doctrine and the Media*. Berkeley: University of California Press, 1978.

Stone, Gerald. *Examining Newspapers: What Research Reveals about America's Newspapers*. Sage CommText Series, vol. 20. Beverly Hills: Sage, 1987.

Tebbel, John. *The Media in America*. New York: Crowell, 1974.

Television News Index and Abstracts. Nashville: Vanderbilt Television News Archive.

Tocqueville, Alexis de. *Democracy in America*. Translated by Richard D. Heffner. New York: Mentor/New American Library, 1956.

Tuchman, Gaye, ed. *The TV Establishment: Programming for Power and Profit*. Englewood Cliffs, N.J.: Prentice-Hall, 1974.

Wanniski, Jude, ed. *The 1989 Media Guide: A Critical Review of the Print Media's Recent Coverage of the World Political Economy*. Morristown, N.J.: Polyconomics, 1989.

Wells, Alan, ed. *Mass Media and Society*. Palo Alto: National Press Books, 1972.

White, David Manning, and Robert H. Abel, eds. *The Funnies: An American Idiom*. New York: Free Press, 1963.

White, David Manning, and Richard Averson, eds. *The Celluloid Weapon: Social Comment in the American Film*. Boston: Beacon Press, 1972.

Wilde, Oscar. *The Annotated Oscar Wilde*. Edited by H. Montgomery Hyde. New York: Clarkson N. Potter, 1982.

Articles

"Accentuating the Positive about Your Union Membership." *Carpenter* (Magazine of the United Brotherhood of Carpenters) 109 (February 1989): 15 + .

"AFL-CIO Plans TV Ads to Boost Labor's Image." *Wall Street Journal*, May 11, 1988, p. 17.

American Enterprise Institute. "Opinion Roundup: Looking at the Union Label." *Public Opinion* 11 (November–December 1988): 21.

Anderson, Jack. " 'Blood Feud.' " *San Francisco Chronicle*, May 5, 1988, p. 59.

Anderson, Pat. "Pictures Never Lie." *Films in Review* 35 (April 1984): 231–32.

Ansen, David. "Which Side Are You On?" Rev. of *Matewan* directed by John Sayles. *Newsweek*, September 14, 1987, p. 82.

Aslakson, Arnold. "Labor Is News—A Reporter's View." *Journalism Quarterly* 17 (June 1940): 151–58.

Aufderheide, Pat. "America Works—But Not on WNET." *Village Voice*, June 12, 1984, pp. 40–41.

Bauer, Charles. "The Media: Labour Reporting in Canada." *Canadian Labour* 31 (July–August 1986):15 + .

Bayles, Martha. "Taking AIM at Biased Documentaries." *Wall Street Journal*, February 24, 1986, p. 8.

Benson, Edward, and Sharon Strom. "Crystal Lee, Norma Rae and All Their Sisters." *Film Library Quarterly* 12, nos. 2–3 (1979): 18–23.

Berkman, Dave. "You Can Fool 48% of the People All the Time. . . . " *Channels* 4 (May–June 1984): 68.

Born, Roscoe. "Madison Avenue Techniques considered by the AFL-CIO." *Wall Street Journal*, February 6, 1958, p. 5.

Brandon, Thomas. "Survival List — Films of the Great Depression." *Film Library Quarterly* 12, nos. 2–3 (1979): 33–40.

Brandon, Thomas, and William Pierce. "A Directory of American Labor Films." *Film Library Quarterly* 12, nos. 2–3 (1979): 88–99.

Breedlove, Lois, et al. "Media Monitors: Most Are Simply Vigilant, but Some Are Vigilantes." *Quill* 72, no. 6 (1984): 16–21.

Brown, Les. "The Law of Unexpected Consequences." *Channels* 6 (June 1986): 19.

Brown, Merrill. "The Shifts in Television Power." *Channels* 6 (September 1986): 20.

Bureau of National Affairs. "Labor Experts Discuss Strike Tactic." *Labor Relations Reporter* (April 10, 1989): 431.

———. "Report on 1984 Work Stoppages." *Labor Relations Reporter* (March 11, 1985): 186.

————. "Report on Public Image of Unions." *Labor Relations Reporter* (January 7, 1985): 1.

————. "UAW Ad Campaign." *Labor Relations Reporter* (April 24, 1989): 509.

Buss, Dale B. "'Gung Ho' to Repeat Assembly-Line Errors." *Wall Street Journal*, March 27, 1986, p. 32.

Canby, Vincent. "America—We're Nobody's Sweetheart Now." Rev. of *Joe Hill. New York Times*, October 31, 1971, sec. 2:1+.

————. Rev. of *Blue Collar. New York Times*, February 10, 1978, p. C5.

————. Rev. of *Bound For Glory. New York Times*, December 6, 1976, p. 47.

————. Rev. of *F.I.S.T.. New York Times*, April 26, 1978, p. C15.

————. Rev. of *F.I.S.T.. New York Times*, May 14, 1978, pp. 11+.

————. Rev. of *Joe Hill. New York Times*, October 25, 1971, p. 44.

————. Rev. of *Norma Rae. New York Times*, March 2, 1979, p. C10.

————. Rev. of *Sometimes a Great Notion. New York Times*, March 2, 1972, p. 34.

————. Rev. of *The Wobblies. New York Times*, November 5, 1977, p. 13.

Clark, Paul F. "Union Image-Building at the Local Level: Labor Education Techniques and Materials." *Labor Studies Journal*. Forthcoming.

Cockburn, Alexander. "Their Miners and Ours." *Nation* 249 (August 21–28, 1989): 195.

————. "Their Miners and Ours—II." *Nation* 249 (October 16, 1989): 410–11.

Corry, John. "TV: Labor Union Problems in the Sunbelt." *New York Times*, March 5, 1983, p. 48.

Cosco, Joe. "Unions Polishing a Tarnished Image." *Public Relations Journal* 45 (February 1989): 16–21.

Craft, James A., and Suhail Abboushi. "The Union Image: Concept, Programs and Analysis." *Journal of Labor Research* 4 (1983): 299–314.

Craig, Berry. "News Media Treats Unions Unfairly." *Labor Notes*, August 1988, p. 10.

Crowther, Bosley. Rev. of *The Devil and Miss Jones. New York Times*, March 16, 1941, p. 21.

————. Rev. of *The Pajama Game. New York Times*, August 30, 1957, p. 12.

————. Rev. of *Racket Busters. New York Times*, August 11, 1938, p. 13.

————. Rev. of *Reaching for the Sun. New York Times*, May 8, 1941, p. 21.

————. Rev. of *Salt of the Earth. New York Times*, March 15, 1954, p. 20.

————. Rev. of *Whistle at Eaton Falls. New York Times*, October 11, 1951, p. 49.

Cuperfain, Ronnie, and T. K. Clarke. "A New Perspective of Subliminal Perception." *Journal of Advertising* 14 (1985): 36–41.

Dennis, Everette E. "Memo to the Press: Let's Have Fair Play." *Vital Speeches of the Day* 54 (June 1, 1988): 499–501.

Douglas, Sara U., Norma Pecora, and Thomas Guback. "Work, Workers and the Workplace: Is Local Newspaper Coverage Adequate?" *Journalism Quarterly* 62 (1985): 855–60.

Dubofsky, Melvyn. "Film as History: History as Drama—Some Comments on 'The Wobblies,' a Play by Stewart Bird and Peter Robilotta, and 'The Wobblies,' a Film by Stewart Bird and Deborah Shaffer." *Labor History* 22 (1981): 136–40.

Eder, Richard. Rev. of *Harlan County U.S.A. New York Times*, October 15, 1976, p. C8.

Farah, Judy. "Writers' Strike Forces Cast to Improvise." *Honolulu Star-Bulletin*, March 25, 1988, p. B2.

Feinsilber, Mike. "Newspaper Comic Page a Serious Matter." *Honolulu Star-Bulletin*, April 13, 1989, p. E5.

Ferguson, Tim W. Rev. of *The Coming Battle for the Media: Curbing the Power of the Media Elite* by William A. Rusher. *Wall Street Journal*, April 8, 1988, p. 13.

Foner, Moe. "Like a Beautiful Child." *Film Library Quarterly* 12, nos. 2–3 (1979): 64–65.

Foner, Philip S. "A Martyr to His Cause: The Scenario of the First Labor Film in the United States." *Labor History* 24 (1983): 103–4.

Gallup Poll. "Approval of Labor Unions Remains at Low." *The Gallup Report*, August 1981, Report No. 191, pp. 6–7.

———. "Long Slide in Approval of Labor Unions Comes to Halt." *The Gallup Report*, June 1985, Report No. 237, pp. 30–31.

Gans, Herbert J. "Are U.S. Journalists Dangerously Liberal?" *Columbia Journalism Review* 24 (November-December 1985): 29–33.

Giardina, Denise. "Solidarity in Appalachia." *Nation* 249 (July 3, 1989): 12–14.

Gliatto, Tom. "It's a Blooming Shame." *Honolulu Star-Bulletin*, May 5, 1989, pp. B1, B5.

Gomez, Joseph A. "History, Documentary, and Audience Manipulation: A View of 'The Wobblies.' " *Labor History* 22 (1981): 141–45.

Grimes, John A. "Are the Media Shortchanging Organized Labor?" *Monthly Labor Review* 110 (August 1987): 53–54.

Hall, Mordaunt. Rev. of *The Power and the Glory* directed by William K. Howard. *New York Times*, August 17, 1933, p. 13.

Handman, Edward. "DC 37 News Watch Proves TV Puts Koch on a Pedestal." *Public Employee Press*, May 29, 1981, pp. 5–7.

Heeger, Susan. " 'Ed Asner' Starring Lou Grant." *Channels* 2 (April–May 1982): 38+.

Henniger, Paul. "Victims Get Revenge." *San Francisco Chronicle*, February 10, 1985, p. 45.

Higham, Charles. "When I Do It, It's Not Gore, Says Writer Paul Schrader." *New York Times*, February 6, 1978, reprinted in *New York Times Encyclopedia of Film, 1977–1979*. New York: Times Books, 1984.

Hill, Michael. " 'Act of Vengeance' Tells the Jock Yablonski Story." *TV Week*, April 27, 1986, p. 15.

Howe, Irving, and Michael Kinsley. " 'Special Interests' and American Politics." *Dissent* 31 (Summer 1984): 270–74.

Hoynes, William, and David Croteau. "Are You on the Nightline Guest List?" *Extra!* 2 (January–February 1989).

Hoyt, Michael. "Downtime for Labor: Are Working People Less Equal Than Others—Or Is Labor Just a Dead Beat?" *Columbia Journalism Review* 22 (March–April 1984): 36–40.

———. "Is the Labor Press Doing Its Job?" *Columbia Journalism Review* 22 (July–August 1983): 34–38.

———. "Sticking It to the Unions." *Channels* 6 (November 1986): 42–45.

"HSTA, NEA Set to Broadcast Election-Year TV Commercials." *HSTA Teacher Advocate* 17 (September 1988): 5.

Hughes, Kathleen A. "Zowie! Newspapers Poll Readers on Comic Strips." *Wall Street Journal*, June 15, 1988, p. 25.

Ignatius, David. "The Press in Love." *Columbia Journalism Review* 16 (May–June 1977): 26–27.

International Association of Machinists. "Network News Fails Union Viewers." *Labor News*, August 30, 1980, p. 2.

Jensen, Klaus Bruhn. "News as Ideology: Economic Statistics and Political Ritual in Television Network News." *Journal of Communications* 37, no. 1 (1987): 8–27.

Johnson, Candice. "Union Yes Message Stresses Valued Role of Labor." *AFL-CIO News* 33 (May 14, 1988): 1–2.

Johnson, Ralph Arthur. "World without Workers: Prime Time's Presentation of Labor." *Labor Studies Journal* 5 (Winter 1981): 199–206.

Jurovich, Tom. "Anti-Union or Unaware? Work and Labor as Understood by High School Students." *Labor Studies Journal* 3 (Fall 1991): 16–32.

Kalaski, Robert J. "TV's Unreal World of Work." *AFL-CIO American Federationist* 87, no. 12 (1980): 16–21.

Kanabayashi, Masayoshi. "Japanese Unions Slipping at Workplace, Emerge as an Intriguing Political Force." *Wall Street Journal*, July 8, 1989, p. A4.

Kirkland, Lane. "Labor's Part of the First Amendment." *Carpenter* 108 (February 1988): 7.

Krahling, William D. "Labor's Charge of 'Unfair': A Libel Risk for Newsmen." *Journalism Quarterly* 38 (1961): 347–50.

Kwik, Phill. "Pittston Power." *Nation* 249 (October 16, 1989): 409.

Lasch, Christopher. "Archie Bunker and the Liberal Mind." *Channels* 1 (October–November 1981): 34+.

Lazare, Daniel. "State of the Union: The Newspaper Guild under the Gun." *Columbia Journalism Review* 27 (January–February 1989): 43–48.

Leab, Daniel. "Confronting a Myth." *Film Library Quarterly* 12, nos. 2–3 (1979): 8–17.

Lichter, Robert S., and Linda Lichter. "The Once and Future Journalists." *Washington Journalism Review*, December 1982, pp. 26–27.

Lichter, Robert S., and Stanley Rothman. "Media and Business Elites." *Public Opinion* 4 (October–November 1981): 42–46, 59–60.

Lieberthal, Mil. "TV Images of Workers—Reinforcing the Stereotypes." *Labor Studies Journal* 1 (Fall 1976): 162–69.

Lipman, Joanne. "TV Ads' Influence Found Wanting." *Wall Street Journal*, February 15, 1989, p. B6.

Lipset, Seymour Martin. "Unions in Decline." *Public Opinion* 9 (September–October 1986): 52–54.

Lynch, Roberta. "The Media Distort the Value of Labor Unions." *In These Times*, July 15–28, 1981, p. 17.

McManus, John T. Rev. of *Dead End*. *New York Times*, August 25, 1937, p. 25.

Maltz, Albert. "What is Propaganda?" *New York Times*, April 28, 1935, reprinted in *New York Times Encyclopedia of Film, 1929–1936*. New York: Times Books, 1984.

Margolies, Ken. "Silver Screen Tarnishes Unions." *Screen Actor* 23 (Summer 1981): 43–52.

Martin, Everett D. "Our Invisible Masters." *Forum* 81 (1929): 145.

"MCO Enhaces Public Image." SEIU *Public Division Update.* 2 (Winter–Spring 1989): 21.

"Media Watch: What Are They Afraid to Tell?" *People's Daily World* 4 (September 21, 1989): 2.

Midura, Edmund M. "A. J. Liebling: The Wayward Pressman as Critic." *Journalism Monographs*, no. 33. (April 1974).

Mills, C. Wright. "The Trade Union Leader: A Collective Portrait." *Public Opinion Quarterly* 9 (Summer 1945): 158–75.

Moberg, David. "Post-Modern Labor Struggles." *Union* (Magazine of the Service Employees International Union), September 1988, pp. 22–26.

Molotch, Harvey. "Media and Movements." In *The Dynamics of Social Movements: Resource Mobilization, Social Control, and Tactics*, edited by Meyer N. Zald and John D. McCarthy, pp. 71–93. Cambridge, Mass.: Winthrop, 1979.

Mort, Jo-Ann. "The Vanishing Labor Beat." *Nation* 245 (November 21, 1987): 588 + .

Oshiro, Sandra S. "From Bargaining Table to TV Screen." *Honolulu Advertiser*, February 19, 1987, p. C9.

Patrick, Paul. " 'Garment Jungle' True Union Story." *AFL-CIO News*, May 11, 1957, p. 8.

Patterson, Gregory A., and Louis Aguilar. "UAW Blasts Wall Street with Ad Blitz." *Wall Street Journal*, April 19, 1989, pp. C1 + .

Peters, Charles. "A Neo-Liberal's Manifesto." *The Washington Post*, September 5, 1982, pp. C1 + .

Pomper, Gerald. "The Public Relations of Labor." *Public Opinion Quarterly* 23 (Winter 1959–60): 483–94.

Porter, Rockne. "Coors Beer Doesn't Deserve Drake's Business." *Times-Delphic*, December 3, 1982.

———. "What 60 Minutes Didn't Tell You." *Gavel* (Drake Law School), December 8, 1982.

Presser, Jackie. "Does the Press Understand Unions?" *Ohio Teamster* 22 (April 1984): 1 + .

Rabinowitz, Dorothy. "Snap, Crackle and Pop." *Wall Street Journal*, June 23, 1981, p. A8.

Robinson, Michael J., and Maura E. Clancey. "Network News, 15 Years after Agnew." *Channels* 4 (January–February 1985): 34–39.

Robinson, Michael J., and Andrew Kohut. "Believability and the Press." *Public Opinion Quarterly* 52 (Summer 1988): 175–89.

Rollings, Jerry. "Mass Communications and the American Worker." In *Labor, the Working Class, and the Media*. Vincent Mosco and Janet Wasko, eds. Norwood, N.J.: Ablex, 1983: 129–52.

Rubenstein, Harry R. "Symbols and Images of American Labor: Dinner Pails and Hard Hats." *Labor's Heritage* 1, no. 3 (1989): 34–49.

Rukeyser, Louis. " 'Funnies' Having Last Laugh in Advertising," *Honolulu Star-Bulletin*, December 5, 1988, p. C1.

Sawyer, Charles. Rev. of *Silkwood*. *Films in Review* 35 (March 1984): 178–79.

Schlechtweg, Harold P. "When Worlds Collide: Amherst's Progressives and the Picketing of Louis' Foods." *Labor Center Review* 11 (Spring 1989): 25–30.

Schneider, William. "Views on the News." *Public Opinion* 8 (August–September 1985): 6–11, 58–60.

Seeger, Murray. "A Keyhole View: The Press and the Campaign." *AFL-CIO American Federationist* 92, no. 1 (1985): 5–8.

Seltzer, Curtis. "The Pits: Press Coverage of the Coal Strike." *Columbia Journalism Review* 20 (July–August 1981): 67–70.

Sennwald, Andre. Rev. of *Black Fury*. *New York Times*, April 11, 1935: 27.

———. Rev. of *I Believed in You*. *New York Times*, April 11, 1934, p. 25.

Shorto, Russell. "Machinists Tool Up for TV." *Washington Journalism Review* (September 1980): 9.

" 'Skag': TV's Steel Soap a Factual Wipe-Out." *Steel Labor* 45 (February 1980): 7.

Stone, Gerald, Barbara Hartung, and Dwight Jensen. "Local TV News and the Good-Bad Dyad." *Journalism Quarterly* 64 (Spring 1987): 36–44.

Sussman, Leila A. "Labor in the Radio News: An Analysis of Content." *Journalism Quarterly* 22 (September 1945): 207–14.

Tasini, Jonathan. "Lost in the Margins: Labor and the Media." *Extra!* 3 (Summer 1990): 1–12.

Taylor, Clarke. "AFL-CIO Plans Labor Shows." *Los Angeles Times*, October 3, 1983, p. VI:3.

"$13 Million Advertising Campaign Will Be Largest in AFL-CIO History." *Government Employee Relations Reporter*, January 4, 1988, p. 4.

Thomas, Paul. "I Could Have Been a Contender." *Film Library Quarterly* 12, nos. 2–3 (1979): 58–63.

Thompson, Howard H. Rev. of *The Garment Jungle*. *New York Times*, May 16, 1957, p. 28.

"UAW Ad Campaign." *Labor Relations Reporter*, April 24, 1989, 509.

"Union Network." *Business Week*, December 17, 1949, pp. 92–93.

"Union Yes: It's Working." *AFL-CIO News* 33 (July 30, 1988): 4–5.

"Union Yes Spots Aired Widely on Radio." *AFL-CIO News* 33 (June 11, 1988): 2.

U.S. News and World Report. "How Unions Labor Away Cleaning Up Their

Image." *Sunday Star-Bulletin and Advertiser* (Honolulu), October 21, 1979, p. A28.

United Auto Workers. "The Media Business: A Worker's Guide to the Media." *Ammo* 25 (November 1987): 8.

Walsh, Francis R. "The Films We Never Saw: American Movies View Organized Labor, 1934–1954." *Labor History* 27 (1986): 564–80.

Ware, Charles. "Fairness of Advertiser's Rutledge Suit Coverage." *Honolulu Advertiser*, May 6, 1984, p. B3.

Weaver, David, and Swanzy Nimley Elliott. "Who Sets the Agenda for the Media?: A Study of Local Agenda-Building," *Journalism Quarterly* 62 (1985): 87–94.

Weiler, A. H. Rev. of *The Inheritance*. *New York Times*, November 9, 1964, p. 42.

————. Rev. of *Never Steal Anything Small*. *New York Times*, February 12, 1959, p. 23.

Wildavsky, Aaron. "The Media's 'American Egalitarians.' " *Public Interest* 88 (Summer 1988): 94–104.

Wiles, Greg. "Union-Promoting Ads May Be 'Localized' for Hawaii." *Sunday Star-Bulletin and Advertiser* (Honolulu), June 12, 1988, p. B5.

Wilkes, Kathy. "What They're Saying: ABC's *Roseanne*." *Dispatcher* 47 (March 10, 1989): 8.

————. "The House of Labor and the Fourth Estate: Where the Middle Ground Is." *Labor Center Review* 8 (1986): 5–18.

Williams, Maureen. "From Incendiary to Invisible: A Print-News Content Analysis of the Labor Movement." *Labor Center Review* 10 (1988): 23–27.

Zack, Albert J. "The Press Bias on Labor." *AFL-CIO American Federationist* 84, no. 10 (1977): 1–7.

Zagoria, Sam. "Labor News and Labor Relations." Press Release of Remarks at the Forty-Sixth Annual Convention of the National Association of Broadcasters, Chicago, April 1, 1968, pp. 1–8.

Zieger, Gay P., and R. H. Zieger. "Unions on the Silver Screen: A Review-Essay on *F.I.S.T.*, *Blue Collar*, and *Norma Rae*." *Labor History* 23 (1982): 67–78.

Interviews

Edwards, Patricia. United Auto Workers of America. January 23, 1991.

Gagala, Kenneth. Director, Labor Education Program, University of Minnesota. January 25, 1991.

Hayashi, Clyde. Former President of the Federal Employees Metal Trades Council at Pearl Harbor. April 14, 1989.

Kupau, Walter. International Brotherhood of Carpenters, Local 745. December 6, 1988.

Memminger, Charles. Reporter for the *Honolulu Star-Bulletin*. December 1, 1988.

Meyer, Phil. Reporter and feature writer for the *Honolulu Star-Bulletin*. December 8, 1988.

Oshiro, Sandy. Reporter for the *Honolulu Advertiser*. August 18, 1988.

Schneider, Richard L. Grand Lodge Representative, International Association of Machinists and Aerospace Workers. March 1, 1989.

Smith, F. Kirsten. United Auto Workers of America. January 23, 1991.

Turner, Charles. Former reporter for the *Honolulu Advertiser*. November 28, 1988.

Miscellaneous

AFL-CIO. *The Changing Situation of Workers and Their Unions*. Report by the AFL-CIO Committee on the Evolution of Work. Washington, D.C.: AFL-CIO, February 1985.

———. *Proceedings of the Seventeenth Constitutional Convention of the AFL-CIO*. Washington, D.C.: AFL-CIO, October 1987.

Clark, Paul F. "Changing Labor's Image: Unions, Media and Public Opinion." Slide/tape program and "Instructor's Manual." Pennsylvania State University, 1987.

"Deposition of Cher Mungovan." November 1987. U.S. District Court, District of Hawaii. *C&W Construction* v. *Brotherhood of Carpenters and Joiners of America, Local 745*. Civil No. 83–0710.

"Deposition of Walter Mungovan." February 1986. U.S. District Court, District of Hawaii. *C&W Construction* v. *Brotherhood of Carpenters and Joiners of America, Local 745*. Civil No. 83–0710.

Hoynes, William and David Croteau. *Are You on the Nightline Guest List?* Special Report prepared for Fairness and Accuracy in Reporting, February 1989.

International Association of Machinists. "IAM Television Entertainment Report Part II: Conclusions and National Summary of Occupational Frequency in Network Prime Time Entertainment for February 1980." June 12, 1980.

Medoff, James L. "The Public's Image of Labor and Labor's Response." Colloquium co-sponsored by Harvard University Economics Department and Labor Relations and Research Center, University of Massachusetts, 1985.

Menig, Harry W. "Labor Union Films, 1930–1970: Increasing Cinemacy on the Labor Front." Paper presented at the Popular Culture Association Meeting, April 1977, in Baltimore. A "Working Paper" in Film/Video disseminated by Film Research in Progress. Southern Illinois University.

NBC Reports: "Labor in the Promised Land." Reporter, Mike Jensen; writers, Mike Jensen, Tom Spain, and Marilyn Nissensen. NBC, March 5, 1983, 10:00 P.M.

"On Television: Public Trust or Private Property." Narrator: Edwin Newman; writer and producer: Mary Megee. PBS, South Carolina Educational Television Network. Produced at St. John's Television Center, December 1, 1986.

Plumbers and Steamfitters Local 33. "95th Anniversary Video and 6 TV Commercials." Videotape, Des Moines, Iowa, 1987.

Sickler, A. David. "Memorandum To: Coors Boycotters." October 8, 1982. Re: CBS/60 Minutes Coors Boycott Story, September 26, 1982. Coors Boycott National Coordinator, AFL-CIO.

Tasini, Jonathan. "Lost in the Margins: Labor and the Media." Special FAIR Report prepared for Fairness & Accuracy in Reporting, September 1, 1990.

"Trouble Brewing." Reporter: Mike Wallace; producer: Allan Marayanes. *60 Minutes*, CBS-News, vol. 15, no. 38. September 26, 1982, rebroadcast June 5, 1983.

UCLA, Center for Labor Research and Education. *As Others See Us: The U.S. Labor Movement, as Depicted on Stage and Screen*. Study guide prepared by Gloria Busman, project director. October 13, 1990.

U.S. Department of Labor. *Semiannual Report of Inspector General, April 1, 1982–September 30, 1982*. Washington, D.C.: Government Printing Office, 1982.

Index of Film and Television Program Titles

General Index

ABOUT THE AUTHOR

WILLIAM J. PUETTE is on the faculty of the University of Hawaii at
Manoa and teaches at the Center for Labor Education and Research.
He received his undegraduate degree at St. Vincent College and his
Ph.D. in American Studies from the University of Hawaii. His work
has centered on labor relations and the way unions are perceived.